Marshall Fine has been an entertainment writer and critic for more than twenty years, for publications including *Entertainment Weekly, Premiere, Playboy, LA Times* and *USA Today*. He is an entertainment writer for Gannett Newspapers in New York and the author of *Bloody Sam: The Life and Films of Sam Peckinpah*.

MARSHALL FINE

harvey keitel
the art of darkness

HarperCollins*Publishers*

HarperCollins*Publishers*
77–85 Fulham Palace Road,
Hammersmith, London W6 8JB

A Paperback Original 1997
1 3 5 7 9 8 6 4 2

Copyright © Marshall Fine 1997

Marshall Fine asserts the moral right to
be identified as the author of this work

A catalogue record for this book is
available from the British Library

ISBN 0 00 225808 4

Set in Aldus by
Rowland Phototypesetting Ltd,
Bury St Edmunds, Suffolk

Printed and bound in Great Britain by
Caledonian International Book Manufacturing Ltd, Glasgow

To my brother and sister, Richard and Julie

contents

illustrations

THE YOUNG HOPEFUL

Keitel at the beginning of his acting career
Keitel discusses a scene in *Mean Streets* with Martin Scorsese
and Cesare Danova (courtesy Warner Bros.)

THE DIFFICULT YEARS

Ellen Burstyn and Keitel in *Alice Doesn't Live Here Anymore*
(courtesy Warner Bros.)
On the set of *Blue Collar*: Keitel, Richard Pryor and Yaphet
Kotto (courtesy Universal Pictures)
Donning full Napoleonic-era mufti for *The Duellists*
(courtesy Paramount Pictures)
Keitel as the villain in *Saturn Three* (courtesy Associated
Films)

THE MANY FACES OF HARVEY KEITEL

As Roddy in Bertrand Tavernier's *Deathwatch* (courtesy
Delta Films/Gaumont)
As Judas in Martin Scorsese's *The Last Temptation of Christ*
(courtesy Universal Pictures)
As Mickey Cohen in *Bugsy* (courtesy TriStar Pictures)
Quick on the trigger in *Reservoir Dogs* (Corbis/Everett
courtesy Miramax Films)
Going native as Baines in *The Piano* (courtesy Miramax
Films)

THE GODFATHER OF INDEPENDENT FILM

Keitel works through a scene with Quentin Tarantino on the set of *Reservoir Dogs* (courtesy Miramax Films)
At the Cannes Film Festival with Theo Angelopoulos and Maia Morgenstern (courtesy AFP/Corbis Everett)
Auggie Wren in Wayne Wang's *Smoke* (courtesy Miramax Films)
Jim Jarmusch shares his last cigarette with Auggie in *Blue in the Face* (courtesy Miramax Films)

LOCAL HERO

Keitel and daughter Stella at 'Welcome Back to Brooklyn Day' (courtesy Marshall Fine)
Keitel accepts his award (courtesy Marshall Fine)
Fellow Brooklynites actor Daniel Benzali, Keitel, radio legend 'Cousin Brucie' Morrow and jazz drummer Max Roach (courtesy Marshall Fine)

All cover photographs courtesy The Ronald Grant Archive.

introduction

Harvey Keitel is a tough interview. Ask anyone who's tried it. It's not that he won't talk to you. It's just that, for the most part, he will only talk about what he wants to talk about, no matter what you ask him.

The first time I met him, in October 1994, he started by telling me why he didn't want to discuss the character he played in the film he was there to promote because 'I'd like your readers to see the film with their own hearts, to see it without my influence.'

Neither did he want to discuss his work methods or his personal life. Nor would he talk about the taboos on male frontal nudity in films – 'I wouldn't know because I've never done a nude scene.' All evidence to the contrary.

Instead, he wanted to discuss how he had discovered the joys of reading as a young man in the Marines, when, out of boredom, he picked up a book of Greek mythology and transformed his life. And to complain that 'we've lost the art of story-telling for the most part. We've lost the art of sitting around the table and sharing stories about life. We've lost the art of the caveman who painted on walls to express his own fears and desires.'

Most of all, he wanted to discuss the journey inward, the journey to self-knowledge that drives him onward as an actor and as a man. It was the kind of discussion that could have sounded pretentious; well, actually, it *did* sound pretentious. But Keitel also made it sound heartfelt:

I still struggle at times not to escape from the inward journey. I can never weigh for you how hard that is, the temptation away from doing what is right. The problem is we give short shrift too often to the devil in us. We shun it instead of making its voice divine and accepting our goodness. The problem is in accepting the dark side. People don't understand that they can accept it – but they don't have to act on it. There are ways of expressing the dark side without hurting anyone. It can take a lifetime to learn – but it doesn't have to.

Harvey Keitel's journey to self-knowledge and his career as an actor have both been bumpy, sometimes frustrating trips, that eventually led to creative breakthroughs and newfound success in the 1990s.

He came to acting late – in his mid twenties – and was already in his thirties when he had his first burst of fame in *Mean Streets*. But subsequently he couldn't find parts worthy of his talents, playing colorful but small character roles before suffering a kind of career meltdown in the late 1970s that lasted, more or less, through the 1980s. Then, in 1991 and 1992, Keitel was reborn as the risk-taking king of the American (and, indeed, the international) independent film scene.

When I started this book, I assumed I understood Keitel's career, having followed it since he emerged in *Mean Streets* in 1973, the same year I left college and started working professionally as an entertainment writer and critic (after several years of practicing in college). Acting, as it turned out, was an escape from a life so unsatisfying that Keitel had sought refuge in work as a court stenographer, where he could sit without speaking or being spoken to for days at a time. Yet that proved to be the opposite of what he wanted and needed: the ability to explore, understand and express the riot of emotions roiling within him.

To chronicle Keitel's career required watching close to sixty of his films. Though I'd seen most of them when they originally came out, I doubt that even Harvey has seen all of them; many of the lesser outings – the ones he made in the deep, dark eighties with directors no one will ever hear of – are impossible to find on video in the States.

Watching as many as I did, however, was a revelation and an education. The young Keitel of *Mean Streets* or *Blue Collar* was so energized, his potential practically oozing out of his ears, yet with an edge of desperation – he was, after all, almost thirty-five when *Mean Streets* came out. He was playing characters so feverishly caught up in their own lives that he seemed to give off sparks – he created friction and electricity just by walking through life.

Compare that with the older, sadder, more confident Keitel of *Reservoir Dogs* or *Smoke*: here are characters who have lived long enough to know which lines they will and won't cross – and what each of them costs. That smooth, slightly wolflike face has gained wrinkles and lines, making its planes and valleys a landscape of unexpressed emotion. And his always forceful physique has, if anything, become even more solid and formidable.

I've gained what is probably a permanent appreciation for Keitel the actor and the way he has grown and achieved mastery of his craft over the last twenty-plus years. To my mind, there is no one else working today who has the same courage and daring as an actor, the same restless urge to explore uncharted territory of the human soul. No matter how unworthy of his talents a movie might be (and his taste certainly isn't flawless), you can trust him to bring everything he has to whatever role he's playing.

To get a better idea about Keitel's career, I talked to as many of his friends and colleagues as I could, some of whom I can thank by name, some of whom I can't. But I would like to acknowledge, in no particular order:

Ulu Grosbard, Mike Kusley, Yaphet Kotto, Howard Bershod,

Paul Lynch, Gina Richer, John Badham, Anthony Harvey, Chuck Patterson, Stockard Channing, John Sayles, Mike Moder, David Dukes, Michael Dinner, James Gammon, Joel Tuber, Arvin Brown, Tom Reilly, Ian Bryce, John Fiedler, Steve Rotter, Peter Medak, John Pierson, David Proval, Matthew Carlisle, Harry Ufland, Ron Silver, Steve Brenner, Joel Schumacher, Peter Scarlet, Stuart Cotton, Arthur Brook, Giancarlo Esposito, Marc Urman, Ann Wedgworth, Ernie Martin, James Toback, Allen Garfield, Martin Sheen, Ellen Burstyn, Bertrand Tavernier, Tom Davis, David Sosna, Zina Bethune, Jack Mathews, Roger Ebert, Bruce Williamson, Joe Queenan, Harlan Jacobson, Peter Travers, Janet Maslin, Amelia Kassel, Marlin Hopkins, Cynthia Kirk, Andy Shearer, Jeremy Walker, Marian Koltai-Levine, Susan Kaplan, Jennifer Bretton, Marian Billings, Elizabeth Pettit, Scott Siegel, the San Francisco International Film Festival, *The Charlie Rose Show*, the New York Public Library, the New York Public Library for the Performing Arts at Lincoln Center, the White Plains Library, and video stores too numerous to mention.

I also want to thank Alan Rudolph, who didn't ask whether the book was authorized until midway through the interview, and then kept talking provided I mentioned the circumstances.

My gratitude to Dr Emily Stein, my favorite expert.

A big 'thanks for listening' to my colleagues Ross Priel, Georgette Gouveia, Barbara Nachman, Mary Dolan, Elaine Gross, Bill Varner and Ed Tagliaferri.

An added thank you to my friends Larry Sutin and Joey Morris, who provided counsel, humor and the occasional advice to 'Stop whining.'

Finally, all my love and gratitude to my wife, Kim, and my sons, Jacob and Caleb, for giving me their considerable support and understanding while I was writing this book.

'Sometimes a person has to go a very long distance out of his way to come back a short distance correctly.'

Edward Albee, *The Zoo Story*

prologue

Step off the Number 4 subway at the Eastern Parkway stop in Brooklyn, climb the stairs out of the station and hang a quick left. Suddenly you've escaped out of the crush of New York and into Eden: the Brooklyn Botanic Garden.

On this particular Sunday, a week before Father's Day 1996, the garden is suffering from the greenhouse effect as a gaggle of people elbow each other in heat and humidity that have both hit eighty-five, trying to stake out their little piece of paradise on the garden's Celebrity Path. Though the weather is sticky as overcooked rice, many of them are dolled up: suits and dresses and pantyhose – the whole Sunday-best rigmarole. They are milling with a certain impatience.

Yes, they've already spotted actor Fyvush Finkel among the assembled notables. The sight of jazz legend Max Roach, resplendent in a black suit and shirt and red tie, sends a shudder of recognition through the few African-Americans in the largely white crowd. Everyone perks up a little at the appearance of Daniel Benzali, late of TV's *Murder One*, bald head reflecting his blindingly white double-breasted summer suit (worn with white sneakers). But he's not the one they're here to see.

Then the crowd parts and Harvey Keitel joins the procession, his ten-year-old daughter Stella in tow. His hair longish and dark, shot through with gray, his face deeply tanned, he looks fit and natty in charcoal and black, his sportcoat and open-neck shirt complemented by sandals and a small gray suede bag with a knit strap.

The power surge through the crowd is almost noticeable. Harvey Keitel is here – the movie star. The Brooklyn movie star.

Suddenly this unmotivated throng has a purpose. Now they're ready: 'Welcome Back to Brooklyn' day can begin.

A few determined members of the public have wormed their way into this invitation-only ceremony, at which Keitel, Roach, Benzali and two others are being inducted into the Celebrity Path in the Botanic Garden. The Celebrity Path, an idyllic trail through shady pines near a lake, consists of flagstones bearing the carved names of prominent Brooklynites.

The press has been invited and has responded with a slightly pushy band of photographers and cameramen, battling for position around the edges of the crowd as the official procession begins up the narrow pathway. Led by a pompous fellow in a bad straw hat and what looks like a shepherd's crook, the caterpillar-like procession of honorees, their families, the press, and civilians who have slipped past the lax security works its way up the path.

It inches its way along, in part because Mary Tyler Moore, who is being crowned Queen of Brooklyn for the day, is on crutches. But there's also the matter of stopping at each flagstone for an annual ceremonial reading of the names.

'Walt Whitman!' the man with the shepherd's staff calls out, before taking two baby steps to the next stone. 'The Ritz Brothers!' he announces, leaving one to ponder the range of vision possessed by the selection committee.

Holding hands with his daughter, a slim and pretty girl with her father's piercing eyes (in gimlet), Keitel moves with the crowd, trying not to be bothered by all the cameras, the photographers now snapping pictures of his little girl, the cameras constantly clicking at him. His shirt and pants are black, soaking up heat like solar panels; the only cooling effect comes from the sockless sandals he's affected for this walk in the park with a few hundred onlookers pressing closely in on him.

Then, with a final flourish – 'Floyd Patterson!' – the procession stops at Keitel's new marker.

'Harvey Keitel – one of our inductees,' the man with the shepherd's crook enunciates and Keitel steps forward. He looks down at his name chiseled in capital letters in the smooth piece of paving.

After a moment of cameras clicking it becomes obvious that he is expected to say something.

'I'm honored to be included in this walkway,' he says, not quite meeting the eyes of the circle closing in around him, 'and I thank you for having me here today.'

There is a smattering of applause and then it's time to move on to the next stone – 'Gil Hodges!' – as Keitel and Stella fade back into the crowd.

As the procession gathers around the stone of another inductee – early sixties New York radio legend 'Cousin Brucie' Morrow – Keitel stops at a marker and stoops down. The stone is that of Harry Houdini, whom Keitel is getting ready to play in a film for Paramount, *Illumination*. He has already begun doing copious homework, sometimes phoning his researcher at midnight with new ideas he'd like to look into. All in preparation for a portrayal of the great escape artist and mama's boy who spent half his life debunking mediums and spiritualists – and the other half seeking a way to contact his mother in the next world.

He touches the stone, then kisses his hand and offers it with a smile to Stella, for her kiss as well. One stone further and he stops again: 'Look – Edward Everett Horton!' he says to his daughter with genuine glee. 'The Mad Hatter in *Alice in Wonderland*!'

The procession ahead of them comes to a conclusion, stranding the crowd on a narrow path on a peninsula in the lake.

Everyone must now turn around to return to a small amphitheater overlooking the water.

There, Keitel finds himself perched on a folding chair on the edge of the improvised stage, tapping his foot, waiting for the event to begin. Max Roach comes and sits next to him, and Cousin Brucie, his hairpiece looking distinctly younger than anyone on the stage, sits down next to him.

Cousin Brucie leans over to Keitel and Roach and says, 'Isn't it strange to think that that stone will be here after we're gone?' as though he had only this second discovered his own mortality.

If anything, for Keitel, the stone symbolized more about how far he had come since he was the kid who'd managed to make himself unwanted at two Brooklyn high schools, the kid whose greatest aspiration was his own stick at the poolroom, the kid who, out of simple macho boredom, quit high school altogether at seventeen and joined the Marines to escape from Brighton Beach.

To be here in Brooklyn was an honor he couldn't ignore. Still, the photographers are beginning to get on his nerves. Sitting on the folding chair in the cramped amphitheater, he can feel the lenses pointing at him as Stella crawls into his lap and, at age ten, begins sucking her thumb.

Keitel scans the crowd. He spots his older brother, Gerry, and several old friends, who've come to keep him company, to celebrate, and to see their friend and brother receive recognition from the borough where he grew up.

Stella leans against him, her thumb still in her mouth, watching with bored eyes as Daniel Benzali gets up to receive the medal signifying his placement in the Celebrity Path from Borough President Howard Golden. Her free hand pinches her father's ear between thumb and forefinger, as Keitel affects a look of comic pain.

Then Golden begins talking about Keitel and mentions *Smoke* – the Wayne Wang film in which Keitel plays Auggie Wren, the owner of a Brooklyn smoke shop. The film has been adopted as an official Brooklyn film when, in fact, it is *Blue in the Face*, *Smoke*'s rowdier, less self-satisfied companion film, that repeatedly announces its love for all things Brooklyn. Be that as it may, *Smoke* is the film Keitel is associated with on this day of accolades – because it's about Brooklyn and because it's more socially acceptable than, say, *Bad Lieutenant* or *Reservoir Dogs*.

'. . . Our next honoree, Harvey Keitel.'

Keitel gets up and Golden shakes his hand. There's the grip-and-grin moment for the cameras, which snap and whir furiously – the two men shaking hands while Golden holds the medal up between them. Then, as he starts to give it to Keitel, the hand-over is muffed and the bronze medal falls to the flagstones with a clang.

'Ooooh,' says the assembled group, but Keitel saves the moment, picking up the medal and holding it aloft to show it's unharmed. Then he kisses it and offers it to God.

'Remember that?' he says of the gesture. He smiles broadly. 'I think of the words of that Sinatra song: "The house that I lived in, the people I knew." The guy in the poolroom was named Charlie. I remember Mr Levy, the tailor. And my friends, Howie Weinberg and Carl Platt – we joined the Marines together.

'All those people I grew up with, my buddies, my brother. We carved our names in cement all over Brooklyn, notched it in trees and poolrooms. I'm pleased to be here. Thank you.'

Even as Golden is introducing Max Roach, Keitel is spirited away to the fragrance garden by one of the event's press flacks for a stand-up interview with New York's Fox-TV affiliate. As he stands uncomfortably next to a smiling blonde, mouthing the necessary niceties ('I've always loved Brooklyn'), his group of friends have detached themselves from the crowd still watching the induction ceremonies and stand together: Platt, Weinberg, Gerald Keitel, Keitel's long-time buddy Victor Argo (who appears in many of Keitel's films), the women attached to each.

When Keitel finishes his TV interview, he and his friends wander back up the hill to the induction ceremony. As Keitel looks through a batch of pictures of one of his friends' children, an autograph-seeker approaches, obviously prepared for this moment. He offers a color print of Keitel from *Reservoir Dogs* in a manila folder and Keitel signs it.

'Can I take a picture with you?' the fan says and, as Keitel says, 'Well . . .' the thin, T-shirted young man jumps next to Keitel, throws an arm around his shoulder and smiles for a friend, who takes a flash picture.

The flash functions as a signal to the half-dozen or so other fans lurking in the fringe of the crowd near Keitel and his friends. Emboldened, they approach him in twos and threes, asking for an autograph and a picture. He obliges, once, twice – then finally frowns and says to the next request, 'Look, I think that's enough of that.' The frown hits the kid like a bolt and the edge in Keitel's voice is unmistakable. Time to back off.

Yet, moments later, two aging women, husky and begowned, interrupt his attention to the ceremony for an autograph. Without even asking, one stands next to him while he's signing and the other quickly snaps a picture. Keitel can't believe the chutzpah, but all he can do is smile, shrug and look up at the heavens, as if to say, 'Isn't anybody listening to me?'

He pointedly turns back to his friends and begins to discuss plans for later. The combination of the heat and the crowd has made everyone edgy; they'd just as soon cut out now and escape from this whole scene to someone's house where they can kick back and talk about old times.

But obligations must be met. There's still the coronation ceremony for Mary Tyler Moore as Queen of Brooklyn before several hundred people in the rose garden. Keitel and his new colleagues from the Celebrity Path will be introduced and then spend the rest of the ceremony sitting on a platform under an unseasonably intense sun. The applause for Keitel will be the loudest of the day, louder even than for Queen MTM.

'I still have to do this other thing – then we can leave,' Keitel says, taking Stella's hand as the crowd begins to drift toward the staging area for the rose garden coronation.

Then he weighs the chunky medal in his hand, looks at its image of the Brooklyn Bridge, hears his parents saying to him, 'Harvey, be a mensch.' He realizes how ungracious what he's said might appear and smiles sheepishly. 'I didn't mean that like it sounded.'

1

How do you explain a nice Jewish boy from Brighton Beach, scion of an Orthodox Jewish family, quitting high school – turning his back on education – to join the Marines? It simply wasn't done. As one long-time friend observed, 'What kind of Jew goes into the Marines? And likes it!'

One seeking to rebel against and distance himself from a background he found oppressive and limiting. One who could see that his current form of rebellion – hanging out in the poolroom with his friends – was a dead end. But one who wound up substituting one rigid system of behavior (that of the United States Marine Corps) for another (Orthodox Judaism).

Keitel's parents had escaped the rising tide of anti-Semitism in Europe, emigrating to New York where they settled in the Brighton Beach section of Brooklyn. His father, who was from Poland, worked as a hatmaker and a garment worker, meager wages on which to raise a growing family. His mother, who had come from Romania, supplemented the family income by working at a luncheonette.

When Harvey was born on May 13, 1939, he was the youngest of three children, with an older brother and sister. The family all lived in a small apartment in Brighton Beach on Avenue X and Brighton Beach Avenue.

The second-floor walk-up rattled and shook every time the elevated subway, on tracks twenty feet from the window, screeched by. The apartment was small and dark, but it overlooked a colorful neighborhood of immigrant families staking out second-generation roots. Keitel's Brighton Beach blended together Jews, Italians, Irish. 'It was an incredibly colorful place to grow up,' he said. 'Brooklyn was a culture unto itself – Italian immigrants, Jewish immigrants, the music, the dances.'

His turf during his boyhood summers was the ocean and the nearby Coney Island amusement park. Swimming, climbing on and fishing off the rocks – what more could a kid ask for? There were fireworks every Tuesday night in the summer and an annual Mardi Gras at Coney Island, where the young Keitel would sell confetti.

The proceeds would go toward stuffing himself with Nathan's Kosher hot dogs or, occasionally, buying rides on the Steeple-chase. Somehow, though, the high-speed ride was never as exciting as the thrill of trying to sneak in without paying or the fear of getting caught. It was never easy.

As Keitel observed, 'Everything was right there on those streets, in that poolroom. It was limiting only in that we had very few teachers to show us where that elevated train led to. That was our limitation. We didn't know the avenues of possibilities. Manhattan could have been the moon to us.'

If he had fears as a kid, they were more of the movie-inspired kind. He walked around in a state of mild terror, fearful that he might encounter deadly quicksand or molten lava or some other natural disaster he'd seen at a Saturday matinee.

In fact, the worst thing he was likely to run into during those early days of the Eisenhower administration was the occasional fist fight. The toughest decision he had to make was where to hang out that day: the poolroom or the candy store at Avenue U and East 8th Street, where they would sip egg creams and eat Mello Rolls.

Yet even the tough kids understood certain innate rules of respect and discipline, which they made clear to the young Harvey one day in the luncheonette his mother ran on Avenue X. He had been acting the big shot with the help, while a few boys sat and had coffee and talked among themselves. The final straw was when Keitel's mother sat down next to him and asked him if he'd be able to help that day.

'Oh, man,' Keitel said loudly, upset at being pressed into service.

Before he knew it, he had been swatted across the back of the head by one of the more imposing Avenue X boys, who now loomed over Keitel. 'Don't talk that way to your mother,' he told Keitel, who could only rub his head and nod mutely.

Home life was something else: 'I've had many problems in my life that I've had to get through, beginning with being a little boy,' Keitel observed.

Such as the fact that he began stuttering at the age of six or seven, a problem that carried on into his teens. What is a painful and emotionally challenging period in anyone's life became excruciating for a young man who stuttered:

It was a huge, huge, deep, deep embarrassment, the object of humiliation by other children. It took years to go away. I still stutter at times. The stutter is something that occurs as the result of something else. It's sort of a road to your identity. It's a clue about something, it's a clue about disturbance.

It was very painful because I was shy to begin with. Confrontation means asserting yourself. Stuttering is an attempt to stop the assertion of the self. I can't think of anything more frustrating or more detrimental to evolving than not allowing yourself whatever thought comes to mind.

What kind of thoughts? Ones that went against the rigid interpretation of life practiced by his parents, Orthodox Jews in the middle of a secular world exploding with the expanding and engulfing youth culture of movies and rock 'n' roll.

It's not hard to imagine the lectures Keitel must have received from his parents, strict Eastern European people who had escaped annihilation in Europe only to be forced to start all over again – and in a new language. Nor is it difficult to conjure up the grinding combination of Orthodox Judaism and Depression-era economic pressures – which squeezed the neighborhood long after World War II had ended, well into the 1950s, even as the rest of America seemed to be enjoying a much-vaunted post-war prosperity.

'My mother worked at a luncheonette and my father worked at a factory as a sewing-machine operator and they could barely read or write,' Keitel recalled. 'Life demanded of them that they work hard for their family and they did so and I admire them deeply for that.'

Here, however, was Keitel, with all the raging hormones and sexually charged thoughts of a normal teenage boy in the Elvis era, when his peers were rocking and rolling, affecting the hairstyles and attitudes of James Dean in *Rebel Without a Cause* and Marlon Brando in *The Wild One* – none of which had penetrated the world of Keitel's parents.

Undoubtedly the lectures were long and stern: about the forbidden nature of sex and everything else young Harvey deemed most interesting, on the need to remember and honor the old way and resist the temptation of this godless new popular culture. Not to do so was not just wrong – it was punishable. But Harvey found himself irresistibly drawn to what he could see of the outside world and suffered the wrath and disappointment of his parents as a result.

Which may have led to the stuttering, he decided:

Guilt can be insidious, which helps to repress thoughts. You pick it up quickly – in your home, in your neighborhood. Once children are taught guilt, they will stutter in one way or another. If you're ashamed of one feeling, you're going to be ashamed of all your feelings. That's the basis for neurosis. Unfortunately, as a youngster I learned that certain feelings and thoughts were bad. You learn it's wrong to have a certain thought. As a young man, there were thoughts I had and propensities to do certain things, which I was very ashamed of. So if you have that thought, you say, 'I'm bad. I must get rid of that thought.' But how do you get rid of a thought? What do you do as a child? You choke yourself.

A doctor I know said to me, 'You are allowed any thought. Every thought is a worthwhile thought.' You are not responsible for your thoughts. One is only responsible for what he does. It took me a long time to learn what that doctor expressed to me.

Self-satisfaction was unknown to me as a young man. That came late in my life. The pain of my journey led me to satisfaction. Avoiding the pain led to strangulation, to self-loathing. By descending into the pain, I learned satisfaction.

Without that kind of repression and longing Keitel might not be the actor he eventually became: 'I've learned over the course of my life,' he said, 'that memories I once considered painful have been the greatest source of revelation in my life, so it's too simple to say they're positive or negative.'

Obviously, he wasn't the only Jewish kid from Brighton Beach who argued with his parents about dressing like a hood. Indeed, at Keitel's bar mitzvah, the rabbi performing the Jewish coming-of-age ritual booted one of Keitel's young pals out of the synagogue. His crime? Wearing such incipient hipster garb as a checkered cabana-style jacket, peg pants and pointy-toed shoes.

The conflict between Keitel's need to conform to his parents' wishes and his urge to create an identity of his own didn't really come to a head until after his bar mitzvah.

It was a Kosher household, which meant that they followed the Jewish dietary laws prohibiting, among other things, the eating of any pork or shellfish products as well as proscribing milk and meat products at the same meal. Though he moved away from Judaism, the habits of keeping Kosher stuck with Keitel, at least through his stint in the Marines. There, his friends would battle to sit next to him in the mess hall, because he would give away the milk that was invariably served with the meat of the day.

Keitel went to Hebrew school and studied at home with his grandfather, a man whose imposing strictness daunted him: 'I remember my grandfather sitting at the kitchen table in Brooklyn, making me read from my Hebrew book,' he recalled. 'My brother, who is five years older, stuck his head in the kitchen and said, "Aleph bais, gimme a raise, ches tes, kiss mein ess." Then he ran out, with my grandfather hollering at him. I couldn't believe my brother had done that. I was scared to death.'

Once the bar mitzvah was past, however, Keitel began to re-evaluate Judaism, losing faith as he looked at the problems that seemed to threaten the world's very existence in those days of Cold War panic. What kind of God would allow such things to go on?

In his crowd Keitel became known as someone who was willing to put his life on the line and confront God himself: as an act of rebellion, he started spitting on mezuzahs, the little metal sacraments containing a small piece of parchment with writings from the Torah that some Jews attach to the front doorpost. Observant Jews kiss their fingers and touch the mezuzah as they enter and leave their homes.

And Keitel was spitting on them:

I was literally spitting. My friends would say, with great fear, 'Don't do that, Harvey!, don't do that!' I said, 'Why? What's going to happen? Here I am, God – do something!' I wasn't ashamed of being a Jew – I had just lost faith.

There was so much misery and so much deprivation. I didn't understand how God fit into that. I thought God was responsible.

Religion meant nothing to me when I was growing up because it was never made clear to me how the stories and myths in the Bible were relevant to my life. We were simply taught to be fearful. It's a sin religion isn't taught with more feeling for the beauty of the stories.

Back then, someone said to me, 'It's people like you who are the true believers.' I spat on the mezuzah again. That person was right, though. It's been a long journey but I've come back. I would now say that I am a devout believer in the divinity but for a long time I just adopted Thomas Paine's credo, that my religion was to do what is right.

His rebellion extended beyond attempts at blasphemy into his efforts to attain juvenile-delinquency status: the duck's-ass hairstyle, the leather jacket, the peg pants set off by pointy shoes with metal cleats to announce his arrival from a block away. He wanted to be a tough guy because that's the way the guys were.

Not out-and-out gangsters, of course: just wiseguys who caused a little commotion now and then. According to one classmate of Keitel's at Abraham Lincoln High School in Brighton Beach,

We were what was called *trumbnicks*, troublemakers. We were tough but we weren't bad. By today's standards, we were angels. We got into fights, local things. We would go to a dance and end up in a brawl. We'd go to the old Manhattan-Brooklyn Jewish Center. We were Ashkenazi Jews and we'd get into fights with the Syrian Jews. We'd talk to their girls or they'd talk to ours and the next thing you know, you'd have fifty guys fighting in the street. But not with guns or knives — just with fists.

As Keitel recalled it, 'You had to be tough, otherwise you were considered a fag, a sissy. We used to have rock fights with black people. I had some black friends and we'd kid one another. The divisiveness and the rock fights always seemed absurd to us. I threw rocks at them and they threw rocks at me.'

Being tough meant doing things that scared you, things you knew could get you in trouble with the police or worse. Being tough meant never copping to that fear, no matter how over-powering it might become. For Keitel, being tough meant hiding his fear along with all the other unwanted, unwelcome emotions swirling around in his adolescent mind:

> I remember being scared to rob pigeon coops, but you couldn't admit that. There was nothing to be but tough. Now the other kids who were going to school and studying to be something – a doctor, lawyer, an Indian chief – they had a different identity. But the tough guys, their identity was to be tough. It was as if you were living in Africa and you had a tribe. You had to go out and kill animals to survive. Well, in this particular environment, to survive, you had to steal a car, tap a pigeon coop, steal things, wear certain clothing, put on the whole show. Otherwise you would be an outcast.

Which was already an identity Keitel was dealing with in everyday life. As the son of immigrants who resented his ever-more-Americanized worldview, he dealt every day with being an outsider in his own home; outside the house, on the other hand, he knew he would never be the all-American kid. As a Jew, he had grown up with the idea of anti-Semitism, its specter emanating from Europe during the war against Germany. As a teenager, he coped with the mercurial nature of social standing in the ever-shifting world of high school. And the only place he seemed to fit was with the tough guys.

Mark Reiner, a high-school friend, said, 'Harvey was street-wise and tough, but he was never mean. He knew how to handle himself and while he wouldn't back off from a fight, he never went looking for trouble either. He did some things I wouldn't, but he never lost his sense of decency.' And Keitel acknowledged:

I knew, deep down, that I didn't belong with that crowd. I was scared and didn't feel part of it but I couldn't admit that to myself, much less to them. So I played the game. I was not a real tough guy. The Brighton Beach Sinners were a group of friends of mine. The name was created by the press after a serious incident of vandalism at a neighborhood school. We didn't consider ourselves great sinners. We were trying to learn what life was about, we were trying to survive life. I saw myself trying to develop the power to live. I didn't think so much that I could be something as much as I needed to be something.

There was so much energy and talent among those guys. I wish I could have sat down with them and talked about things I was interested in – about feelings, about life, about personal problems. I wanted to do that but I couldn't. That wasn't tough. That was soft.

Yet he was a popular kid with his classmates, being elected by his peers as leader of the eighth-grade honor society, much to the chagrin of teacher Edna Dinkel, who took one look at the grinning juvenile-delinquent-in-training and said, 'I do not consider that an appropriate choice.' She ordered a new election, with different results and, being the teacher, she got what she ordered.

Meanwhile, Keitel was discovering new paradigms for his notions of toughness – in the movies of Marlon Brando and James Dean. Here, too, were misunderstood young men, at odds with both parents and society, trying simply to find out who they were amid a world of misunderstanding and opposition. The films showed the young Keitel that toughness could

be associated with emotional honesty and not simply a readiness
to be quick with the fists:

> I related to James Dean because he was in situations that we
> were in. I never related to his tough guy side. It was always
> his sensitivity and yet that's exactly what I couldn't be. I
> always buried it.
>
> My comrades and I didn't know about being nourished and
> we didn't have the courage to love somebody. That wasn't
> something we pursued. We weren't brought up to nourish
> one another's thoughts, to discuss our deep conflicts. Who
> the hell ever walked over to someone back then and said,
> 'Uh, listen, I really feel very lonely', or 'I feel very scared'
> or 'I'm not sure where I'm at.' We never spoke like that.
>
> I began to get a sense that courage was something other
> than what I thought it was. I saw people such as Dean,
> Brando and John Cassavetes as being heroic. As growing up
> has its difficulties, we look for heroes to help us through
> that shadowy forest. The work these people did represented
> a struggle to cope with the difficulty of being that stimulated
> and gave hope to me and my friends.
>
> They began to take the place of these warrior-like gods
> who had been my heroes. Somewhere along the line I have
> the sense that I was pursuing being tough in the wrong
> fashion. I wasn't really becoming tough. I was building a
> stronger facade because now I see tough as being a whole
> different animal, as being someone who can face problems,
> who can try to solve them without a baseball bat. All those
> guys back in the old days I used to call fags were tougher
> than anybody because they knew how to be scared.
>
> I began to want to be less of a war hero and more of what
> those men were. They gave me courage, they gave me hope.
> The courage to express their feelings, their emotions, their
> thoughts. That was stunning. Frightening. It took more cour-

age than I ever imagined, much more courage than picking up a gun.

And part of that courage had to do with facing his own fears, something Keitel was not ready to do: 'I never thought I could do what [Dean and Brando] did,' he noted. 'I was just glad someone was doing it — the "it" being something so personal and so revealing that it gave me some hope of understanding myself at a time when I was lying to myself with such ferocity. They somehow penetrated my defense, stirred things up.'

2

The sense of hope he gained from watching Dean and Brando act – the realization that men could actually reveal their anguish, anxiety and insecurity without compromising their sense of masculinity – was yet another emotion Keitel hid away as he coped with the pressures of family life and high school.

He entered Abraham Lincoln High School in September 1954, a short, rather young-looking freshman in a school full of lower-middle-class Jewish and Italian kids from the Brighton Beach and Coney Island neighborhoods.

The school had no metal detectors, no security forces, none of the stripped-down, urban-siege quality it possesses today. In this sunny era, the worst kids smoked cigarettes (with an occasional puff of marijuana by the really bad guys) as they hung out at the sweet shop across the street from Lincoln (long since replaced by the imposing edifices that comprise Trump Village housing development).

The school was home to the budding musical talents of Neil Diamond and Neil Sedaka, who both sang in the choir during Keitel's years there. The Tokens, who would have a hit with 'The Lion Sleeps Tonight,' also walked Lincoln's halls.

Gangs were not a problem; the biggest concern of principal Abraham Lass were the intramural scuffles between members of rival cellar clubs, local dance haunts. Keitel and his friends frequented a club called the Raleighs; they wore sharp red-and-black jackets with an image of Sir Walter Raleigh on the back.

So Lass finally banned the wearing of club jackets to school to stem the spate of scuffles they seemed to invite.

For most teenagers at Lincoln, the biggest concerns were social: having dances and meeting girls; hanging out at the beach and Coney Island. None of which did much for the confused existence of Harvey Keitel, as he explained:

Growing up, success for us was what? Money. Very simply: Money. Whoever had the most money at the end of the day was the most successful person. We grew up believing that, because that was the message given to us – and to our parents, and through our parents to us – and directly to us from the movies we saw and the television we watched.

There was a huge concern over material things. Having a car, a new car. Buying a girl a diamond engagement ring. A friend of mine would buy a new car and I would immediately spit on it. I would say, 'Why are you so caught up in this? It's only a piece of machinery.' The same thing I thought about buying a diamond engagement ring. Guys were like humiliated that they couldn't afford a carat ring or a carat-and-a-half diamond ring for an engagement. And something about that struck me as wrong, that people were being judged by the amount of money they had, as opposed to who they were.

Keitel, who had good enough grades to be a member of the honor society in middle school, suddenly found himself struggling in the face of high school's educational demands. He wouldn't pay attention even to the work in front of him. Outside of school, he was rebelling against his family's demands for better performance, running with his friends to the poolroom rather than keeping up with his homework.

'I didn't like anything except hanging out with my friends,' Keitel remembered. 'I didn't want to read. I didn't want to study. I didn't have the concentration, I didn't have the focus.

I was just upset, upset with those familiar things that perhaps any young person would have been upset about. And being upset doesn't afford one the patience necessary to learn anything. I failed everything but I thought I was a great student.'

He hid that emotional turbulence behind bravado, behind the tough-guy, wiseguy persona. Yet there was also something straightforward and ingenuous about the bantam Keitel, as Principal Lass found out on his first day at Lincoln, in the fall of 1955. Patrolling the halls, looking for stragglers after the first bell, Lass ran across a diminutive sophomore, peg pants stopping just short of his pointy, shiny black shoes, metal taps scraping restlessly on the floor. And, when asked, the underclassman couldn't produce a hall pass.

'What are you doing here, young man?' Lass asked, giving Keitel a baleful look.

'I'm waiting to see what our new principal looks like,' came the reply.

Lass fixed Keitel with a no-nonsense look. 'I'm your new principal.'

'How do you do?' the young man said, extending his hand seriously. 'I'm Harvey Keitel. I'm your new student.'

He lost interest in the classroom, falling further and further behind, barely scraping by. Outgoing and funny with his friends, he became withdrawn and unresponsive in class. Thirty years later, visited by a high-school classmate backstage during the Broadway run of David Rabe's *Hurlyburly*, Keitel found himself confronted by a woman who asked him, 'Harvey, what happened to you? You were so quiet.'

'Who's really quiet?' he replied.

None of the things that would prove to be his salvation later in life – literature, the arts – seemed available to Keitel and his friends. Movies? Sure, they went to westerns, horror films, gangster movies. The theater? Reading a book? Fuhgeddaboutit: 'There was no involvement in the arts at all. Zero,' Keitel said.

'We were taught we could not be something different. They'd say, "How could I be anything but what my father was?" In Brighton Beach, I mainly tried to look tough and having a book under one's arm doesn't make you look tough.'

Nor was there anyone to take the young Keitel in hand and say, 'I see potential in you. Let me help you.' A young man desperately searching for a mentor, Keitel couldn't look to his father for advice:

The important things to a man like my father were having food to eat and a roof over your head – with good cause, because he had mouths to feed for twenty years. I had trouble in high school. I was disoriented and I didn't know who I was. I needed guidance and I didn't get it. Here I was, so choked with internal conflict that I had a serious stuttering problem and there was nobody I could talk to. I had potential; my marks showed that. But there was nobody to say, 'Hey, it's alright to have these feelings and thoughts.'

What were my fears? Fear. Fear of us talking, fear of what's going to happen later, fear of tomorrow, fear of death, fear of not succeeding.

In desperation, after his sophomore year he changed schools, moving from Lincoln in Brighton Beach to Alexander Hamilton High School in Brooklyn's Bedford-Stuyvesant area. He did it, he said, 'seeking another road. I wasn't doing well at Lincoln and I thought maybe if I changed my physical circumstances, I would do better. I wanted to do better. So I went to vocational school.'

As a vocational school, Hamilton was hardly an academic hotbed. Keitel wasn't interested in being channeled into a manual vocation that offered him the same life of tedium and stress he'd seen in his own father. He found the curriculum dull and unchallenging.

When he tried to re-enroll at Lincoln, however, officials there found a technicality to deny him admittance: 'I was seventeen,' Keitel said, 'and the irresponsible idiot of a dean said I was too old.' Rather than return to Hamilton, he chose the poolroom over the schoolroom. His chronic absenteeism eventually caught up with him near the end of his junior year:

> I had a very good average but I was absent too many days. I just lost the desire to do anything. They called me down and told me they were going to throw me out. This history teacher went to bat for me. But he couldn't do a thing about it. There was some law about truancy, and they put me out. The dean at the time was a jerk, because he didn't pay attention to what was going on with his students' lives – one student being me. To this day, it's something that irks me.

3

It was 1956, a year when the hated Yankees beat the beloved Dodgers in seven World Series games, including a perfect one pitched by Don Larsen – and still more than a year before the Dodgers abandoned Brooklyn for sunnier climes. Elvis Presley was exploding out of the South and into American homes. *Peyton Place* was top in the ratings. An oral polio vaccine was making America breathe easier. Even as Dwight Eisenhower and Richard Nixon were once again turning Adlai Stevenson into a sacrificial Democrat in the race for the American presidency, a young senator from Massachusetts named John F. Kennedy was topping the best-seller lists with *Profiles in Courage*, which would win him the Pulitzer Prize in history the following year.

In 1956, Harvey Keitel was seventeen, unemployed and broke, with an incomplete education and limited job prospects.

From that vantage point, the military looked like a highly viable option: a job with training and travel – not to mention getting away from Brighton Beach and Brooklyn and being on his own for the first time in his life. He had, after all, just been expelled from one high school for repeated truancy – after being denied admittance to another.

In a moment of clarity, Keitel realized that he couldn't just spend the rest of his life hanging out in the poolroom. If he wanted a future, he needed a fresh start – and the military provided that. 'For me at that time it was a good move,' he remembers. 'It broke the roll I was on, the roll of the neighborhood poolroom, family; it cut the cord. When I went away, I was on my own, completely on my own.'

The only question was: which branch? With his best friends, 'Pittsburgh' Carl Platt and Howie 'the Moose' Weinberg, he decided to join the Navy: 'We were three young men in search of an identity, in search of heroes, trying to become our own heroes. There's that great line in Dickens's *David Copperfield*: "Whether I shall turn out to be the hero of my own life or whether that station will be held by anybody else, these pages must show."'

Before they could actually enlist, they ran into Joey Brodowski, a guy from the neighborhood a year or two older, who came into the poolroom at Brighton Beach and 5th Street in his Marine Corps uniform.

'Hey, Joey,' the trio told him eagerly, 'we're gonna join the Navy. What do you think about that?'

He looked straight at them and said, 'Nothing, if what you wanna be is the Marine Corps' little sisters.'

And so Harvey Keitel of the Avenue X Boys and the Brighton Beach Sinners became Private Harvey Keitel, USMC: 'When my friends and I joined, it was to play some war. What do seventeen-year-olds know about war? Nothing. About starving and dying children? Nothing. But we knew about the quality of being a Marine because we had heard about and read about it.'

What he found instead was discipline, both physical and mental. The Marines gave him a physical regimen that built his short, wiry physique into something well-muscled and impressive, despite his compact size. He gained a new sense of confidence from the training itself. Here was little Harvey Keitel from Brooklyn, shooting guns, learning hand-to-hand combat – and both enjoying and excelling at it. 'As a young Marine, I was more than willing to kill for my country and die,' he recalled. 'At times, I believe that's very worthwhile to stand up for what you believe in. If I had been a young Marine at Kent State, I would have fired had I been ordered to fire. I would have fired upon those students myself. Back then, I was an ignorant young man.'

That, in turn, gave him the courage to give education another try. After basic training, he began studying and taking classes, in pursuit of the high-school degree he had abandoned when it had abandoned him. And, before he left the Marines, he had earned it: 'I learned things there that were the beginning of a spiritual journey. In the Marines, I learned that the guys who were really tough were not necessarily the best fighters or the biggest bullies. They were the guys who would endure, who would be there when you needed them and who were not afraid to admit they were scared.'

The night that changed Keitel's young life forever came with no forewarning of its importance. Before it was over, however, his entire view of the world, himself and everything he faced in his life would be different. He gained an insight that would prove crucial to his way of thinking – and to his way of delving into the world of the characters he played as an actor – forever.

If Harvey Keitel has gained a reputation as an actor who is willing to confront his own darkness at its most stark and penetrating – to take his most frighteningly human fears and impulses and turn them into art – he gained the keys to that kingdom on a moonless night in 1956 near Jacksonville, NC, at Camp Lejeune, where he was a private in the Marines.

The incident, as he would later recount, was one of two lightning-bolt moments that would affect everything that came after. A direct line could be drawn from that particular night in 1956 and his breakthrough performances thirty-six years later in *Reservoir Dogs* and *Bad Lieutenant*. Indeed, an entire career may have been shaped by one night-combat class in the

Marines. The Keitel persona can be traced to that exercise: the edgy young (or middle-aged) man, whose way of dealing with the world is to lash out at it in spasms of violence – or worse. The good man confronted with his own attraction to what is forbidden – or coping with guilt at his inability to resist temptation.

When Lt, the character he plays in *Bad Lieutenant*, stares into an abyss of drugs, sex and numerous forms of spiritual corruption and faces his own pitiable disintegration, he is looking through Harvey Keitel's eyes. And those eyes say, 'I know these thoughts. I understand this way of thinking.'

The comprehension dawned on that dark night in North Carolina when the young Keitel, barely seventeen and newly sprung from basic training, showed up for night-combat training. It was an inky night and Keitel was nervous and skittish. He had played the tough guy for years, learning it early on the streets of Brooklyn. But this was the Marines – and he was hardly the only tough guy who wanted to prove just how tough he was by joining the Marines.

He had the kind of approachable hard-boiled quality of a young John Garfield. Mixing for the first time with people from all parts of the country, he'd found other Brooklynites and hung out with them, if anything emphasizing his own Brooklyn origins.

But this was different: even though it was peacetime, even though he was armed and wearing combat gear, even though it was only an exercise and not actual combat conditions, standing out here in the dark was creepy. He was a Brooklynite through and through, used to corners with streetlamps and traffic and people. This was darkness one can only find far from city lights, darkness like he'd never experienced except, perhaps, while hiding in a closet as a child: 'It was pitch-black out. You couldn't see your hand in front of your face. We were sitting in the darkness, me and hundreds of other Marines, huddled together, about to go through this course in night combat. And I was scared. And I didn't want to tell any of my fellow Marines that I was scared. But I was scared.'

Then, out of the darkness came a voice: calm, reasonable, all-knowing. It was the voice of the instructor, an aged veteran of, perhaps, twenty-five or twenty-six who seemed like a mystic ancient to this still-raw batch of shaven-headed seventeen- and eighteen-year-olds. 'You're all afraid of the dark,' he said, without judgment, 'because you're all afraid of what you don't know. I'm going to teach you to know the darkness, so that you're no longer afraid of it. So that you learn how to live in it.'

'My introduction to mythology and philosophy,' Keitel called it. 'In the years that came, that is one of the essences of all the mythology and philosophy I have read. He could tell us those words because he had experienced the darkness. He had experienced that terror in a war. But that was the first time I had heard words like that.'

That notion – of dealing with fear by confronting it and learning about it – struck a chord that resonated with the seemingly easy-going Keitel. It remained with him and became a credo of sorts: to explore the darkness in order to better understand the light, to examine wrong in order to better know what is right. It became the source of Keitel's journey as an actor – the inner journey to explore his own darkest, least-acceptable feelings and ideas, then using that self-knowledge while creating his film and stage characters – to plumb his own pain for his characters' reality:

That is probably the most important philosophical question to ask oneself. What is the darkness? How do I learn to live with it? I heard that when I was seventeen years old and I never forgot it. It appealed to me. I wanted to learn to live with the darkness. What the Marine was teaching – it's not that you are not scared in the night time. It's that you learn about your fear and the darkness. That fear becomes different and you can work with it.

At that time I didn't know what the extension of that idea was. I know now. It took me years to understand it, but I sensed it.

Eventually, Keitel would find the same thought echoed in the Gospel of Thomas, as he researched the role of Judas in Martin Scorsese's *The Last Temptation of Christ*: 'If you bring forth what is within you, what you bring forth will save you. If you do not bring forth what is within you, what you do not bring forth will destroy you.'

'There,' Keitel said, 'is the whole foundation of self-analysis.'

4

Keitel was more excited and curious than scared when America decided to intervene in Lebanon in 1957, to provide a peace-keeping presence while American and Soviet diplomats conferred and tried to resolve the dispute between Lebanon and the Soviet-backed forces in the region. 'Jews weren't normally allowed to be sent to the Middle East then,' he said, 'but it was an emergency situation – the threat that some Arab states were going to invade Lebanon – so they didn't separate me from my unit.'

Once they got to Lebanon, they carried rifles in the name of their country when they were on duty and, when off duty, explored Beirut, where they were stationed, as much as the politics of the moment would allow. Keitel was fascinated by Beirut's blend of the modern and the biblical, but appalled by the poverty that he saw. American Marines always drew a crowd of children; Keitel found himself moved by the squalid conditions in which they existed. Though it was against regulations, he and his friends began filching rations in order to give them to the children they encountered.

As he patrolled Beirut, Keitel – who only a couple of years earlier was spitting on the mezuzah at every opportunity – began wearing a Star of David on a chain around his neck, in plain view, as a note of defiance aimed at the people he was there to protect, people he knew would wipe out him and all the Jews in Israel, given the opportunity.

Inevitably, it led one day to an encounter with a Lebanese

civilian, who dropped a remark in passing – along the lines of 'Jewish dog' – that Keitel wouldn't let pass. Springing suddenly into action, the nineteen-year-old Marine, eager for combat, grabbed the transgressor by the throat and applied a choke-hold long enough to make it clear that he disapproved of the remark. Keitel walked away, satisfied that the young man would keep future opinions about Jewish jewelry to himself.

It wasn't Keitel's first run-in with anti-Semitism in the Marines. Still, the prejudice he'd found in the Marine Corps had a somewhat less emotionally charged context: 'I was called a kike once by a sergeant when we were alone. I called him a guinea. He said, "Don't call me that." I said, "Don't call me a kike." He never said it again and we were OK.'

His three years in the Marines remain a touchstone of his life, from his lifelong devotion to working out to the sense of self-esteem it instilled:

> That was the first time I had a real sense of pride about myself, a sense of belonging to a group that's special. To this day, I'm proud of being a Marine.
>
> There was a spirit. We were on a journey, albeit the creativity was directed to a place none of us wanted to go to – war. But you understand, if you are in the middle of that, why the group is unstoppable. There is a spirit at work there, a support system, where you know you will never get left behind. I'm talking about being there for someone. Semper fidelis. That says it all. Always faithful. It means you'll never let the other guy down. It means if he needs you, you will be there. Every experience I have affects my choices in life and the Marines was one of those experiences. Certainly the elevation of spirit that I encountered in the Marine Corps influenced me.

Yet what he came away with – that pride in being a Marine – was hardly what he had gone looking for:

I volunteered because I was looking for a war. And in retrospect, I see that it was all because of my inability to suffer, to be sad, to be lonely. I ended up being a Marine for three years and I know now that it's easier to go to war than it is to face your own inner violence.

I think I was probably looking to be tough, to be part of something where I could say, 'I'm not afraid of anything.' To hide the fear. But now I know where that's at. The only way to protect yourself is to know fear and to accept it.

It was on the return boat from Beirut to the United States that Keitel had the second revelation that changed his life forever.

Bored and restless, having exhausted the ship's supply of magazines and other forms of recreation, Keitel turned as a means of last resort to something he had studiously avoided for much of his life:

He picked up a book and started to read.

'I read a book for the first time. I wasn't exposed to literature as a young boy. I'm not well-educated. I left school when I was seventeen. I went into the Marine Corps and I hadn't read a book in my life. I was slow to come to it. It took me many years before I became something of a reader.'

It is fitting that the book Keitel wound up with in his hand was about mythology, in which the stories provide moral lessons about the most basic sins: hubris, greed, jealousy, treachery, betrayal. Keitel seems to have built his entire career around telling stories – creating modern myths – dealing in the same issues that have attracted story-tellers from the most primal mythology to the most sophisticated: man's quest to discern right from wrong, to resist evil even when doing good involves deep sacrifice, to learn the penalty – both internal and external – of embracing the dark path.

I was aboard ship and somehow I picked up a book of Greek mythology and began reading. I had a desire to understand this chaos that I was experiencing in my body. And books were a guide. I don't find that my reading has given me something I didn't know so much as it's made me more aware of what I do know but hadn't permitted to enter my consciousness. Sometimes reading makes something clear to me. I'm reading Dostoyevsky, say, and I read a thought, and I say, 'I know that thought; that thought is already in me and he just uncovered it.'

I can think of no more important endeavor than reading. To be a little dramatic, it's saved my life in many ways.

5

Keitel returned to Brooklyn from the Marines in 1959, facing an uncertain future. He had no discernible job skills but now was equipped with a high-school equivalency diploma and an honorable discharge.

For a while, he tried living at home. Pressured by his parents, he began working for them at an Atlantic Beach concession stand they now ran. But, after the relative freedom of the Marines, after being on his own for three years, the confines of the old apartment and the close quarters of working at the concession stand quickly began to chafe.

He hooked up with an old friend from the neighborhood, Mark Reiner, and the two of them found an apartment in Brooklyn. After a brief employment search, Keitel took a job on 34th Street in Manhattan, selling shoes. But he didn't like the work; given his shyness, he found it excruciating to put on the phony salesman's smile and try to sell people shoes. The monotony and mundanity rapidly drove him wild. 'I thought I did not want to be what I was,' he recalled.

Yet what else was there for him to do? He had no training in anything other than carrying a rifle and, now, measuring and trying shoes on people.

Then someone from the neighborhood suggested court reporting. It was well-paid, steady work that offered variety on a daily basis, but without the need to interact with anyone. All you had to do was listen and transcribe to the stenotype machine. Keitel saved money from being a shoe dog and enrolled on a course to learn to be a court stenographer. 'To learn it is easy,' he said. 'To get your speed up is difficult. I was good.'

He landed a job in Manhattan Criminal Court, an imposingly tomblike building at 100 Center Street, near City Hall. It suddenly offered him a chance to be invisible.

To Keitel, a young man still unsure of how and where he should fit into the life that swirled around him, the job promised a particularly clever way to elude the world while seemingly being a part of it. Working as a court reporter meant being present without ever being called upon to participate, except in the most passive way possible: listening and transcribing.

'It's solitary,' Keitel said. 'Something about the aloneness of it attracted me. You're silent all day. It seemed to appeal to me because I didn't have to talk. I was just looking to be left alone, really. I could just be quiet and type. Even now, I have this fantasy when I pass office buildings at night or banks and see a solitary worker in there. I feel it's a job I might like to have.'

Sometimes, the job provided unexpected reunions with faces from the past. One day, during a massive arraignment of drug defendants (mostly for heroin), Keitel looked up from the flow of transcribing and recognized one of those charged with a crime. He knew the young black man from Marine basic training. They'd been friends, part of a group of friends. It had been Keitel's introduction to the state of American racial relations, hanging out with a black Marine in the South Carolina of the mid 1950s. They would travel around off-base together, where Keitel saw, for the first time, public facilities marked "WHITE ONLY". He was incredulous when, accompanying his friend into a "BLACK ONLY" coffee shop, he was told that he wasn't allowed in. As he put it, 'We laughed, because we were from Brooklyn and we didn't know what the hell all of this was.'

And now his fellow Leatherneck and he connected again

under these circumstances: 'Here's this guy, years later, busted on a drug rap. We just looked at each other and he smiled and shook his head, as if to say, "Wow, this is what you're doing." I couldn't talk to him because I was up there working. Then they took him to the holding pen. On the break, I went back to see him but he was gone. Gone.'

The job held its satisfaction for a while – until about year three, out of what would prove to be an eight-year career.

After the confusion of adolescence and the strictly organized Marine lifestyle, he'd thrown himself into a job in which he sat as a silent spectator to other people's misfortunes, whether the crime was committed by them or against them. He could never comment on the misery and venality he saw, never offer an interpretation or connect it to the larger picture. As he'd continued to read and work, he could feel a need to express the increasingly powerful feelings he had no place to sublimate or exorcise. Hiding in his job no longer offered the kind of solitary satisfaction it once did, a feeling that lasted 'only a short time, a couple of years, before I felt the need to speak.'

Even though he had attained civil-service tenure as a court stenographer – giving him, essentially, lifetime job security – Keitel grew so unhappy at how bad things were that he found himself standing in front of a local Marine recruiting center, poised to re-enlist.

Here was the answer to his dilemma. It wouldn't be like he was quitting a new job but returning to an old one, one he already knew and was comfortable with.

Suddenly he also remembered clearly the tedium of drilling and working at the base all day, when there was nothing else to do but clean and reclean every inch of a barracks, of the rank and the routine and the rigidity.

And he turned round and walked away.

6

Then, one day in 1962, one of his colleagues in the court-reporter pool – of all unlikely sources – offered Keitel an invitation he didn't know he'd been waiting for.

A co-worker asked if he wanted to take acting classes, just as a kick, as something to do in their spare time. The idea, though it had occurred to Keitel, had been squashed and banished, like all the other inappropriate ideas he'd managed to squeeze away into his subconscious. In fact, the friend had to talk him into it.

Keitel didn't believe he fit the picture of an actor. He was self-conscious about his lack of a college education and worried that he might not be smart enough, that he lacked the polish to make himself believable as an actor: 'I had it drilled into my head that a guy like me couldn't be an actor. Someone who came from a lower-middle-class family, who wasn't well-educated, well, this wasn't something they could do.'

He finally agreed to attend the class, though he was nervous that his friends in Brooklyn might find out he was taking it. They might surmise that he harbored secret dreams of being an actor which, when he was honest with himself, was in fact true. He did want to be an actor.

Until he went to his first acting class, he never knew just how much. Keitel stayed; the friend who invited him went back to the world of court stenography.

So, for that matter, did Keitel. It took him several more years

– court reporter by day, actor by night – before he finally gave up court reporting for good.

He knew he'd found something he wanted for himself: 'I was attracted to these people who were creating stories and telling them,' he said. 'A powerful dynamic was going on that I didn't know anything about. I had never even seen a play. There was something about acting that put me in touch with forces that I felt aligned to and were important to me to know, to own. It gave me hope that I could become a member of a group of people who know themselves, people like Dean, Brando, Kazan.'

Suddenly here was something that seemed to tap directly into his need to express himself, to externalize feelings that he had no outlet for. He no longer had to sit silently in court, transcribing pain and unhappiness without being able to work it out in another way:

> The reason I became an actor was to get closer to the mystery of understanding myself. Acting lessons filled a need; I had no idea of anything except a need. A need to do it. I was stiff and rigid; I had great doubts that I could do this. But the need was there. I wanted to be an actor out of a whole desire to get the inside out, to express myself.
>
> When my friends would call me 'Hollywood,' I'd laugh along with them because I didn't want to reveal how much I liked it and wanted it and feared that I wouldn't be good enough for it.

Granted, up to that point, Keitel had never set foot in a theater to see a play. But he had studied the acting of Brando, Dean, Cassavetes and others at the movies. If he'd never seen live stagecraft, he had seen Kazan's *A Streetcar Named Desire* – and *East of Eden* and *On the Waterfront*. They all made an impression, shaping the kind of actor Keitel wanted to be. He knew there were untapped, volcanic emotions inside him, feelings that had been stored away for years, just waiting for the moment to make themselves useful – or to drive him crazy. Acting was a way to go a little crazy without ever straying outside of society's boundaries of acceptable behavior.

He began taking classes with Frank Corsaro and studying at the Actors Studio (though he wouldn't pass his audition for membership until after he made *Mean Streets*, almost a decade later). As a novice actor in this Mecca of serious method acting, as someone who was unsure of his ability to measure up before the gurus of the acting craft, Keitel approached each class with determination, willing himself to overcome his fears as he attempted to *be*, rather than to act, in his scenework for Corsaro:

> I was petrified. I didn't get up on the stage for months. Later, I used to stand outside the Actors Stage on East Fourth Street before I had to do a scene. And I used to tell myself, 'Now all I'm trying to do is get what I feel here, on the street, in through that door, walk up the stairs and go on the stage and do it, as real as I am here.' That was my preparation: Go out on the street and try to bring this human being in from the street on to the stage. Well, it wasn't easy. I realized this was going to take time and patience, which I didn't have much of.
>
> It was a struggle. It was the same with my reading. I had the desire to learn, but I didn't have the patience. I remember reading, 'The reward of patience is patience.' I wanted to tear that page up, because I didn't have the patience to even contemplate those words. I was in a hurry to run away from the suffering that was required to sit still. I was lucky to meet a teacher like Frank Corsaro, because he was such a nurturing man; he nurtured what I had to offer.

Gradually, he began auditioning and finding work, in tiny off-off-Broadway venues. He read the show-business dailies, working as many auditions as he could into and around his work schedule. 'Acting was remote to me and to my upbringing, my environment in Brooklyn,' he said. 'It was something I came to very slowly and very painstakingly, with great uncertainty and fear.'

For one thing, there didn't seem to be any money in it. As he started being cast in small roles in one-acts at Café LaMama and Café Cino, places where the off-off-Broadway theatrical revolution of the 1960s was taking place, he still had to work full-time to pay for the rest of his life. You simply couldn't make a living as an actor by working on the off- and off-off-Broadway stages.

According to actor and teacher Allen Garfield, a friend from those scuffling days of the 1960s who appeared with him in two films, 'It was a gritty, very self-sacrificing time because none of us had too many bucks financially. How much did you get paid if you did an off-off-Broadway play? Zero. It would cost you money because of car fare and food. But it was our training ground. You'd have fifty plays happening at the same time. You were being seen while you were emerging.'

Keitel made his official debut in summer stock in Nantucket, where he apprenticed and appeared in Edward Albee's *The American Dream*: 'I was doing everything from acting to cleaning toilets – in other words, I hadn't gotten paid. I acted in places that didn't even have a name. A lot of them didn't even have a ceiling.'

Summer stock was an American theatrical tradition. They were small theaters, usually in resort towns up and down America's East Coast, which paid scale and sometimes provided barracks or summer-camp-like lodgings for its actors. In return for a summer of work – doing mostly light comedy, musical comedy or melodrama, with a new show opening virtually every week or every other week – the actors often pulled double and triple duty, as Keitel did: building and painting the scenery, cleaning the theater, taking care of their own costumes and make-up.

But there was also a romance to it: working in the theater, living in a resort town. Here was Keitel, actually being paid to be an actor. Not much, to be sure, but enough to live on. And he was in close proximity to young women, also caught up in the romance of the experience, as well as the headiness of summer. According to friends of the time, Keitel cut a wide swath.

Returning to New York, he opened off-Broadway, at the Cherry Lane Theater in Sam Shepard's *Up to Thursday*, in February 1965. He also developed a fascination with and appreciation for the films of John Cassavetes, whose raw, improvised style and independent spirit attracted him. He'd been particularly struck by the blunt, cinema-vérité quality of Cassavetes' film *Shadows* and by a scene in the film in which one member of a group of friends has the self-confidence to admit that he likes abstract sculpture, to say that 'It is whatever it is to you. And that to me is art.'

'I know what that scene was about, because I was the kind of guy afraid to venture an opinion,' Keitel said. 'From lack of self-worth. But after that I had to know what this was all about. One little comment like that in a Cassavetes movie opened an avenue of thinking to me that was closed before.' Cassavetes was 'a guy who sustained me for a long time – not personally, but his work did. I used to look forward to his work. He influenced us all. He inspired me and moved me a great deal into wanting to be an actor.'

Steve Brenner, a friend from that period (whose father would distribute Keitel's first film), recalled running into Keitel one Saturday night in late 1968, at a place called the Third Avenue El on East 59th Street in New York. Brenner and his date began telling Keitel and his date about an awful movie they'd just seen. Keitel was almost equally vociferous in praising the film he had just come from. It turned out they had both seen the same film: Cassavetes' *Faces*.

Keitel finally met the director a number of years later when he was invited to accompany Martin Scorsese to visit Cassavetes at his home in Los Angeles, after *Mean Streets*. Cassavetes regaled them with descriptions of scenes from *Minnie and Moskowitz*, a film he'd made a couple of years earlier starring his wife, Gena Rowlands, and Seymour Cassel. 'He was laughing hysterically,' Keitel remembered. 'My cheeks were hurting me because I was so nervous, I was trying to smile because he was laughing so much. I could not laugh for the life of me.'

As Keitel continued to pursue roles and take classes, he found a theater community in Greenwich Village that was vital, providing fertile ground for the burgeoning off- and off-off-Broadway scenes that had exploded a few years earlier. Keitel would make the rounds of auditions, while taking classes at the Actors Studio. When he wasn't working or acting, he was talking about acting with other actors.

Yaphet Kotto, Keitel's co-star in *Blue Collar*, recalled, 'I used to pass him in the street in lower Manhattan when we were all struggling to be somebody. He and James Earl Jones had a working-actor reputation.'

'We would all talk about our dreams,' Garfield remembered, 'and about how much acting meant to us. The sixties were a lively, intense time. I remember walking the streets late, talking about theater. We had no thought of doing film or leaving New York. It was a real, exciting, passionate time in the off-off-Broadway movement. It was the most thrilling time to be an actor.'

7

Meeting Martin Scorsese was like encountering a soulmate Keitel knew and understood instantly, though they'd never met and shared different ethnic backgrounds. The chemistry was instantaneous and, seemingly, lifelong. They would make five films together over the next twenty years and their names would forever be associated with each other. According to Keitel:

> When Marty and I met, it was like two comrades meeting on the way somewhere. I asked him where he was going and we discovered we were trying to get to the same place, so we held hands and got scared and walked along together. Marty and I discovered when we met and became friends that we shared a very similar life. It didn't matter that I was raised Jewish and that Marty was raised Catholic – our place was beyond local religion.
>
> I think it's no different than when a man sees a woman or a woman sees a man and all of a sudden you're taken by that person. You sense something. Then no matter what happens in the years that follow, you remain family forever, because you're bound by some inexplicable things that no action can destroy.

Scorsese, small, asthmatic and hyperactive, saw a surprising doppelgänger in the bristling young ex-Marine from Brooklyn: 'I found him to be very much like me, even though he is a Polish Jew from Brooklyn. We became friends and found we had the same feelings about the same problems. Both our families expected us to achieve some sort of respectability.'

The meeting took place one day late in 1965. While reading the casting notices in the trade papers – *Backstage*, *Show Business* – Keitel came across an ad seeking actors for a student film at New York University. Assuming that any film experience would look good on his still woefully brief acting résumé, Keitel turned up for the casting call.

The director was a fast-talking young Italian-American, short on stature but in all other ways indefatigable. Scorsese, then a film graduate student at NYU, had put together funding to make a student film, which would eventually grow into his first feature release, *Who's That Knocking at My Door?* He asked Keitel back to read for the role a second time, then called him back a third time, before finally casting him as the lead in his film.

The role, J.R., was an alter-ego for Scorsese: a young man in Little Italy trying to find direction in his life, even as he kindles a romance with a young woman he meets (known only as 'the Girl' and played by Zina Bethune) by earnestly explaining his love of John Wayne. They become romantically involved, but he cannot bring himself to have sex with her. When she confides to him that she had, a short time earlier, been the victim of date rape, he is disgusted. To J.R., the fact that she's not a virgin makes her unacceptable; he must wrestle with his confused and conflicting feelings about her and about women in general.

It was like tumblers clicking into place in a safe: the combination of the passionate young director with a highly personal film vision, the passionate young actor looking for the key to an acting career – and a passionate time, when movies and acting had suddenly become a vehicle through which one could comment on society as a whole. For Keitel, mightily frustrated by the limitations of court stenography, the chance to make a movie seemed like his ticket to the big-time. 'He was working with some friends on a student film and it was the most glorious thing to him,' Garfield recalled. 'Harvey was on top of the world because of being in a film and working with a young director that he was so excited about.'

In the film Keitel looks so impossibly boyish, so positively Christian Slater-like, that it's easy to forget he was almost thirty when he made it. Although one can see the dark, brooding Keitel of the future lurking beneath the surface, this is still a relatively happy-go-lucky Harvey in the early scenes: easy to laugh, easy to joke, just plain easy to be, still unaware of or unable to tap into the inner torment that would mark so many of his roles. His anguish at finding out that the Girl is not a virgin is painfully self-centered: How could she do this to him? Keitel brings brilliant opaqueness to the film's key moment, when he decides he can live with her past and tells her so by saying, 'I forgive you and am willing to marry you anyway.'

This precursor to *Mean Streets* has Keitel playing J.R. like the younger, more callow brother of Charlie Cappa: coping with feelings he can't quite express or understand even while trying to ignore them. He doesn't have as much on his mind as Charlie but he's similarly confused and willing to exist in a state of denial. The film also contains Keitel's first nude scene, though without frontal nudity on his part.

For Keitel, part of the pleasure lay in his ability to plug in so completely, almost automatically, to Scorsese's vision:

It was right there when we met: a recognition of a sameness of purpose, of a need to discover and explore what's meaningful to us and hopefully to become better men. I was asking myself the same questions he was: What is courage? What is fear? The ultimate fear is of being adrift, abandoned and not being able to cope with it. One's ability to cope with these darker elements will determine the heights one will reach.

The heights for *Who's That Knocking . . . ?* included frequent trips to the depths as well, as funding for the film came and went. Everyone had other jobs, so shooting was done on weekends. Even then, given weather, schedule conflicts and the ebb and flow of funding, momentum was hard to build. 'Harvey was very upset because he was working as a court stenographer and we were wasting his time,' Scorsese recalled. 'He kept having his hair cut at inappropriate times, so the scenes we shot never matched. I would say, "Harvey, how can you do this?" and back came the answer, "But I have a life, too." '

According to Zina Bethune, 'The story was supposed to take place over the space of three weeks. But Harvey looks different throughout the film. He laughed about the fact that he looked like he had aged quite a bit during the course of the film.'

Bethune, who was nineteen at the time, had been working as an actress since childhood, most successfully on the TV series *The Nurses* when she was fourteen. Her agent, Harry Ufland, who was at William Morris and had just begun to represent Scorsese (and who would later represent both Keitel and Robert De Niro), persuaded her to take the role in the up-and-coming director's film.

She met Keitel at a screen test and found him a little shy. As she got to know him, however, she said, 'He struck me as a very sweet individual, a very dear person. That always amused me because most of the characters he's played are anything but sweet. He has an interesting edge on camera that's anything but sweet.'

The film was shot during the frigid 1966 winter: 'I remember we started shooting in January or February,' Bethune said. 'It was bitter cold and there was a lot of outdoor shooting. I don't ever remember being warm.'

Scorsese had written the script as the second in a trilogy of films about young Italian-American men (the first, a script called *Jerusalem, Jerusalem*, was never made; the finale, a script

Scorsese called *Season of the Witch*, was later rewritten and retitled *Mean Streets*). But this script was sketchy, full of ideas for scenes with suggestions, but in which improvised dialogue was encouraged. As Bethune recalled,

> I kept asking Harvey, 'What do you think this will mean? How do you think this will finally play out?' A lot of times he didn't really answer and I'd have to wait and see how it evolved. A lot of Martin's direction is through the lens and in the editing room. He creates an environment and lets it evolve and Harvey seemed more used to that. He was always very willing to try whatever Marty wanted. I couldn't tell what he felt about that.
>
> Harvey had a kind of unsureness that worked for the character. The character is totally unsure and not able to come to terms with anything because everything doesn't fit in his puzzle, which is what the character is about. Harvey had those qualities sitting right on him.
>
> That whole first scene, with the discussion of the magazine and John Wayne, was totally improvised. There was no script. Martin created an environment and a scenario and wanted it to evolve. Harvey seemed to go with that mode and never questioned it. After a while, I started understanding how they devised the scenes and let the art happen. It was exciting but unnerving.

Scorsese was excited to have found in Keitel an actor who was willing to go for it, to reach for the kind of emotions few actors are capable of: 'Harvey travels into very forbidding regions of his soul for his work and he's able to have the experience and put it on the screen in an absolutely genuine way I find very touching,' he said.

Keitel's connection with Scorsese made him believe in the scrappy young director: 'I always knew *Who's That Knocking . . . ?* would get done. I vividly recall sitting down together to watch a scene that had been cut. It was inside the church, when the title song is played and I was aware of being in the midst of some extraordinary experience. I was deeply stirred by a whole cacophony of emotions and I felt I was in the right place. I knew that I was with somebody special.'

According to Scorsese, 'What struck me about Harvey was his tremendous passion and that's the quality that's carried me through with him on each of the five films we've done together. He pays scrupulous attention to the smallest detail of a role and is always intensely supportive of the project as a whole.'

Between the pauses in filming and the extended process of editing and then selling the film, it was 1968 before *Who's That Knocking at My Door?* saw the light of day at the Carnegie Cinema, after drawing a strong review from Roger Ebert of the *Chicago Sun-Times* when it was shown at the Chicago Film Festival.

Scorsese had found Joseph Brenner, a distributor of skin films, through his mentor Haig Manoogian, who was a friend of Brenner's from their Army days. Brenner had agreed to distribute the film on one condition: Scorsese had to insert a nude scene. Scorsese, who was working in Amsterdam when Brenner's offer came through, flew Keitel over and shot a dream sequence involving J.R. and several fantasy girls, with whom he is having sex. Brenner booked the Carnegie Cinema.

The opening at the Carnegie was delayed by the extended run of *The World of Laurel and Hardy*, recalled Steve Brenner, who worked for his father and was a friend of Keitel's. And, unexpectedly, *Laurel and Hardy* was doing enough business to keep extending the run. When the film finally did open, Keitel, Scorsese and Steve Brenner were out on the street, distributing handbills.

The audience, however, was small for this gritty black-and-white story of a confused young man in New York: 'It was not that successful,' Bethune remembered. 'It played arthouses but didn't go a heckuva lot further. Now it's this cult classic that's on cable all the time.'

Brenner said, 'Harvey was excited. We were all excited when it opened. But we were disappointed because we expected a lot more than it delivered. It had good runs in certain parts of the country. But when you're not Warner Bros. without all that money behind you, you have to take pictures and release them independently.'

Which left Keitel exactly where he had started: as an actor forced to support his art by working as a court stenographer. But he felt compelled to make a choice once and for all, to follow acting as the journey he wanted to commit his life to. 'Being a stenographer was something he really didn't talk about,' Bethune recalled. 'He'd just say, "Yeah, well, that's what I'm doing right now."'

He'd already taken some steps toward creating this new life. Rufus Collins, a black actor with whom he had studied, had told him, 'Harvey, you'll never be an actor unless you leave Brooklyn.' So he'd moved into a Greenwich Village apartment on Bedford Street, which he later traded for a tiny apartment in Hell's Kitchen.

But Keitel still needed to make the separation from the courtroom job, which had become both a lifejacket and an anchor in his life. 'It took me five years to really commit myself to be an actor,' he said. 'It was a little bit of a joke to the guys on the block and it really took me a long time before I said, "Well, the hell with all of them and what they say. I'm going to do it." And that's when I quit my job and went to summer stock.'

8

Even though Keitel had resigned from his civil-service job, he found he still had to take on free-lance court-reporting jobs to pay the rent and put food on the table. For a time he took assignments from the Doyle Reporting Co., transcribing depositions while barely containing his impatience with the job.

'He appeared to be one of those stage actors who was never going to make it,' recalled attorney Stuart Cotton, who was a young associate at a law firm where Keitel was occasionally assigned. 'During cigarette breaks, he'd talk about how he was pursuing acting and was being a court reporter to make money.'

Arthur Brook, an associate at the same firm, remembered, 'He would say, "I'm an actor, I'm doing movies," and we'd figure, "Yeah, right." It's like every waiter and waitress in New York is actually an actor. When he worked as a court reporter, he was very good. But it was obvious he didn't enjoy what he was doing. He was always very dour.'

An old girlfriend, Gina Richer, put it more succinctly in remembering Keitel's on-going frustration about not being able to put court stenography in his past: 'Who would have thought he'd actually make it as an actor? He was working as a court stenographer and living in this tiny apartment in Hell's Kitchen,' she said. 'This was a man with a lot of rage.'

Yet he did manage to find work as an actor on an increasingly regular basis, working summer stock, finding extra work in films. He recalled landing a spot among hundreds of extras playing a soldier in John Huston's overwrought adaptation of

Carson McCullers's sexually ambiguous *Reflections in a Golden Eye*, which starred one of his idols, Marlon Brando. He even worked up the nerve to approach the bewildered star and tell him he was about to have his audition for the Actors Studio, to which Brando could only say, 'Hmm,' and shake his hand.

He also began working at regional theaters on the East Coast. Though he was nearing thirty, he was frequently cast in juvenile roles, playing the son in Frank Gilroy's volatile family drama, *The Subject Was Roses*, at the Pittsburgh Playhouse in January 1968, and one of the menacing teenagers in Israel Horovitz's *The Indian Wants the Bronx* at the Long Wharf Theater in New Haven, Conn., as he was about to turn thirty.

For Arvin Brown, who directed the Long Wharf production, Keitel brought menace to the stage, but also innocence, playing a dangerous young hoodlum who, together with a friend, threatens the life of a lost tourist from India who is trying to use a pay phone:

> I had seen it with Al Pacino and it was really quite different with Harvey. Harvey had a lot of the same street quality that Al had, but there was a slightly more ingenuous quality. Al registered street cunning. But for all the repressed violence about his portrayal, there was an innocence in Harvey. As I've watched Harvey over the years, that's the one quality that's remained a constant. There's an ingenuousness, no matter how decadent, how violent, how disturbing the world he moves in.

Keitel, Brown found, was very open and still inexperienced, eager for direction. And he was willing to try anything, a trait that would become a trademark. He was an actor in the midst of learning his craft – and of learning the importance of the craft itself. Always an intense presence onstage, he tended to depend on that innate electricity, according to Brown: 'Back then, he relied on a tremendous natural energy. But he was definitely a driven actor.'

He may have had presence, but he had still not developed his voice for the stage: 'One of the acting problems he had to combat at the start was that he was limited vocally,' Brown said. 'His voice did not have tremendous range or power. That's why film was a great medium for him from the beginning. By the time I saw him in *Hurlyburly* [in 1984], his voice was much more flexible and assured.'

Zina Bethune remembered that, during the filming of *Who's That Knocking at My Door?*, Keitel seemed to be 'in a stage of evolving. I got the sense he was searching for what kind of actor he was, searching for an identity.'

For a long time, though he loved the sense of emotional freedom and expression acting gave him, he tried to convince himself that it was merely a seemingly easy route to riches and fame. He would tell his friend Rufus Collins, 'I just want to be an actor to make money. That's my only interest: to make money.'

To which Collins would reply, 'You're not telling the truth, Harvey.'

Which, of course, he wasn't. If anything, the opposite was true: here was the thing he'd been seeking all his life, an art into which he could pour all the feelings he had struggled for years to hold in check. If he could convince himself that he was just doing it to make a living, he wouldn't have to face the fact that it was the most important thing in the world to him. And that, so far, he wasn't making much of a dent as an actor. Yes, he was working semi-regularly. But he worried endlessly to his friends and numerous girlfriends over every part he didn't get, agonizing over whether he really did have talent. Had he made a colossal mistake? Was he exposing his most secret self merely to be humiliated?

The apparent proof that he had chosen the wrong direction

slapped him in the face every time he had to accept a part-time job as a court reporter. Every time he sat down at a deposition to transcribe the proceedings, he was plunged back into the world of uncertainty: If he was an actor, why was he here? Why couldn't he support himself with his art? Would he ever be able to escape permanently, out of this drudgery and into the realm where his thoughts and emotions could guide and shape him? Too many days, it seemed as if that would never come, that he had foolishly dreamed and hoped for something that could never be his; that, like Icarus, his wings had melted because he'd dared to fly too close to the sun and would forever be plunged into the dreariness of life that had all but consumed his father.

But he began to feel that all the risks he had taken had been worthwhile when he began studying at the Actors Studio with Lee Strasberg and Ernie Martin, who taught for Strasberg. Working with Strasberg opened his eyes to what acting could be about if you thought about it and applied yourself. According to actor Ron Silver, who shared the Strasberg classes with Keitel:

> When Strasberg taught, what he was saying always seemed so simple. Like you almost didn't know whether to take him at his word. At the same time, he could be very abstract. He'd say, 'Just be, just exist for a minute. Just have a real moment.'
>
> Some pupils took what he said to an extreme. He was never one for indulgence, never one to dispute a director's authority. He was never someone who would insist on substituting his own truth for the character for the playwright's truth. At the same time, you also had to have respect for the actor as the author of the authenticity of the line.

The bulk of the teaching focused on sensory work as it applied to doing scenes. The idea was to work on each of the five senses, to teach the actor to expand on his imagination – to be personal in the work by drawing upon his own experiences to revisit emotions comparable to ones being felt by the character. The emotions, Keitel was taught, were already there; now he had to learn to free them when he did the scene.

It wasn't the same as planning what to do in the scene; rather, the actor unleashed the emotions and applied them to this character. Keitel was taught to create an imaginary life for the character; the scene was a moment out of that life that was happening now, spontaneously and freely.

Keitel, already consumed by the love of acting, immersed himself in this new way of thinking, discussing it in class and outside, with whomever he could get to talk about it. Martin remembered about his former student:

> There's always been passion for the work. His choices were always big choices. He works to be in the moment and he doesn't allow other things to interfere with the creative process. He's always discussing the work, wanting to understand more of it.
>
> In the past twenty-five years, I've seen a lot of people go for results, rather than the work, and you can make good money doing that. There are a few, however, who truly, truly have the passion and the love to work and rehearse, who love to go through the process. Some people want to get there as soon as possible. Harvey is one of those people who love the process.

The process: that method by which an actor discovers, develops and comes to embody a character. To Keitel, it became a meticulous regimen involving the various kinds of rehearsal exercises he'd learned, finding a physical key to the person as well as an interior emotional design: 'This is my way of working, but it's not as if I made it up myself. It's part of the way acting is taught now in New York, based on the Stanislavski system. It's part of the teachings to "fill the part".'

Doing the homework, for Keitel, means analyzing the script and extrapolating an entire life for that character, a framework in which to set his actions in the script:

Stella Adler, who's a great teacher, remarked that the analysis of the text is the education of the actor. So you get the script and you dig into it, to discover where the character is coming from, where his background is, what he does, what his desires are, what his fears are, how he lives – analyzing what the author had in mind.

I must know what his mother and father were like together, what his childhood and home life were like. I have to know if he didn't go to college, or only stayed one year, or graduated. I have to know what his views are about many different things: the actor creates the character's past. Before you shoot, you have rehearsals, where you find out what the other actors are going to do, what works best. Once the cameras roll, there's always that little something that is improvisational, spontaneous.

For him, it became part of the spiritual framework of his life: 'Acting is religious,' he said. 'Great acting can be worshipped because it descends into the subconscious, into the soul. And somewhere in there must be God.'

Yet, as much as he loved the work he was doing at the Actors Studio, Keitel remained frustrated in one major pursuit: membership of the prestigious organization, something that could be attained only by auditioning for and being selected by a rigorous membership committee. You were allowed to audition only once a year. But each year from the mid 1960s on, Keitel would find himself passed over for new membership: 'I kept failing. I was so humiliated, so miserable that I couldn't get in.

It had tradition – something was being passed on. There was a standard that was aspired to.'

Keitel persevered, another quality that would serve him well in the career to come. Finally, in 1974, after he had appeared in *Mean Streets*, he was accepted as a member of the Actors Studio in his eighth year of auditioning. One of the Studio stalwarts told him later that she'd threatened the committee, saying, 'Either let him in this time or I'm telling him not to audition again. Don't put him through this anymore.'

'It was a great day for me,' Keitel said. 'I felt I'd accomplished something I'd always dreamed of.'

In the spring of 1970, anti-war protests on American college campuses resulted in the killings of four Kent State University students by overzealous Ohio National Guardsmen. The event upset Keitel; when he phoned Scorsese, he learned that anti-war forces were taking over the film department at NYU and making short films to be shown on college campuses around the country. So Keitel helped out and even appeared in *Street Scenes*, the documentary shot that spring during the height of anti-war sentiment. 'I see the movie we did as more than entertainment,' Keitel said. 'I resolved then to try to choose roles that have social meaning.'

By the end of 1970 Scorsese, on the strength of his work as assistant director and editor on the movie *Woodstock*, had moved to Los Angeles to try to edit Warner Bros.' mess of a rock-concert film, *The Medicine Ball Caravan*. Eventually, Keitel followed him out there and lived with him for a while as he looked for work. But the pickings were slim, both in terms of work and women: 'No one would go out with either of them,' observed one friend from the period, 'because the women thought they were a couple of losers.' By the beginning of 1972

Keitel had moved back to New York, convinced he was going to have to go back to court reporting.

Keitel could barely contain his frustration. Acting had been a kind of salvation, one that lifted him spiritually even as it challenged and nourished him intellectually. But he was getting absolutely no encouragement; he seemed unable to put two paying jobs back to back. The movie he had made had gone nowhere and done nothing for him; nor had he been paid for it.

Then Scorsese called with the news that he had the money and the backing of Warner Bros. to make a movie and would Keitel be interested in playing the lead?

9

Most people chart Harvey Keitel's career from the release of *Mean Streets* in October 1973. In fact, by the time it was released, he'd been acting for more than a decade. He was thirty-four years old.

As Charlie Cappa, a would-be wiseguy, he was playing someone years younger than he was. The confused young man was supposed to be 'the Graduate,' Mulberry Street-division: a young man about to begin in life, torn between conflicting demands for loyalty, torn by feelings of religion-driven guilt on all fronts.

Keitel looked the part of the feral young climber trying to advance within the crime family, even as he tortured himself with guilt about the morality of what he was doing. The interior life, however, came from the additional years of experience Keitel brought to the role. He understood Charlie so well because he had already lived the life Charlie was struggling with: trying to balance the pull of family expectations with dreams of his own liberation, clambering to gain a foothold in a profession that offered the cold face of rejection significantly more often than one of warm acceptance.

'Perhaps I got the part of Charlie because Marty sensed that I came from a similar background,' Keitel ventured. 'I was new, I was raw, I hadn't much experience. I don't think it was my experience at acting that landed me that work, but the experience Marty saw in me. Our neighborhoods said to a young man, "You have a place and you will not go beyond this place because you do not belong anywhere beyond this place." Marty and I rebelled against it.'

Scorsese maintained, 'Nobody was better suited for his part and nobody could have played it better, with more honesty, power and sweetness.'

Except that he almost gave it to someone else.

Consider Charlie Cappa: a young Italian-American in Little Italy. Sharp dresser and aspiring operator. Still a deep believer in the powers of God and the devil, as set out by the Catholic Church. Unable to reconcile that with the criminal life he is positioning himself for, running a restaurant for his uncle, a Mob capo. Troubled by his uncle's demand that he stop spending time with his crazy friend Johnny Boy, equally troubled by Johnny Boy's penchant for wild behavior that invariably gets him into trouble.

Now imagine the clean-cut, all-American WASP Jon Voight playing the part. 'Marty approached Jon about playing Charlie in *Mean Streets*, with Harvey as Johnny Boy,' remembered actor Richard Romanus, who played Michael. Coming off Oscar nominations for both *Midnight Cowboy* and *Deliverance*, Voight was a star. And he was interested in this story of sin and redemption set against the criminal backdrop. To get his film made, Scorsese was willing to swallow hard and cast him.

Then Voight decided to do something else (*Conrack*) shortly before Scorsese was supposed to start production. Scorsese was in New York to take advantage of the scant two or three days of location shooting in Little Italy that was budgeted for the production. He thought of Keitel and decided that, as he had done in *Who's That Knocking at My Door?*, Keitel would serve as his alter ego in *Mean Streets*. He called Keitel and filmed him walking through the conveniently timed San Gennaro Festival in Little Italy, footage that went into the film.

Even as Scorsese began rehearsing Keitel with de Niro, the

casting question remained somewhat up in the air – because de Niro wasn't sure he wanted to play Johnny Boy.

De Niro had appeared in more than a half-dozen films at that point, including a trio of Brian de Palma's early efforts (among them *Hi Mom!* and *Greetings*, both of which also starred Allen Garfield), as well as working with Shelley Winters in Roger Corman's *Bloody Mama*. He'd just completed a supporting part as a doomed catcher in *Bang the Drum Slowly* – and now he wasn't sure he should be playing a supporting role again. 'I ran into Harvey on the street and he was going to play Charlie,' he remembered. 'I told him I thought maybe at this stage of my career, I should hold out for something else. I felt the logical part for me was Harvey's part, but he already had it. But I wanted to work with Marty.'

In de Niro, Keitel saw a compatriot, a fellow actor who relished the process of discovering the characters in the same way he did: 'We looked at each other and we just laughed,' Keitel recalled. 'That was it, we just kept laughing. Looking back I see that we recognized each other. I knew he was a great actor.'

Finally Keitel hit on a solution: he would switch roles with de Niro. De Niro could have the lead, the central role of Charlie Cappa. Keitel would play the supporting part of the volatile Johnny Boy. But Scorsese put his foot down: the casting would stand as it was.

Later, Keitel would say to de Niro, 'I can see you doing Johnny Boy.' To de Niro, it was the nudge he needed for the role that would launch his career: 'I hadn't thought of playing him at all,' he admitted. 'But Harvey somehow made me see it in another way. I couldn't see Johnny Boy at first, but in a way, it was a good thing. When you play a role you don't see yourself doing at first, you can get things from yourself that you ordinarily wouldn't get.'

The role of Charlie was the film's anchor. The entire movie

is his story: his wrestling with the disparate forces trying to dominate his life. He is the film's eyes, its heart, its conscience. Scorsese was being autobiographical in examining the questions that dominated in his life – and Keitel was the actor who understood exactly what Scorsese was talking about. The two of them shared an interest in the big questions: God, faith, redemption, what makes a man good in relation to other people and to God. They would hash it over and over: How should you act in a certain situation? Was there such a thing as situational ethics?

They talked about their families, with Keitel, the baby of his family, discussing family pressures with Scorsese, the babied only child. Expectations on both had been great; each, in his own way, had turned his back on those expectations.

And they debated religion: Keitel, the guilt-ridden Jew who once spat on the mezuzah; Scorsese, the guilt-ridden Catholic who had once entertained ideas of being a priest. 'We are both very religious people and we have experienced the same conflicts with religion,' Keitel observed. 'He's Catholic, I'm Jewish but we both belong to the Church of Struggling to Do What's Right. It's a personal moral code rather than a formal religion.'

As Scorsese and Keitel saw it, Charlie was a modern urban saint, struggling to keep possession of his own soul, torn between decisions that will affect the rest of his life. 'Marty understands that sainthood isn't like the movies,' Keitel said. 'He was out to make a real story about a real saint, one who had fears, obstacles, doubts, who knew pain.'

In their discussions, Scorsese told Keitel a story about religious retreats he went on as a kid. The priests would discuss the idea of purification through pain, demonstrating this by holding their hands over candles. It was a gesture Keitel adopted as Charlie, constantly testing his resolve with candles and matches. 'It had to do with the idea of understanding the physical pain of hell,' Scorsese remembered. 'On religious retreats, this was a technique used by some of the priests who would give you a hell-and-damnation sermon. Harv went right with it.'

Keitel was still learning the craft of screen-acting, of building the character, then stepping into the reality of that moment of the character's life when the camera rolled. But as he studied the script and imagined Charlie's life (and found parallels in his own experience), he developed strong ideas about how Charlie should be at any given time. Scorsese, recognizing Keitel's commitment to the character, let him run with it.

'Marty and I always discussed a scene and, usually, he trusted me to do what I had in my mind to do,' Keitel recalled. 'Mine was a gut, root, raw experience of trying to express myself and express the character of Charlie, and trying to discover what it meant to express yourself in a character. I was learning my technique, learning how to apply it.'

Scorsese trusted Keitel to let the moment evolve, something they'd done together on *Who's That Knocking at My Door?* Now, working with de Niro, another Actors Studio member, the three of them found a groove that couldn't be shaken by the brevity of the shooting schedule or the smallness of the budget.

Though more scripted than *Who's That Knocking . . . ?*, *Mean Streets* offered opportunities for the actors to develop scenes for themselves. According to Scorsese,

Much of the improvisation in the film was taped at rehearsal and then scripted from those tapes. A few scenes, like the one in which de Niro and Keitel fight each other with garbage pails, were improvised during shooting. I remember that, at the end of one take, Bobby threw the thing at Harvey and Harvey threw it right back and I said, 'Great, we'll do that in the next take.'

In the scenes in the back room between de Niro and Keitel after they meet in the bar, I thought it would be fun to improvise and show more of the characters. We realized that we liked Abbott and Costello a great deal, their language routines with inverted word-meanings done with wonderful timing. We tried to keep as much of that as possible, although it had to be shot very quickly. And the result is so structured that if you only see that one scene, you know more about their way of life from it than from anything else in the film. We see the shifting of trust, how Johnny trusts Charlie but, God, he's got his problems; and Charlie trusts Johnny but he's using him. The scene was Bob's idea and since he and Harvey are not afraid to try things, I said, 'Why not?' When I shot it, it was about fifteen minutes long, hilarious and clarified everything totally. It's like the betrayal of trust, one character taking advantage of the other, that I enjoy in the Hope-and-Crosby movies.

David Proval, playing Tony, who owned the bar where Charlie and Johnny Boy hung out, was making his film debut, having been cast after Scorsese saw him at an actors' workshop with Voight. 'For me, it was a real experience to watch Marty and Bobby and Harvey just jamming,' he recalled. 'They were like jazz musicians up there. I remember thinking, "I'd love to be able to jump into this." And every once in a while I tried to jump in.'

The sparks that Keitel and de Niro were giving off on the set led Romanus and Proval to rethink their approach to their characters, in dealing with the hyperactive Johnny Boy and the fast-talking Charlie. Romanus remembered,

I chose to be laid-back with my character because Bobby and Harvey had a bristling energy I hadn't seen before. David Proval and I decided that since Harvey and Bobby had such energy, we should take the low-energy road so that we could be a contrast to them. Harvey is totally organic, fast on his feet. He's not the kind of guy you can sit down and discuss the part with. But between action and cut, he's like a broken-field runner. He's fast, he's very instinctive. And very solid – boy, you couldn't trip him up if you wanted to.

Proval found Keitel 'intense and demanding. It's few and far between, the actors with that level of commitment.'

That commitment had to do with the quality of the work as a whole, and not just his own performance. While filming Proval's biggest scene, in which Tony explains to Charlie why believing in the Catholic Church is a sucker bet, Proval was nervous and unsure. As they played the scene after a preliminary rehearsal, Keitel's attitude shifted – he began to shut Proval out, purposely turning away from him, instead of listening to what he had to say. Proval pushed a little harder at Keitel, giving the scene an added frisson of friction and life. That night, Keitel phoned Proval and told him how good he'd been. 'I was so grateful for that,' Proval recalled. 'He saw doing that was the only way to really get me into the scene. A lot of actors come on with a lot of social bullshit on the set. But Harvey was calling me to say how well he thought I'd done and it meant a lot to me.'

Mean Streets had its debut at the prestigious New York Film Festival in September 1973 before its opening in October. The film drew reviews that hailed Scorsese's emergence as a welcome and distinctive new voice, dealing with issues of morality and human frailty while re-imagining the gangster film. Keitel, in his major studio debut, received the kind of reviews most actors would kill for. With, perhaps, the exception of de Niro – who parlayed the flashier Johnny Boy role and a sensitive comic turn in *Bang the Drum Slowly* (as a slow-witted but lovable Southerner, a sort of proto-Forrest Gump) into a New York Film Critics Circle Award as the best supporting actor of 1973.

Newsweek's Paul D. Zimmerman called de Niro's Johnny

Boy 'beautifully realized in all his self-destructive flamboy-
ance.' Still, Pauline Kael observed in the *New Yorker*, 'Keitel
makes de Niro's triumph possible; Johnny Boy can bounce off
Charlie's anxious, furious admiration. Keitel, cramped in his
stiff clothes . . . looks like a more compact Richard Conte or
Dane Clark, and speaks in the rhythms of a lighter-voiced John
Garfield, Charlie's idol.'

Roger Ebert would later write, 'Keitel was an actor unlike
other leading men. He seemed vulnerable, needy and driven –
but in a fundamental way, not in a mannered way, like James
Dean. His character introduced the theme that would be central
to Scorsese's work and to Keitel's: guilt and its redemption.'

Keitel was gracious about de Niro's burgeoning movie career,
even as he himself had to hustle to land TV roles: 'When you
really love someone, and they have success, that love only
allows you to be happy for that person. Nothing else is permitted if the love is true. Would I have liked to have had other
roles? Yes. Because I didn't work for a long time after *Mean
Streets*.'

10

The critical success of *Mean Streets* earned Robert De Niro an Oscar-winning role in *The Godfather, Part II*. For Harvey Keitel, it meant a guest-starring shot on the first episode of *Kojak* and one on *The FBI*.

Proval, who was also cast in the *Kojak* episode, played a cop who was being held hostage by a gang of thugs, led by Keitel: 'I remember he made a choice to call Telly's character "Kojik" instead of Kojak. He's inventive and daring.'

'He was the hot new actor from New York,' recalled David Sosna, who was an assistant-director trainee on *The FBI* when Keitel appeared as a guest star. 'I remember hearing it was really important that they got this hot young kid. But he was somebody I'd never heard of. I remember that he didn't know there was a bathroom in his dressing room.'

And then – nothing. As much as he auditioned, he couldn't find movie work, though more TV work beckoned. TV, however, was fast and unsparing. There was, as one long-time director observed, 'no time for a performance.' Which grated on Keitel – and didn't make him popular with the TV directors he worked with.

Keitel had been spoiled by his work with Scorsese. Even with a limited budget, Scorsese was able to let Keitel and de Niro explore a scene through multiple takes until all were satisfied that they had found what they wanted to. It might take anywhere from six to twelve weeks to shoot a ninety-minute or two-hour feature film. But a one-hour TV drama is shot in slightly more than a week. Which means the director's main concern is not helping an actor reach perfection but, frequently, just achieving adequacy.

'It's good enough for television,' however, was not a sentiment that Keitel wanted to hear. In being able to fully apply his art in his work with Scorsese, Keitel felt he had dined at the table of the gods. Now he was being offered a drive-thru meal from McDonald's.

It wasn't that he was the only one with complaints. Everyone else he was working with, after all, had similar aspirations. They knew they were settling for what they could get, biding their time with a job that at least paid the rent until something better came along. Keitel, however, was vociferous in his dissatisfaction and fought for his vision, even in circumstances where he could not win. Those arguments with the director – about motivation, about getting another take to try a different interpretation – ate time. Time, as always, was money – and no matter how good Keitel might be, he wasn't worth going over budget on a TV show that would have to crank out another episode again the next week without him. So word got around that he was difficult – that he wouldn't, in other words, get in, give it his best shot and then move on.

For Keitel, however, it was a case of an industry that seemed to be conspiring to stifle his creativity, to force mediocre work on him when he was capable of so much more: 'I went back to New York and the Actors Studio because I wasn't being fulfilled. It was almost a year later that Marty offered me *Alice*.'

Indeed, the most attention he received came in January 1974, when he attended the 39th New York Film Critics Circle awards dinner at Sardi's to present de Niro with his supporting-actor award. A star-dotted crowd – including Paul Newman and Joanne Woodward, Lillian Gish, Elia Kazan and François

Truffaut – had packed the show-business landmark on West 44th Street for the usual meal of a faintly recognizable steak in a thin Béarnaise with tepid steamed vegetables.

Suddenly Joan Alpert, the wife of *Saturday Review* film critic Hollis Alpert, began choking on a piece of meat and turning blue. Dr Heimlich had not yet discovered the universal maneuver for dealing with this situation, but Keitel leapt into action and saved the day, startling the choking woman by grabbing her ankles and turning her upside down, then shaking her. Out popped a piece of meat. She was able to finish the meal and Alpert promised only positive reviews for Keitel from then on.

Eventually, Scorsese landed another assignment from Warner Bros.: *Alice Doesn't Live Here Anymore*, a dramatic comedy about a widow and her pre-teen son coping on their own in the American Southwest after the death of her husband. Scorsese had been chosen by the film's star, Ellen Burstyn, who selected him after watching *Mean Streets* on the recommendation of Francis Ford Coppola. 'At the end of the movie,' Burstyn recalled, 'my friend said, "Isn't he terrific?" I said, "Which one?" She was talking about Bobby de Niro. But I liked the other guy – Harvey. So we hired Marty and he brought Harvey aboard.'

But not without a fight from Warner Bros.

Scorsese wanted to cast Keitel as Ben, whom Alice Hyatt meets in Phoenix, where she and her son have moved and she has found a job as a piano bar singer. Ben and Alice become romantically involved; he seems like the miracle she needs after the death of her boorish truck-driver husband. In fact, he's already married, though Alice doesn't know it; when his wife turns up at Alice's and asks her to stop seeing Ben, Ben arrives, almost on her heels. He breaks in, beats his wife as he chases her out, then threatens Alice and her son, pointing to the scorpion in the ornamental slide on his string tie: 'See it? You bother it and it'll kill you. So don't mess with it,' he warns her, in lines Keitel improvised.

When Scorsese mentioned Keitel, all the Warner Bros. executives could see was the tightly wired young hoodlum of *Mean Streets*. They could not believe that Keitel, whom they assumed was an Italian from Little Italy, would be convincing as a seductively easy-going and smooth-talking Westerner.

It was a problem Keitel would have over and over throughout his career. Even critic Janet Maslin admits, 'He made that character so indelible that it took a while to see who the actor was.'

Scorsese held firm, convinced Keitel could bring an explosive quality to the character. The studio finally agreed – but only if Keitel would take $3,000 for the role, instead of the promised $10,000. Keitel agreed.

It only took a week or so to film Keitel's part. He shows up almost an hour into the film as Ben Eberhart, a young Phoenix hotshot who's developed a hankering for Alice Hyatt (Ellen Burstyn) after he hears her singing in a local bar. His openness and youth trigger something in her and his sexual vitality is a welcome change from the perfunctory gropings of her late husband.

But later he turns into another creature altogether, exploding in a powerfully realistic display of brutality, toward both his wife and Alice. Like a jolt of nasty-edged adrenaline in the midst of what was apparently an enjoyable domestic comedy, he comes on like the aggregate viciousness of her late husband incarnate, condensed into one frightening outburst.

When Keitel was finished with the first and only take, Scorsese said, 'He terrified me. That rarely happens between professionals on a set, but it happened then.' Scorsese had rehearsed the scene with the actors for the handheld camera that would cover the scene. When they got on the set and Scorsese said, 'Action!' however, Keitel abandoned himself to the moment to a degree that startled everyone in the cramped location. According to Mike Moder, first assistant director, 'When he came busting in, he broke the glass in the door and actually cut his hand. It was just a little motel room and he went wilder than anybody thought. He scared the hell out of Ellen Burstyn. She didn't expect him to get that ferocious.'

Burstyn, another Actors Studio alumna, found it

terrifying. We were both really in the scene. They shot it handheld and he sort of tore up the place. I got really scared and, after it was over, had a crying jag for a couple of hours. What you do in rehearsal is one thing. But when it's a take, it jumps two levels. It got really intense.

I wasn't afraid of Harvey. I was afraid of the character. Harvey's very centered and in the moment. He plays a scary character and, when he lost his temper, it was very real. The fact that he was in the scene that intensely only spoke well for him.

Even Keitel himself was affected by the scene:

I remember a sense of repugnance about what I saw. He was a repugnant character. My girlfriend certainly responded that way at the time. She wouldn't talk to me.

The first time I saw it on the screen, it scared me. I think it was because Ben is a part of me that I hadn't really expressed, in terms of putting it all together and having it emerge as a character. You have to search to find him in yourself. I was in denial of that. That's why I think I scared myself when I saw it. Maybe scared is the wrong word. I didn't like him, meaning I didn't like that part of me.

As he was discovering, making the emotional journey to that dark part of his soul promised the greatest reward for the questing young actor: 'The craft is a way to penetrate emotions and the only way to be fearless is to go through fear. I'm talking about fear in terms of existing, of having to wake up in the morning and saying, "What do I do now?""

11

What to do now? What could he do? The movie parts didn't come.

And while some of the reviews of *Alice* were warm, others were scorching. Robert Hatch, writing in the *Nation*, referred to Keitel as 'a charming Jack Nicholson type, who turns out to suffer, when cornered, from hysteria with homicidal overtones.'

Which meant that he liked him more than the ever-acidic John Simon in *Esquire*, who refers to him as 'that boring actor Harvey Keitel' and then makes a point of noting 'how dreadful he was in *Mean Streets*.' Keitel, Simon wrote, 'has a crudity that sometimes fits the setting.'

Now forget for a moment that most other critics think of Simon as a sour old crank whose influence is as minimal as his opinions are contrived to be mean. Imagine that you're a sensitive and insecure actor whose career is sputtering – and then imagine how devastating it would be to read that kind of line about yourself in a national magazine. The assumption you make while reading that in those circumstances is simple: Not only is everyone reading it – but they're reading it and saying, 'You know, he's absolutely right.'

What's worse, Keitel seemed to be getting proof that he was being typecast by the people who were making the decisions about his career. Asked at the time if he would like to play a few sensitive-guy roles after so many tough guys, Keitel said, 'Yes, I would love to be playing those roles now but a lot of people are blind and can only see an actor for what he's doing at that moment. Had Marty not let me play this character from the Southwest in *Alice*, I would have been typed as an Italian for the rest of my career.'

If the studios weren't beckoning, the TV networks were. Keitel agreed to play Bugsy Siegel in an NBC made-for-TV movie, *The Virginia Hill Story*, a film built around actress Dyan Cannon, whose movie career had peaked and then plummeted five years earlier after the success of Paul Mazursky's *Bob and Carol and Ted and Alice*. 'After *Mean Streets*,' Keitel remembered, 'I was offered all the gangster roles around and I played some of them because I had to get work.'

Keitel played the hair-trigger Jewish gangster who helped to create Las Vegas for the New York Mob, while Cannon played the bit-part actress who became his lover. Allen Garfield played another mobster, who was Virginia Hill's boyfriend before she met Siegel. The whole thing was written and directed by a first-timer, a former art and costume designer named Joel Schumacher, who would go on to a movie-directing career that included some of the most commercially successful films of the 1980s and 1990s, including *The Client*, *A Time to Kill*, *Batman Forever* and the upcoming *Batman and Robin*. Schumacher recalled,

> The film was a soap opera NBC wanted to do as a vehicle for Dyan Cannon. It was one of those nineteen-day movies. It's over before you even start.
>
> It was the first directing I'd ever done. Marty had shown me a clip in the editing room of Harvey in *Alice Doesn't Live Here Anymore*. Bugsy Siegel was very violent: charming, handsome but violent. Harvey seemed perfect.

Keitel became a stickler for detail as an actor early on. He paid attention to the smallest facet of his character, no matter how minor the role or how hurried the production. According to Schumacher, 'He did tons of research and had lots of interesting questions and notions. He was much more interested in the depth and interior of the character. He was willing to do anything to do a good job.'

That included stripping to the buff for a scene set in a steam room, before putting on his towel: 'Most of the actors had underwear on under their towels but Harvey insisted on being naked,' Schumacher said.

Keitel had made a point of staying in shape since his Marine days and worked out regularly, which was apparent to Schumacher: 'I'd never seen his body. A lot of women on the crew were kind of struck at what a sexual presence he was. His body, when you see him dressed, he can play ordinary, asexual characters. And he doesn't have a face you'd ordinarily associate with a Calvin Klein guy. But his body is so masculine, so forceful. I thought he was like a young John Garfield.'

Keitel brought great compassion to the soundstage. Schumacher explained that 'Dyan was going through a bad period. She was very insecure and considerably older than Harvey. And he was very helpful to her – and to me. The seeds of his sensitivity and support for a new director – he was very kind to me. He never made me feel like an amateur, which I was.'

There was some question about Keitel's age. Though he was now thirty-five, he still looked like a recent college graduate. His fresh-faced quality might have made him unsuited for the trigger-happy gangster known as Bugsy. But, Allen Garfield remembered, 'Even though some said he was too young, he took it on like a champ. He delivered a bravura performance. It was a kick to watch him. He captures the magnetism, the ballsiness and the sensitivity of the character.'

Ironically, almost twenty years later, Keitel and Garfield found themselves competing for a role in another movie about Virginia Hill and Bugsy Siegel: Barry Levinson's *Bugsy*. The two ran into each other in the parking lot outside Levinson's office on their way to read for the role of gangster Mickey

Cohen; Keitel wound up with the role and eventually received both a Golden Globe and an Oscar nomination. As they walked in, Keitel joked, 'Can you believe this, Allen? We're both going in to read for this, to lower ourselves to go in and meet instead of just being offered the role. And I'm not even going to play Bugsy Siegel!'

After the TV movie, Keitel got the kind of invitation he'd been waiting for, hoping for; the kind of job offer he always assumed that a film like *Mean Streets* would land him: the chance to play one of Willie Loman's sons in George C. Scott's revival of Arthur Miller's *Death of a Salesman* at the Circle in the Square Theater in New York, to open in June 1975.

And, shortly after that, more good news: Scorsese would be making his next film, *Taxi Driver*, in New York during the summer. There was a part for Keitel and the shooting schedule could be built around his availability from the play.

Arthur Miller's classic was being directed by Scott, who was also playing Willie Loman. Teresa Wright was playing Linda Loman, James Farentino had been cast as the troubled older son, Biff, while Keitel would play the younger son, the callow Happy. Chuck Patterson, a young black actor from the Midwest whom Scott cast as the son of the Lomans' next door neighbor, recalled that

> Early on, my first take was that, just in terms of their natures, the roles of the sons should have been cast the other way around. Harvey was a quiet, introspective person, while James Farentino was very gregarious and out-going. But that may have been the reason George cast them that way; he cast against type.
>
> Still, early on in rehearsal, George wanted Harvey to be expansive as Happy and James to be moody, dark and poetic

as Biff. But he was getting the opposite thing from each actor. That worked itself out in rehearsal. But coming out of the blocks, it was a challenge for Harvey to be this very gregarious, frivolous character.

Keitel knew the role pushed him in new directions: 'He's different than anything I'd done before. He's not a tough guy, a beat-'em-up kind of guy.'

In the end, Scott achieved the effect he sought, according to Long Wharf Theater's Arvin Brown, who saw the production: 'It created a kind of tension because they were playing against type. That made it really interesting.'

If anything, Keitel was serious to the point of earnestness backstage, always focusing on the work and improving his own concentration, in order to have real moments, to be present in the moment instead of acting the part. He kept to himself, not palling around with Farentino or any of the other cast members. He would attend the morale-building rounds of dinner and drinks that Scott would occasionally host: 'It was a very friendly company,' Patterson remembered, 'with a family quality. George was the big daddy and everybody was in awe of George.'

Patterson was also somewhat in awe of Keitel, particularly for his physical vigor: 'Two things set him apart from the other people in the cast. His seriousness and focus and concentration on the work – and his physical fitness. He was the perfect picture of health and physical fitness. His body was like a sculpture of a Greek god. He really took care of himself.'

So Patterson was surprised when Keitel told him one day backstage that he'd been mugged the day before, jumped by two or three guys. 'I thought, "Who'd mess with this guy?" But it shocked him. He said it was very frightening.'

In fact, Keitel was giving new definition to the idea of frightening a few blocks away from the Broadway theater where he was appearing. As Sport, the pimp who controlled the young prostitute played by the twelve-year-old Jodie Foster in *Taxi Driver*, Keitel couldn't have been farther from outgoing, all-American Happy in *Death of a Salesman*.

The reviews of *Death of a Salesman* were laudatory, with both Clive Barnes and Walter Kerr raving in the *New York Times*. The play became one of that summer's hottest tickets, with a particular jolt of energy the night Jacqueline Kennedy Onassis turned up to see it. Though the reviews mentioned Keitel (Kerr: 'Handsomely acted'; Jack Kroll in *Newsweek*: 'Farentino and Keitel play the brothers affectingly'), Keitel was too busy to notice.

For a couple of weeks, every night he'd leave the Circle in the Square and head downtown, to the location where *Taxi Driver* was shooting.

The film, from a script by Paul Schrader, is a haunting document of its time, a career-making film for both de Niro, as the increasingly mentally unbalanced loner, Travis Bickle, and Scorsese, as a director announcing his style and themes with a bold, provocative work. And there was Keitel, the star of *Mean Streets*, all but unrecognizable in the small but memorable role of the pimp, Sport (also known as Matthew).

Scorsese had given him the Schrader script to read, assuming that Keitel would want the role of the campaign worker who is a colleague of the Cybill Shepherd character, a part that eventually went to comedian Albert Brooks. But Keitel, who was still living in Hell's Kitchen, saw something in the tiny role of the pimp, whose crude, insinuating sex talk to Travis about Iris triggers something in the troubled loner.

When he told Scorsese that he wanted to play the pimp, Scorsese said, 'Why? The other role is bigger.'

'I have no idea,' Keitel replied, later explaining, 'Originally the description of the character was an Italian guy standing in the doorway. But I knew these characters from where I was living at the time. And Marty could tell I had something in mind.'

Keitel found a pimp in his neighborhood and began working with him a couple of weeks before filming started. They would meet at the Actors Studio, then spend hours improvising scenes and discussing the pimp's life and way of business, recording the conversations. Some of the scenes they improvised involved Keitel playing the hooker and the pimp being himself; other times, Keitel would be the pimp and the pimp would play the girl.

Keitel presented his work to Scorsese, who, perhaps guiltily, suggested the pimp have another scene. Keitel recalled,

> So I had the idea of me and Jodie dancing to a song I wrote with the line producer, 'I Love You Baby, Come to Me.' It showed that he genuinely cares for this girl and will do anything for her, an extraordinary relationship I'm not sure I comprehend even today.
>
> Here was a man who is doing the job of a pimp and a girl who is working as a prostitute. It's monstrous. It's horrible. But that wasn't my approach to it. My approach was as a working man. The guy I worked with taught me about how the girls were treated.
>
> There is great humanity in a pimp. I don't mean humanity in the benevolent sense. I mean humanity in its suffering sense. They come out of a place of great need, usually of poverty, of broken homes, of never having opportunity. What comes out of an environment like that is often a pimp, a thief, a drug addict, a mugger. What the hell does someone like that know about giving love, caring for, supporting, being the most you can be? They're trying to eat, keep the rats out of their food.

Keitel turns three scenes into a memorable supporting role. When first encountered by de Niro, he reels off a list of sex acts that young Iris will perform as though he were a waiter running through the specials of the day. He is next seen dancing with and providing seductive comfort to Iris in one of the film's creepiest and most haunting scenes. In the bloody finale, he is impatient and all business, trying to shoo away the determined de Niro before de Niro dispatches him with a couple of bullets to the chest.

When he first appears, Sport is wearing a pair of suit pants and a sleeveless undershirt, with a jaunty, wide-brimmed black hat perched impeccably above a head of flowing, shoulder-length hair. He has an earring and one red fingernail. 'In *Taxi Driver*, just the appearance of him and you know there's trouble,' says Jack Mathews, *Newsday* film critic and former film editor of the *Los Angeles Times*. 'Physically, he always seems imposing. You put him in a scene and you get tension.'

Keitel had put together the entire look for the part, including the shoulder-length hairpiece: 'I had seen a lot of pimps in my neighborhood; I just put a number of them together and out came Sport,' he said. The producers, however, didn't want to spend the extra money on the wig. But Scorsese put his foot down and Sport became one of the film's most memorable elements.

Jack Kroll wrote in *Newsweek*, 'As Sport, Harvey Keitel is a kind of perverse Puck, the sleazy muse of the film – long-haired, tight-muscled, jackal-shrewd, forever jittering in a syncopated sweat.'

The film, however, was de Niro's, a tour de force that confirmed his stardom, earning him another Oscar nomination. When it was released, it triggered a national debate about the role of violence in film as it affects society as a whole, a discussion that took a bizarre turn five years later when a deranged young man from Colorado shot President Ronald Reagan after becoming obsessive about Jodie Foster, following repeated viewings of her performance in the film.

Keitel, however, was barely part of the discussion. While his acting colleagues applauded Keitel's daring and craft in *Taxi Driver*, and while playing Sport satisfied Keitel's craving for dark, complex work, it was hardly the kind of role – such as Travis Bickle, for example – that drew the attention of major directors and studios.

'Harvey fought the second banana thing for a while,' admitted his former agent, Harry Ufland. 'There's a broody intensity about him, but there are a lot of reasons his career went the way it did; a lot of it has to do with luck. And Harvey was always attracted to much darker things, things that endeared him to his cult, but not to people who don't go to the movies.'

Later that summer, after finishing *Taxi Driver*, Keitel left *Death of a Salesman* before the end of its run to head for Calgary, Alberta, Canada, to film Robert Altman's *Buffalo Bill and the Indians*. His replacement in the role of Happy was Martin Sheen who, ironically, would replace Keitel again – in the Philippines.

Sheen remembered, 'He was very helpful for my getting ready to take over. I came to New York and saw the show twice. He helped me to prepare for it and was very sweet and helpful. And it was one of the great experiences I ever had.'

Keitel, however, looked back on that experience with bittersweet memories. Here was his first appearance on Broadway, in a great American play with a great American actor. But, as he recalled it, he was not yet an actor capable of giving his best in the situation. He had yet to confront the deeply conflicted feelings he had about his own family, particularly his father. He had yet to go through psychotherapy, something he would do a decade later where he would confront those emotions, identify them, learn to use them. And so, though he couldn't articulate it, he knew as an artist that he hadn't been absolutely truthful in playing a young man who has significant problems with his father and brother:

I didn't handle myself very well. It was painful. I was lost.
I was not intimidated. It just wasn't a good time for me. I
was running adrift. I had nothing to hang on to and I was
uncertain about my technique. It wasn't that I didn't know
what I was doing. I knew as much as I would ever know. I
needed to work on where I was from – the streets of Brooklyn. I needed to know that. It was my steps on the street
where I grew up that I needed to walk again in order to own
myself.

12

By the time 1976 began Keitel had several films in the can – none of which did enough business or drew enough attention to give his career the kind of commercial boost he might have liked.

And yet he was often working with intriguing and adventurous directors, doing work that compelled him much of the time. Certainly, he put himself fully into the service of *Mother, Jugs and Speed*, in which he played the third member of that trio, opposite Bill Cosby and Raquel Welch. But even he admitted that he did it for the money.

Keitel was cast as the fresh-faced young romantic lead. He plays Speed, a Vietnam veteran who is now a police officer on suspension while unfounded charges of corruption are being investigated. So he takes a job with a low-rent ambulance service as a driver and paramedic. Initially paired with the irredeemably sex-crazed Larry Hagman, he beats Hagman senseless after finding him molesting a gorgeous but unconscious woman in the back of the ambulance on a run.

Speed is the only one at the ambulance service who is able to crack the veneer of the receptionist, Jennifer (nickname: Jugs), played by Raquel Welch. Keitel looks alternately amused and perplexed to be playing a coy, post-coital dialogue scene with Welch, the reigning sex symbol of her generation. For the rest of the film, he seems disappointed in himself for being involved in this non-linear and mostly unfunny mainstream piece of Hollywood product. 'For me, it was done as a commercial venture,' he said. 'There was less to work with, yes, but I approached this role with as much seriousness as any other, and Peter Yates [the director] and Tom Mankiewicz [the writer] were very helpful.'

That's the Way of the World was one of the tough-guy roles he didn't turn down. Still, it's a tough guy who's also an artist fighting for his principles. Though the film is poorly shot, lit and directed, Keitel is effective as a hot young record producer in New York, who is forced to compromise his artistic integrity to satisfy the suits at the record company, which is actually controlled by the Mob. Keitel, as Coleman Buckmaster, was dealing with issues that would plague him through much of his career: the conflict between the artist, trying to express his soul, and the businessman, who needs to sell what the artist expresses.

Despite such attractions as Bert Parks singing bubblegum music, Keitel boogying at a roller-disco, and performances by Earth, Wind and Fire, an overblown rhythm-and-blues act of the time, the film flopped, dying a quick and luckless death in limited release in July 1975. It turned up again in April 1977, rechristened *Shining Star* but otherwise unchanged. Despite an ad campaign attempting to sell it as a film 'they'd' tried to repress, audiences resisted the temptation once again.

Robert Altman's *Buffalo Bill and the Indians, or Sitting Bull's History Lesson* put Keitel in heady company: Paul Newman, Burt Lancaster, Geraldine Chaplin, Joel Grey, Pat McCormick, Kevin McCarthy. The large and talented ensemble gathered near Calgary and filmed Alan Rudolph's deconstruction of Arthur Kopit's play. Wearing ridiculously lacquered bangs plastered to his forehead and with a bowler hat perched precariously on top, Keitel plays Buffalo Bill Cody's nephew, a prissy dude who serves as Cody's factotum and toady. He follows Paul Newman around like Radar O'Reilly in Altman's *M*A*S*H*, calling a plaintive, 'Uncle Will! Uncle Will!' Though Keitel can be seen in a number of scenes – and, at one point, utters with total ingenuousness, 'There ain't no business like the show business' – there is barely a character there to play, beyond the hair and the clothes (a couple of outrageously checked and tight-fitting suits).

Granted, it's an ensemble film, with the other stars battling for screentime with Newman. In that crowd – and given his character's tangential relationship to the film's actual plot (about Cody's efforts to turn Sitting Bull into a star attraction without ceding him the spotlight, while struggling with centuries of guilt over the treatment of Native Americans) – Keitel is mostly atmosphere and comic relief, but has very little chance to be the latter.

'The character he played was fictional but came out of research,' Rudolph said. 'Altman always says that casting is 80 percent of a movie. And Harvey's name was there before I wrote the character. I don't believe he's ever been funnier than he was in *Buffalo Bill*. He always says that Altman is the only guy who let him do comedy.' (When Altman asked him during casting which part he was interested in, Keitel replied, without missing a beat, 'Buffalo Bill.')

Unfortunately for everyone concerned, Altman's cutting commentary on the US Government's treatment of Native Americans over the years was trotted out – after a lavish press junket in Calgary – on July 4, 1976, the American Bicentennial. According to Rudolph, 'One of the reviews said Altman and everyone in his shadow should be arrested for sedition, that it was anti-patriotic, that we should be arrested as communists. And that was the best review.'

The main benefit for both Keitel and Rudolph from *Buffalo Bill* and its box-office débâcle was Altman's sleight of hand in getting Rudolph a deal to direct a film of his own after *Buffalo Bill*. As Rudolph explained,

> Altman got all the people responsible for financing *Buffalo Bill* in a hotel room in Calgary. It was two nights before we began shooting with Paul Newman and Burt Lancaster on location. And Altman got all these people in a room and said, 'I'm going to make you a proposition. We're going to make this movie – and for a million dollars more, Alan can make another movie.' And they said OK. I'll never make as audacious a film as that.

Welcome to LA, which Rudolph also wrote, was an ensemble film very much in the mold of Altman's landmark *Nashville*, in which a group of barely connected people interact in a variety of ways. The film's central character was Carroll Barber (Keith Carradine), an itinerant singer-songwriter who returns to LA at Christmas from London, where he's been living, ostensibly to oversee a pop star's recording of his new suite of songs. In fact, his visit has been manipulated by his estranged father, Carl (Denver Pyle), a dairy products magnate.

Keitel plays Kenneth Hood, an extremely button-down executive who is Carl's right-hand man and, being about the same age as Carroll, his surrogate son as well. Hood has an unhappy marriage to an extremely flaky woman (Geraldine Chaplin); he's having an affair with a young woman who likes to clean house topless (Sissy Spacek); and he's about to launch a fling with a desperate real-estate woman (Sally Kellerman). Yet, as he gets a raise and promotion, he finds the one person he wants to share it with is his wife, who is debating a tryst with Carroll Barber.

In a sense, it was a modern version of the character he played in *Buffalo Bill*: an apple-polishing suck-up. Keitel pushed it to the limit, tinting his hair blond, like a young Californian who chalked up plenty of beach time. Then he dressed in fussy little three-piece suits and, for good measure, found a mod-looking pipe that appeared to be made of white Bakelite, like a post-modern meerschaum. It was a chance to distance himself significantly from gangster and tough-guy roles. As Rudolph commented:

> He was completely out of character, right down to that white pipe he smokes. He was extremely intense about the things that made his character interesting. He made himself into a type of person we meet in society, a young, upwardly mobile, career-oriented businessman. And he made him so complex and uncomfortable with himself because he's a very indelible actor and person. The young Harvey was a very impressive person. He had all the intensity and he didn't look like anybody else. He still doesn't.

Rudolph encouraged his actors to improvise. Ron Silver, who pops up in the film's opening minutes in a wordless cameo as a masseur (and who got the film work through Keitel, who recommended him after working with him at the Actors Studio), remembered, 'I did a whole monologue and was quite brilliant, but it was cut from the movie.'

Rudolph, who was working on a tight budget, found he couldn't include all the moments of inspiration his large cast came up with: 'There was too much for an ensemble picture,' he said. 'But when Harvey sees the final cut, he always thinks his best stuff has been cut. In *Welcome to LA*, a lot of the stuff that was missing wasn't necessary to the film, but it sure was good. The whole film could have been about Harvey's character.'

Keitel, who discovers so much about a character through improvising in the rehearsal process, ultimately went in the opposite direction to salvage a scene that was threatening to push the film over schedule. 'It was the kind of movie where,

if you went over schedule today, it was canceled the next day,'
Rudolph said.

The scene was a seduction moment, in which Kenneth Hood,
who is at a loose end, finds himself together with the voracious
realtor, played by Sally Kellerman. As pleased as he is with
himself – with his promotion and this woman's obvious attraction to him – he is preoccupied with his suddenly distant wife.
He can't throw himself into the sex and winds up rejecting
her.

Rudolph had avoided finishing the scene because he wasn't
sure how it should end and wasn't at ease directing Kellerman
in a sexual situation. 'It was my first sex scene and I was
uncomfortable, even though I'd written the damn thing,' he
said. 'She was supposed to go down on him. So we finally
confront the scene and I'm making all these suggestions: Why
don't you try this? Let's try that. Say this.'

On and on, to Take 22.

Finally, Keitel said, 'Alan, this isn't working.'

'What should we do?' Kellerman chimed in.

'Why don't we look at the script?' Keitel suggested.

In his effort to improve the scene, Rudolph found, he'd dis-
torted it completely, lost its focus, until he couldn't even
remember what he'd written initially. So they took out the
script, reread it, then ran the scene as written: 'One take and
we're out,' Rudolph recalled.

Keitel expected to be allowed to collaborate with Rudolph. It
was the way he worked with all his directors; the better ones
understood how to handle all the questions Keitel brought to
the set every day; they let him try things his way before
attempting to shape and direct his performance. Rudolph
observed, 'His thoroughness and ferocious instincts are, for any
director, the best writing his characters can ever receive. I don't
care what the script says. Harvey's quest is really why you
want to work with Harvey.'

Not all directors felt the same way, however, as Keitel's agent discovered. For one thing, not all directors work in a collaborative way; there are those who go so far as to demonstrate for actors how they want the lines read, instead of letting them find their own interpretation – anathema to Keitel, who wants a director to work with him in allowing him to create and shape a characterization. He is always full of questions for a director: about intentions, motivations, story themes.

But the director is at the center of the storm on the movie set. Everyone has questions for him or her; ninety percent of the job is answering those questions. What color should this be? Which lens do you want to use? Should the couch be here or over there? Should the actor enter before or after the moment where the special effect will be? And on and on.

Given that constant barrage of inquiries and the constant pressure of time and money on a movie production, then, there are those directors who would rather not have to deal with an actor demanding such undivided attention for long stretches of time, particularly an actor who is playing a supporting role – or smaller.

For a director who is willing to work the way Keitel does, 'Harvey is inquisitive in a wonderful way,' Harry Ufland said. 'If he wasn't talented, you'd think he was a pain in the ass. But he wasn't asking questions just for the sake of asking questions but because he really wanted an answer. But he had a reputation for being demanding, for being a perfectionist.'

Keitel's performance in *Welcome to LA* won him some nice notices; he was singled out in *Time* magazine as being particularly good (by critic Jay Cocks, a friend of Scorsese's and Keitel's). Pauline Kael, on the other hand, wrote in the *New Yorker*, 'Harvey Keitel looks half asleep. Keitel needs his meanness and blowups; miscast here, he's bland and wooden.'

Welcome to LA vanished from theaters quickly. The quirky, sketchy character comedy was simply outgunned in a year when box offices were swamped by the hype of *Smokey and the Bandit*, *Star Wars* and *Close Encounters of the Third Kind*, not to mention *Annie Hall*, *Saturday Night Fever*, *The Goodbye Girl*, *Julia* and *The Turning Point*.

Yet the film had an incredible buzz among Hollywood insiders prior to its release, while Rudolph finished editing it. The cast included a batch of rising stars, including Keitel, Spacek, Carradine, Kellerman, Chaplin and Lauren Hutton – all convinced that they were doing some of the best work of their careers, and therefore making a point of getting their agents to pass the word to the current hot directors that the *Welcome to LA* editing room was the place to be. 'There were never more directors parading through an editing room than on *Welcome to LA*,' Rudolph remembered. 'I had all these actors who thought this was their best work. James Toback, Ingmar Bergman, John Boorman, Ridley Scott – all came to see what was going on.'

Scott, a British director of commercials, was about to make his film debut with *The Duellists*, an adaptation of a Joseph Conrad story. Watching the editing of *Welcome to LA*, he said to Rudolph, 'Your film gave me a good idea. I'm going to use big close-ups. And I like those two guys.'

'Those two guys' were Carradine and Keitel. Urged on by producer David Puttnam, he told Rudolph he wanted to cast them as the leads in his first film.

'Remember,' Rudolph told him, 'one is thrust and the other is parry.'

One other director found his way to the *Welcome to LA* editing room: Francis Ford Coppola. Stymied by the high asking-price of Steve McQueen (who, despite not having carried a film since 1973's *Papillon*, was looking for $3 million, unheard of at the time), he was still casting about for someone to play the central character in a Conrad adaptation of his own: a reworking of *Heart of Darkness*, set in the Vietnam war.

Watching Keitel in his scenes for Rudolph, he knew he'd found his Corporal Willard.

13

Keitel's reputation for being difficult was cemented for years, based on what was reported about his work on *Apocalypse Now*. Yet it was, if anything, a case of an actor caught in the middle between two massive egos: Coppola's and that of the elusive Marlon Brando.

If anything, Keitel was glad simply to have won the role, given the list of people who had turned down the part, beginning with Steve McQueen. Despite Coppola's success with the two *Godfather* films and *The Conversation*, he faced rejection from actors as diverse as Robert Redford, Jack Nicholson, Al Pacino and James Caan, all of whom passed on Coppola's invitation to spend several months playing war in the steamy jungles of the Philippines.

And the film was only the tip of the iceberg of what Coppola was anticipating. He envisioned making his Vietnam epic, then taking the inevitable profits and plowing them into an idea for an expanded Zoetrope Productions: his own mini-studio, where he and his friends could make the movies they wanted to, without studio interference.

He was frustrated by his dealings with McQueen (who initially wanted the $3 million to play Willard, then offered to take the same amount to play Kurtz, the part that ultimately went to Brando) and other high-priced talent. He longed for the day when he'd have his own studio and could sign his own company of actors, much like Orson Welles had tried to do with the Mercury Theater Players in his early films. And Keitel, he assumed, would be one of his first recruits.

For his part, Keitel desperately wanted the role in *Apocalypse Now*. He was, after all, an ex-Marine, whose unit had spent time in places such as Lebanon and Crete. He had served prior to Vietnam but, as a one-time hawk who had changed his point of view about the Vietnam war as the 1960s had progressed, he was anxious to be part of what was obviously an important story about the politically charged conflict.

As an actor, he wanted to explore the art of darkness in *Heart of Darkness*. And, as someone who understood the commercial fundamentals of the business he was in, he also knew the kinds of roles he was being offered. As much as he learned working with Altman and Rudolph, he was anxious for another chance to carry a movie, to play a leading role.

He was nagged by thoughts that, just perhaps, *Mean Streets* had been it – his one and only opportunity to play the lead in a film. All the good parts he was being offered were small ones, or part of an ensemble; the big parts were for lousy projects, things he could do in his sleep – variations on Charlie in *Mean Streets* or Ben in *Alice Doesn't Live Here Anymore*. Bruce Williamson, *Playboy*'s film critic, recalled, 'For a long time, it looked like he would wind up playing New York thugs. He was an actor who looked destined to be in a rut.'

Now, suddenly, here was an offer to play the lead in a prestigious, big-budget epic, in an adaptation of a literary work that spoke to him exactly where he lived – the big questions about good versus evil, about man's inability to resist temptation and the price for transgressing. He would be acting with one of his idols, Marlon Brando. And he would be working for a director who was positioning himself as the giant of his generation, after twice winning the Oscar for best picture for the two *Godfather* films, taking home another as best director for *Godfather II*.

'The only way you get work is by working,' Keitel said. 'And the only way you get your choice of work is by being in successful movies. You pay a price for not being in the successful movies.'

He had misgivings; he had heard elsewhere that Coppola tended to be autocratic on the set, that he was less interested in an actor's exploration of a role than in the ability to deliver a performance on time and under budget. So he insisted on auditioning for Coppola, in order to discuss the role with him so that they would both head for the Philippines ready to make the same movie and clear about how they would do it.

As it turned out, Keitel's instincts were correct. He and Coppola were a nervous fit: 'I don't think we communicated well. We clashed. It was a matter of a young actor who was an ex-Marine out of Brooklyn meeting up with a talented director who was out of UCLA and some fraternity.'

Yet Keitel managed to convince himself that Coppola would let him interpret the role in his own way. So he accepted Coppola's assurances that they'd work it out on location. But once they reached the Philippines, Keitel found that things had changed.

For one thing, the actors were housed like soldiers, in a barracks, while Coppola lived and worked in a lavish villa. What was worse, right from the beginning, Coppola was rewriting the movie, even as he made it. Under pressure because he had so quickly fallen behind schedule, Coppola tried to drive the actors, to get them to deliver on cue when order could be established out of chaos long enough to get the shot. According to some reports, Keitel was playing the role with a greater dynamism than Coppola liked, making Willard less the observer and more the participant.

Things were so disorganized that, on the first day of shooting, the camera crew accidentally left Keitel and the other actors stranded in the middle of a river. Keitel, armed with a walkie-talkie, couldn't raise anyone from the crew: 'Hello, hello, this is Harvey Keitel. This is Harvey Keitel.' He paused for a moment, then said into the walkie-talkie, 'You wouldn't do this to Marlon Brando.'

Even as Coppola was trying to rewrite the script and cope with the price-gouging by the Philippine Government and unions, as he was trying to shepherd sets and helicopters and actors, here was Keitel, asking for his time to discuss questions he had about the role of Willard.

In addition to their conflict on the set, Keitel and Coppola also had a suddenly escalating disagreement about Keitel's contract. Coppola wanted Keitel to sign an undertaking that would tie him to Coppola for the next seven years, as the first of what Coppola hoped would be the Zoetrope stable of actors.

Keitel began to rethink that long-term provision when he heard, during the second week of filming in April 1976, that Coppola now planned to suspend production for the summer because Brando, who had agreed to play Kurtz, wanted time to be with his children while they were out of school. *Apocalypse* would close down for the summer while sets were built, then resume in the fall when Brando was available.

Keitel had a movie lined up for the fall, fixed in his schedule for the time after his commitment to *Apocalypse* was supposed to be completed. He had had assurances from Coppola before they left the US that he would be released in time to make the other film. But it was an oral contract, the same oral contract that included the seven-year option. If Coppola followed his plan, Keitel would be forced to forego the other film he had committed to.

Keitel dug in his heels – about the scheduling and about his contract. He asked Coppola for a meeting to resolve the situation: 'Had I known then what I know now, I would have kept my mouth shut longer and had them shoot so much they couldn't fire me.'

By that time, however, firing Keitel was exactly what Coppola had in mind. 'Harvey wasn't happy – Francis wasn't happy. But that stuff happens,' Ufland said. 'But Francis is a megalomaniac and he had to have his whipping boy.'

He also wasn't getting the Willard he wanted from Keitel. As Coppola's wife Eleanor wrote in her journal:

> Last night Francis saw the assembly of the first week's rushes. They were the scenes with Harvey Keitel, who plays Willard. Afterward, he sat down on the couch with the editors and Gray Frederickson and Fred Roos, the producers. He said, 'Well, what do you think?' I went upstairs to say good night to Roman and Gio and when I came down about fifteen minutes later, they were already on the phone, making plane reservations for flights to LA. Today Francis has made the decision to replace Keitel, his leading man. Gray said, 'Jesus, Francis, how do you have the guts to do it?'

The story ran on the front page of *Variety* on April 26, 1976, under the headline, KEITEL FIRED; WON'T WAIT FOR BRANDO. 'That's not what happened, but it's a nice souvenir,' Keitel said.

Variety reported:

> Harvey Keitel has been fired from lead role of Francis Ford Coppola's *Apocalypse Now* in what Keitel's agent, Harry Ufland of ICM, says is a contract dispute over possibility that filming may be shut down all summer to accommodate Marlon Brando.
>
> Coppola returned to Hollywood late last week from Philippines' location of the Vietnam war pic, while shooting was stopped for Easter holiday period and fired Keitel in a letter Friday (16) from his attorneys to Ufland. Ufland, angered at the turn of events, said, 'I had to call Harvey [in the Philippines] and tell him; they didn't have the decency to call him.'
>
> Keitel had been highly touted by Coppola as one of his five

initial contractees in the producer-director's much-publicized attempt to counteract the high-priced star syndrome ... Keitel has had his long-term contract understanding voided by Coppola.

'When anybody is fired from a picture, it's a problem,' said Ufland. 'Francis was very visible. There was a headline in *Variety* and Harvey was dealt with in a bad way.'

Martin Sheen was in Rome, making *The Cassandra Crossing*, when he got a call from Coppola, who had chosen him to replace Keitel. He flew to Hollywood to meet with Coppola, then on to the Philippines to take over the role. About four days of reshooting were required to cover the scenes with Keitel. Before it was over, *Apocalypse Now* would lose its sets to a typhoon and would almost lose Sheen to a heart attack.

'I never knew what happened between Harvey and Francis,' Sheen said. He and Keitel worked together three years later on a western called *Eagle's Wing*, but the topic of *Apocalypse Now* never came up between them – nor has it since: 'Harvey and I have never discussed it. I imagine it was a painful and deeply personal thing with him.'

Keitel spent his last night in the Philippines at a bar, struggling with the thoughts and fears that continued to nag at him about his career, the little voice that told him, 'See? You're a failure as an actor. You can't act and that's why you were fired. You have no talent.'

Then a female singer got up and belted out the hoary 'My Way' as Keitel listened, nursing a drink. Paul Anka's overripe paean to rugged individualism struck a chord with the unhappy actor:

I sat there, being encouraged by that song. I thought, 'If people could see me now, they wouldn't believe it.' That scene seemed like such a set-up, you know. But I still kept thinking, 'Yeah, yeah.'

I made a choice. I could not let someone dictate to me. I could not give what was demanded, which was someone saying, 'I'll give you this job, then I will control your life for the next seven years.' The price of my freedom would have cost me more.

I was trembling but I knew I had done the right thing when I stood my ground. I couldn't sell myself out to anybody. Not for money or for the opportunity to be successful. It was hard but my freedom was worth more than becoming an international name.

Though it was at heart a business dispute over contracts and shooting schedules, the initial flare-up on what would become a highly publicized and troubled production hurt Keitel's reputation. It was, at first, cast in the terms usually associated with bad behavior: 'creative differences.' The implication was that, somehow, Keitel wasn't up to the job. Then stories began to circulate about Keitel, about his uneasiness in the jungle and his supposed phobia about snakes and insects.

When Keitel heard that story a couple of years later from director James Toback, he was incredulous. 'I was the only person there who *did* know how to handle the jungle – I was the only one who had even been in the Marines,' he said.

It wasn't the first time an actor had been publicly fired from a film. De Niro, in fact, was fired the same year from a Mike Nichols picture, *Bogart Slept Here*, written by Neil Simon. Nichols even made what seemed like a career-limiting remark at the time – that de Niro simply wasn't funny.

It had no effect on de Niro's career, perhaps because no one equated de Niro with Gene Wilder, one of the leading comedy stars of the time. More to the point, de Niro had other films in the pipeline: Bernardo Bertolucci's *1900*, Scorsese's *New York, New York*, Michael Cimino's *The Deer Hunter*. With the lingering glow from *Taxi Driver* and the plaudits he would collect (including another Oscar nomination for *The Deer Hunter*), *Bogart Slept Here* became little more than a footnote in his career.

Keitel's prospects were iffier. For Keitel, *Apocalypse Now* threatened to turn into a defining moment, forever casting him as an actor so difficult that he had to be fired from a major motion picture. 'It wasn't like Harvey was on top of the world,' Ufland commented. 'So all these things had an effect. Given the brooding, dark roles and his difficult reputation, it didn't help.'

The price of his freedom, Keitel later said, was 'less work. You get fewer offers. I wasn't spoken about very nicely in Hollywood. You know the way it goes.'

Regrets? He had a few. But then again, too few to mention. As he later told a colleague, 'If I have one god in my life, it's not going to be Francis Coppola.'

14

Keitel and Robert De Niro had bonded on *Mean Streets*, a bond that was strengthened during *Taxi Driver*. Keitel felt only affection for his friend, pride in his success and warmth about the rare time they got to spend together when they both happened to be in New York at the same time.

Still, Keitel couldn't help but be struck by the way their careers had diverged. While he had struggled to find meaningful work after *Mean Streets*, de Niro had already won his first Oscar (for playing the young Vito Corleone in *The Godfather, Part II*) and been nominated for two more (for *Taxi Driver* and *The Deer Hunter*).

According to one long-time Hollywood insider, 'At the time that Harvey came along, everyone fell in love with de Niro. That's the way the cookie crumbles. It has nothing to do with his personality or his talent; it's the way life is. I was under the impression that Harvey would never become a superstar because he was so good an actor that he was not commercial.'

Allen Garfield, who knew them both from working in New York theater, said, 'I think the most frustrating thing was that, for years after *Mean Streets*, Harvey was an actor in Bob's shadow. When they did *Taxi Driver*, Harvey was second or third banana to Bob, with Bob about to take over [Al Pacino]'s mantle as foremost American actor. Though I think Harvey was thrilled to do whatever he did, there was an aspect of "Is it ever going to be Keitel time?"'

Keitel thought *Apocalypse Now* would do the trick. Instead,

it contributed to his reputation in Hollywood: that he was difficult to work with, an actor who demanded too much of a director's time. Yet he believed that he'd recovered from any possible
career apocalypse by returning from the Philippines to make
three movies – all with first-time directors – back to back, three
films that all opened within the same six-month period.

For some critics, these films contain some of Keitel's best
early work, performances that, had they come in popular, commercial films, might have turned Keitel into a star. For Keitel,
they provided what he believed would be an antidote to the
kind of dictatorial directors he'd been working with – especially
Francis Coppola. The films – Ridley Scott's *The Duellists*, Paul
Schrader's *Blue Collar* and James Toback's *Fingers* – were all
debut efforts. Each of the directors saw in Keitel an experienced
actor with whom they could collaborate. And if collaboration
was a foreign concept on a big-budget Hollywood picture, it
seemed to be the order of the day with these newcomers.

Given a choice, Keitel had decided, he would rather skip a
part in a possible Hollywood hit if it was only going to frustrate
his creative impulses. He would rather take less money and be
given the opportunity to form a creative partnership with a
director in a riskier venture.

The Duellists marked the feature debut of British commercial
director Ridley Scott, who would vault to prominence with his
next film, *Alien*, and would later direct Keitel in *Thelma and
Louise*. A visual stylist to whom imagery often seems more
important than content, he approached Keitel for the role of
Gabriel Féraud, a French officer under Napoleon who begins a
duel-inducing feud with another officer that lasts for more than
fifteen years.

Scott sent a reel of his commercials to Ufland, who offered
the project to Keitel – who promptly turned it down. 'I'm not

interested in working with a commercials director,' he told Ufland. But Ufland was persistent, bothering Keitel mercilessly until the actor finally agreed to watch Scott's commercial reel.

'I realized each one was like a little well-made film,' Keitel said. 'When I saw them, it made me aware that I must not be stubborn; I must look everywhere. I learned not to be so quick to judge people, that I owed it to them to sit down with them, so I've never made that mistake again.'

Keitel immediately immersed himself in the film's period: France in the early nineteenth century. He read Will and Ariel Durant's *The Age of Napoleon* and other books, watched films, such as *Désirée*, with Marlon Brando and Jean Simmons, and Sergei Bondarchuk's 1968 Russian adaptation of *War and Peace*, to get a feeling for the French military discipline of the time. He also began studying fencing and the etiquette of the period, for this was a part built entirely around the concept of defending one's honor.

He also built a character biography, imagining Féraud as a peasant who joined Napoleon's army to be all that he could be, who rose through the ranks on the strength of his courage and initiative, as opposed to his wealth and influence. He asked the costume designer to add a Légion d'Honneur ribbon to Féraud's uniform, to show that the soldier had worked his way up through acts of bravery.

When he arrived in France to film, however, he discovered that, though he and Scott had had long discussions about the complexities of Féraud and what drove him constantly to pick fights, the structure of the movie made the character more of a plot device: the nemesis who keeps turning up to foil and spoil the life of his rival, the high-born d'Hubert (played by Keith Carradine).

I accepted that the focus was going to be the other character, yes [Keitel said]. But I hoped that my character would be rounded out a lot more. Ridley saw what I wanted to do and was very helpful. It was never my intention when I got involved with the project to just play a nemesis. I felt that in the original script, the characters were pretty much one-dimensional. I told him my exact sentiments about the screenplay and he agreed. We worked very hard to give the character depth, and a good deal of new material was added to the script. Somehow, after the film was edited, the character came out more as a black-coated nemesis. But all an actor can do is create his part. Once he creates it, it's in the hands of the director and the editor.

Keitel found Scott an open, collaborative director with a sense of humor, willing to let Keitel shape a moment, without actually ceding him authority. During one scene, in which Féraud, by now a general, was discussing strategy with his colonels, British actor Edward Fox was supposed to enter and offer new information. As they rehearsed, however, Fox began entering the room, then sitting on the general's desk as he delivered his line.

Keitel called Scott aside: 'He shouldn't sit on my desk,' he said, 'because he's a colonel and I'm a general.'

Nodding thoughtfully, Scott discreetly took Fox aside to relay Keitel's concern. After a moment of discussion, Scott returned to Keitel. 'Well, Harvey, in those days, they did that,' he told him.

'How do you know?' Keitel countered. 'Were you there? I was in the military and I'm telling you it's not done.'

Scott took charge, or so he thought: 'I feel we should do it,' he said. 'Edward needs it.'

Keitel replied, 'OK, go ahead,' and they returned to their original places to shoot the scene. Scott called 'Action!'; Keitel began explaining strategy to his colonels; Fox entered, saluted and said, 'Sir!' then sat on the desk.

At which point Keitel swelled with superior-officer bluster, turned and glared at him, then barked, 'Get your ass off of my desk!' Fox leapt to his feet and finished the scene from a non-reclining position.

Though critics praised the film's visual sweep and painterly images, the central characters were taken to task, for an obvious reason: here were two naturalistic American actors, trying to hold their own in the midst of a classically trained British cast that included Fox, Albert Finney, Tom Conti, Robert Stephens and Jenny Runacre.

'Keitel and Carradine are so perversely cast as French hussars that, whenever they speak, the splendid illusion of nineteenth-century Europe is shattered,' wrote David Ansen in *Newsweek*. 'The problem is aggravated by surrounding the American stars with a supporting cast of sterling-silver British actors ... who feast on their cameo parts like starved epicures at a banquet. The discrepancy trivializes a stylish attempt at serious entertainment.'

But Rex Reed, writing in *Vogue*, took up their defense: 'Lest you think two urbanized American actors like Keitel and Carradine might strain credulity as French cavalry officers, a major surprise awaits: They achieve a driving, aristocratic force that looks right and shows real thought behind the facade. Rarely have I seen a movie so drenched in persuasive style soar so brilliantly above its trappings into first-rate entertainment.'

While Pauline Kael wrote that Keitel could have made Féraud more than he is ('Implacability may come a little too naturally to Keitel; it narrows him as an actor'), she also cited the 'great concentration' of his performance: 'Keitel is potent, though, and at the end his Féraud is a marvelous image, in his crow's black coat and black tricorne, with his thinking processes hidden and warped – a man devoured by bitterness.'

As Robert Asahina pointed out in the *New Leader*, however, Keitel's fears had once again been realized: 'His star billing notwithstanding, by having to prop up Carradine, he is in a supporting role again. In the meantime, he is not getting any younger.'

Keitel later dismissed his work in the film. But people who know him disagree. 'I'd always loved his work since I saw him in *The Duellists*,' said director Peter Medak, who cast Keitel in his film *The Men's Club*. 'He had this incredible charisma. Very few American actors can disappear into period films. I didn't realize that, with his background, he was really Russian.'

James Toback also liked him in the film: '*The Duellists* is my favorite performance of his, though he'd violently disagree with that. It was a tremendously difficult role. He did it with a dimension that no one imagined. The story comes out of Conrad, but it was a Dostoyevskyan portrayal.'

The Duellists was a relatively peaceful shoot. Working with Scott had been collaborative and fulfilling, even if the final film wasn't.

Blue Collar, on the other hand, was a battle almost from the beginning. Paul Schrader found it 'the most unrelentingly unpleasant experience I have ever had.'

Actor Yaphet Kotto, who co-starred in the film with Keitel and Richard Pryor, was even less reserved in his judgment: 'On *Blue Collar*, Harvey and I were both suffering under a director who was misdirecting us – and we were both having a problem with Richard. I don't know how that film got done. We both wanted *Blue Collar* to be over with.'

Written by Schrader, who had also written *Taxi Driver*, and set in an auto factory in Detroit, *Blue Collar* is the story of three friends who work in the same plant: Smokey (Kotto), Zeke (Pryor) and Jerry (Keitel). The factory is trying to screw them; the union is screwing them worse. They all have heavy economic burdens. So they decide to rob the union office.

The robbery yields no cash, but they do get away with a ledger detailing union payoffs and kickbacks. When they try to blackmail the corrupt union boss, however, he uses the robbery to tear their long-standing friendship apart: Zeke sells out his friends (and his fellow workers) to become a stooge of the union boss in exchange for money and a soft job. When Smokey is murdered, Jerry turns informant for the FBI.

Keitel was attracted by the prospect of playing an average working man, trapped in an untenable situation:

> He's not a revolutionary; he's not a tough guy; he's not a well-educated man. He's an honest man, a guy who will not think of doing anything against his neighbor. He wants to work and bring home the pay and enjoy his life – go fishing, play softball, go bowling, have his friends. He was a working-class man who was taught to put the bread on the table. He was never taught to fulfill himself as a human being, to use his mind to its capacity, to be ambitious.
>
> It helped to tell myself that his father worked in the factories just like he did, that his father was a hard-working man whose job also was to put the bread on the table – which was a line I said in the movie, that I improvised in the movie – and that this will probably be the story of the next generation of the character's family.

Keitel appreciated the fact that robbing the union was an act of desperation for a man who had never even considered breaking the law. 'It's a struggle for him to join in on that robbery,' he said. 'He doesn't do it to get ahead; he does it strictly for survival. He's trapped. He no longer feels like the man of the family because he can't care for his own daughter. He does the robbery because he wants the money to get his daughter braces for her teeth.'

The film ran into trouble before filming even began, when the auto factories in Detroit tried to freeze the production out.

Detroit's city fathers were no friendlier. Ten days before they were due to begin, Schrader still didn't have an assembly line to use as a location to make his picture. Finally, the owner of the Checker Cab plant in Kalamazoo offered his factory for Schrader to shoot in.

At which point the trouble truly began. Most of the initial tension was between Pryor and the duo of Keitel and Kotto. Pryor, who had a serious cocaine and marijuana habit at that point in his career, didn't trust anything that prevented him from getting a laugh. He relied on instinct, rather than acting technique, as he worked his way through repeated takes. Sometimes those instincts were blurred by substance abuse – but the drugs never clouded Pryor's sense of his own rightness, even when he was raving with paranoia.

At one point, Keitel and Kotto were acting together in a scene in a bar, which called for them to look over the bar at the end of the dialogue and react to what they saw behind it. Some prankster on the crew took an issue of *Playboy* and opened it at the centerfold, then laid it out on the floor behind the bar.

Keitel and Kotto, who had worked themselves into the serious moment, completed the scene, looked over the bar – and broke up laughing when they saw the *Playboy*.

Pryor, who was out of the scene but sitting on the other side of the room, immediately thought that, for some reason, Kotto and Keitel were sharing a joke at his expense. He exploded out of his seat and stalked across the room to them. 'What are you laughing at?' he demanded.

Keitel and Kotto, still laughing, looked at Pryor in disbelief. Keitel said, 'Not at you, that's for sure.'

Pryor wasn't finished: 'I'm over here on my side of the room and I think you're laughing and talking about me,' he yelled. Kotto and Keitel were eventually able to calm Pryor down and reassure him.

According to Kotto, 'Harvey and I became tighter friends

after that because we both realized this was a guy who didn't have all of his fucking marbles.'

As if to prove the point, Pryor attacked Kotto a few days later. Kotto looked up to see Pryor coming at him with a chair in his hands, saying, 'I'm sick of you, Yaphet.' Fortunately for Pryor, who would have been spotting Kotto at least six inches and about 100 pounds in a brawl, Pryor's assistant snatched the chair from the enraged comic before he could reach his target.

'At that time, he was a very confused individual,' Kotto said. 'I was disappointed. I only took the job because Richard asked me to one afternoon in LA, when I was jogging. I respected his talents. But if he'd touched me, he would have been in the hospital for a while.'

Keitel and Kotto hit it off almost instantly, recognizing in each other a dedication to the craft of acting: 'Harvey comes in character, ready to go,' Kotto commented. 'You can depend on the fact that, when you do something, he'll give you something back. He finds a creative spark that helps him lift you up in what you're doing in a scene.'

The two actors rapidly developed friction with Schrader: about Pryor's tendency to stray from the script and about how much freedom the two of them had to improvise on camera. Pryor would stick to the script for the first two or three takes, then lose interest in what he was saying. So he would begin improvising lines, often changing the scene completely. As Kotto described the situation, 'Harvey would say the lines as written and Richard would come back with any old thing he wanted to say. He was really getting to Harvey.'

It was a clash of acting styles: Kotto and Keitel, classically trained, developed the scene as they worked on it, gradually finding its heart, until they had massaged it into exactly the shape they wanted. Pryor, on the other hand, was working purely on instinct. He was a genius as a stand-up comedian and had begun to make the move into acting with well-chosen comic parts, his reputation growing out of a stage act in which he created characters as part of his comedy. He was as believable playing an old lady as he was a strung-out junkie, a scorned woman or even one of his own pets. His comedy evolved out of improvisation – but improv with a different goal. Kotto and Keitel improvised to discover truth about a character. Pryor started riffing in search of new punchlines.

In *Blue Collar*, he was playing a serious role without a comic net to fall back on. Though Zeke had his share of wisecracks (most of them added by Pryor), the role was a straight one: a family man caught between pressures at work and pressures at home, with nowhere to turn.

Pryor's ad libs were often calculated solely to get laughs, no matter what that did to the dramatic thread of the moment. Keitel and Kotto were actors trained to improvise in character to give their scenes added life. And Schrader had told Keitel and Kotto when he signed them, 'This is my first picture so I'd like to hire director-proof actors. So feel free to do the things you need to at the moment.' But when they did something extemporaneous, Schrader would crack down and tell them to stick to the script.

According to Kotto, 'We kept saying, "You're the guy who told us to feel free." I don't think either of us would want to get into a situation like that again. Schrader was lucky he had us in his picture.'

Schrader, however, didn't feel lucky. The combination of the demands of directing his first film and the strife between his stars and the arguments with his actors devastated him: he broke down in tears one day on the set in frustration over everything that was going wrong.

They constantly rewrote lines, and they came to blows. There were fist-fights. It seemed that every day we had to close down for an hour or two while they battled it out. I tried to conciliate but if I'd really attacked one of those actors, he'd have walked off the picture and we'd have had to close down.

Richard, Yaphet and Harvey were like three young bulls locking horns every day. Each one was determined that every line of dialogue in every scene would belong to him and him only. The ego competition was constant. Richard would say, 'You're making an anti-black movie.' What he really meant was that in the scene we were doing, I was giving Harvey more attention. When Harvey would say, 'You're making an anti-white movie,' he meant that I was throwing the scene to Richard. It was hell working with these guys, a life-or-death struggle between actors. But the tension ensured that they put real feeling into the racial conflict in the scenes.

Did I see the guys after shooting? No, I didn't. I didn't want to.

The feeling was mutual. Kotto had taken a percentage of *Blue Collar* as part of his salary, but he found a screening so disappointing that, when he met some investors who expressed interest in a piece of the film, he quickly sold his chunk to them 'for a lot of money, because I thought I would not make anything. I invested the money in real estate and made a fortune. And a good thing, too: that movie never made any money. That's the only satisfaction I can take away from the experience. The trauma I went through, I won't forget.'

The film drew mixed to tepid reviews, typified by Richard Schickel's observation in *Time* that Schrader 'has trouble finding the heart of a scene, trouble keeping the overall tone and tension of his film consistent. There is a power in this story [Schrader] simply does not realize.'

Pauline Kael dunned Keitel for being 'glum. He doesn't seem to use his instincts; all we see is his determination to act with integrity ... Keitel produced the veneer of someone who's meant to believe that his life is terrible; he holds on to the idea so hard his face is pinched in concentration.'

Released in early 1978, *Blue Collar* quickly disappeared without a ripple at the box office. It was strike two for Keitel in that fateful year. He'd get one more swing at the ball a few months later with James Toback's *Fingers*, a film that continues to polarize critics and film lovers.

15

In 1977, James Toback was a relatively unknown screenwriter with one produced screenplay to his credit and a sometimes uncontrollable gambling habit. But he had written a script that he believed in – and when he ran into Harvey Keitel in the Beverly Hills Hotel, he sprang into action.

He quickly waylaid Keitel and persuaded him to come up to his hotel room. Once he got him up there, he looked Keitel in the eye and said with an almost evangelical fervor, 'The reason you were put on Earth was to do *Fingers*.'

'Thank you for telling me,' a politely bemused Keitel replied.

Then Toback began telling him about the film, explaining the story and the character of Jimmy Angelelli. He wanted Keitel, merely on the basis of his instincts and the sense of connection between the two of them at that moment in a Beverly Hills hotel room, to agree to be in *Fingers* – without actually reading the script.

Keitel smiled and said, 'Well, I appreciate all that. But I still want to read the script.'

Toback had failed in his attempt to dominate by sheer force of will. But he had succeeded in that he had avoided the entire agent-submission rigmarole which means that weeks and months elapse before a script gets from writer to star. Here was the script in Keitel's hand – and he'd uttered the crucial words, 'I want to read it.' Even better, he came back the next day and told Toback he wanted to play Jimmy.

'*Fingers* is Keitel's movie all the way and it is on *Fingers* that the actor's hopes must turn nowadays,' the late Stuart Byron wrote in *Film Comment* in 1978. It's not hard to understand what Keitel saw in the film. It provides exactly the kind of submersion into a soul's darkest reaches that must have appealed to him at this point in his career.

It was, he had decided, the journey that meant the most to him. He wasn't sure why yet – he had still not read much psychology or begun seeing a therapist to untangle just what it was that drew him to confront his darkest impulses. He possessed these thoughts, these urges, though he knew he could not act upon them. Playing these roles allowed him to let his demons loose in a way that was safe and acceptable – and to make a living doing it.

And here was a script that called for him to be a sensitive classical pianist, a fast-talking ladies' man, a Mob tough guy – and a tortured and confused soul who can't figure out who or what he really wants to be. In short, an actor's dream, chock-a-block with operatically emotional scenes.

More to the point, it offered Keitel the central role in a film for the first time since he played Charlie Cappa in *Mean Streets* five years earlier. After the débâcle of *Apocalypse Now*, after the embarrassment of not being able to repeat that initial success, after several years of playing small or ensemble roles, here finally was an opportunity to carry a picture by himself.

In the end, *Fingers* was a ludicrously gritty film, in which Keitel acts up a storm in service of a movie that is poignant mostly for Toback's obvious ache to emulate Scorsese. Keitel plays Jimmy Angelelli, a young New Yorker trapped between two worlds: his desire to be a concert pianist and his obligation to his father, a fading Mob boss who uses him as a debt collector.

Even as he is trying to ready himself for an audition that could put him on the concert circuit, Jimmy is also roughing up small-time hoods who won't make good their debts. He also walks around with a perpetual chip on his shoulder, in the form of a boombox in which he keeps a tape of fifties rock, like 'Summertime Summertime' by the Jamies: 'The most musically inventive song of 1958,' as Jimmy condescendingly informs someone who complains about the noise. Indeed, the boombox serves as a source of more conflict than almost anything else in the film: Jimmy has a propensity for playing it at full volume in smart restaurants, then picking fights with anyone who asks him to turn it down.

And there's much, much more: Jimmy agonizes over which of the two worlds he travels in is really for him, because each side represents one of his parents. His mother, now in a mental institution, was a famous pianist who wanted Jimmy to follow her. But his father, a small-time mobster, sees being a pianist as feminine and soft. Jimmy, aching to please both parents, can't choose which parent to please and winds up a wreck by the finale.

Toback's whole milieu is so overblown and unbelievable that it's hard to know whether Keitel's scenery chewing is intentional or the product of direction that pushed him to be emotionally overwrought. Given the quality of the rest of the film, the latter seems most likely. Keitel gives a performance that is like a showcase for the many moods of an extremely highly strung young man. He obviously has great emotional range but seems almost unable to control the effect he achieves.

'His Toback years were a big problem because Toback encouraged him to overreach, in terms of delving into his private pain,' *New York Times* critic Maslin said. 'He didn't have the control that Abel Ferrara did.'

To Keitel, however, Toback was a dream come true: 'I couldn't have done *Fingers* with a director who wasn't as sensitive and understanding as Jimmy. He's one of the best directors I've worked with – astounding. He has such perception, such insight into a character, a story. He establishes an extremely creative atmosphere to work in.'

Keitel and Toback developed a friendship based on a mutually shared sensibility. They look at life in the same way, in their feelings about women, love, sex and romantic obsession. And their sense of themselves as Jews.

To Keitel, Jimmy Angelelli was 'a man who has no identity. He does not know who he is. He's struggling to be somebody but he doesn't understand that what he wants to be is someone who's trying to please his mother and please his father. But he never tries to please himself. He's not capable of it. He's someone who would do anything to be loved.'

The part obviously called up feelings in Keitel about his own family background: about his parents' disapproval, from the time he had forsaken Judaism for juvenile delinquency. They had continued to disapprove when he gave up a solid career as a court reporter for the uncertainties of acting. This gave him a vision for the film, one he wanted to be sure Toback was committed to: 'I told Jimmy immediately that I didn't want to come near this film unless we did it as completely and as honestly as we could. I wanted it to be a total commitment. No lies. Because so many of us go through an identity crisis because of that need to be loved. We're not taught to seek our own place in the world.'

For the role, Keitel, who didn't play the piano, began taking lessons before he left for France to make *The Duellists*. One of his conditions for the latter film was that he should have a piano in his hotel room; he would return from location or the set and immediately sit down and practice for two hours. 'I couldn't play the piano,' he said. 'So I studied a lot. I practiced a lot.'

Ultimately, he did not play the music that was heard in the movie. But he had learned enough to be convincing when his hands moved over the keys. He also threw in a fillip of his own, humming, singing and otherwise vocalizing as he played – added after Toback had given him some recordings of Glenn

Gould: 'Glenn Gould did that when he played. I thought it right for the character because I thought the character was a bit eccentric.'

A bit? At various points, Jimmy becomes a near rapist and an unwilling voyeur while a black man has sex with Jimmy's girl. According to Keitel, 'The acts of sex which he's substituting for love represent in his mind his only moments of feeling secure. That's why he's constantly involved with sex. This is a very desperate character. And he finally begins to crack up because he's not getting any of the love he's seeking.'

Toback, however, saw something else in Keitel's performance, particularly in the relationship between the aggressive sex scenes and a sequence in which Jimmy undergoes a proctological examination. 'In the sex scenes, he looks like this Toulouse-Lautrecean, agonizing shrimp. He looks the way he did with a urologist's finger up his ass, writhing in agony. That was the agony he brought to the role.'

Yet the agony was not significant enough to induce Keitel to cry on cue in the film's most critical emotional moment: Jimmy sits alone in his apartment, having flunked his crucial audition for the concert tour. Meanwhile, he has also failed in one of his father's assignments – but knows he is now condemned to a life collecting debts for his father, thus disappointing his mother. He breaks down and cries.

Keitel worried about the scene all through the production, telling Toback, 'I can't just sit down and cry.' As the appointed day arrived, he found himself the victim of a self-fulfilling prophesy.

Then, in a moment of inspiration, he asked Toback to get him a recording of Peggy Lee singing 'Is That All There Is?' He began playing the self-pitying song of opportunities missed and life wasted: once, twice, three times.

By the tenth time, members of the crew were muttering under their breath to each other. As the record recycled for the fifteenth time, Keitel signaled Toback, who quietly called, 'Action!' As Peggy Lee once more lamented about how little life had left to offer her, Keitel's shoulders began heaving and then they came – long, racking sobs and spasms of sorrow, which Toback captured for the film.

'Cut!' Toback said finally.

'If he'd put that song on one more time, I would have fucking killed him,' a crew member whispered.

Keitel would have to recreate the sounds of his emotional breakthrough later in a dubbing studio; because he had Peggy Lee playing in the background, a song Toback had no intention of using on his rock 'n' roll soundtrack, the entire vocal track had to be dubbed in post-production.

Several years later, while making *Exposed* with Toback, Keitel marveled at his co-star Nastassja Kinski's ability to summon tears at will. 'I can't believe this girl can cry on cue,' he said to Toback, adding to Kinski, 'You don't know what I had to go through to cry for *Fingers*.'

A few days after principal photography was finished, Keitel ran into Toback and caught him off-guard with a question: 'How can you stand to be in that kind of pain all the time?' He went on to explain that, to get into the role, he had dug down to a level of psychological and spiritual darkness deeper than even he realized, until he'd finished the role and tried to shake it off. 'Then I realized that you're there all the time,' he told Toback. To which Toback replied, nonplussed, 'Well, if so, I don't know it because that's my world, I guess.'

Analyzing the exchange later, Toback understood: Keitel had touched on dark, unexplored feelings of his own, perhaps about his parents and their expectations, about his rebellion and the emotions that he had denied – to a level of despair Toback hadn't even imagined. And then he'd applied it to the role of Jimmy Angelelli.

Keitel actually thought the film would help to get him back

on track in Hollywood. When he was asked, shortly before *Fingers* opened, whether this was the kind of role he'd like to be doing, he said, 'Of course I want the bigger roles. I'm not interested in being a star, if all that means is making money and having a name. I want to get as much control as I can get, and I want to reach a bankable plateau only so that I can do the kind of work I want to do. I'd like to work with people like Kazan.'

Blue Collar and *The Duellists* had come and gone without making much of a dent. It didn't speak well for Keitel.

But they weren't nails in the coffin of his career in the way *Fingers* was. Though it received a couple of positive reviews, it was almost universally vilified at the time of its release. It virtually disappeared from theaters before its first week was finished, the response was so stark. The combination of the very visible misfire with the lack of commercial muscle of the earlier two films dealt a devastating blow to Keitel's career that he wouldn't recover from until the end of the 1980s.

Fingers opened to carnivorous reviews that seemed to take the movie as a personal offense, such as the one by Robert Hatch in the *Nation*, which said, 'I have contempt for this overwritten, confused and distasteful picture, but don't extend that feeling to Keitel. He is a serious actor, though a fallible judge of script, and the present disaster is more his misfortune than his fault.'

And Frank Rich's in *Time* magazine: '*Fingers* never amounts to more than a flamboyantly neurotic drive-in movie . . . Keitel gives the first terrible performance of his career.'

Or, as Toback later assessed the critical assessments: 'A handful of presciently idolatrous reviews were drowned out by middle-brow vitriol.'

Harry Ufland believes Keitel could have survived *Blue Collar* and *The Duellists* – but points at *Fingers* (as well as *Exposed*, a later Toback film in which Keitel appeared) as work that pushed Keitel out of the mainstream for the next dozen years: 'Those movies were something he shouldn't have done. James Toback is a nightmare; he's full of shit.'

Asked before its release if he'd be devastated if *Fingers* failed, Keitel said, 'No. Disappointed. I think *Fingers* is going to stimulate thought. If that's Freudian, maybe we all need a little more Freud. What do they want? Mary Poppins?'

Yet the film has had a surprising half-life, one that came back to touch Keitel years later – when a young *Fingers* fan named Quentin Tarantino approached Keitel about appearing in his film, *Reservoir Dogs*. Indeed, shortly after *Pulp Fiction* opened in New York, Toback and Keitel ran into Tarantino at de Niro's Tribeca Grill. Tarantino looked at Toback and, with a big grin, quoted a line from *Fingers*: 'Any motherfucker tells you that in certain situations his dick ain't worth a shit is lyin'.'

Keitel looked bewildered.

'It's from *Fingers*,' Toback told him. 'Jim Brown's line to you.' Keitel shook his head in amazement at Tarantino's prodigious memory.

Then Tarantino surprised them both by quoting verbatim a Toback story about where he'd heard the line: from Jim Brown himself, in the midst of a wild orgy scene at Brown's house. Toback had written it into *Fingers* for a character Brown would play. And when Brown read the script for the first time, he looked up at Toback and said, 'That's a good line. That's true.'

Though *The Duellists*, *Blue Collar* and *Fingers* drew mixed to negative reviews when they were released within the first quarter of 1978, they have grown in stature among critics, thanks to the kind of revisitation permitted by videocassette.

Jack Mathews of *Newsday* said, 'His definitive movie is *Fingers*, a character at odds with himself. The dark side is trying to overcome. There's this internal conflict which creates chemistry that's explosive and surprising.'

And Roger Ebert maintained, 'It's one of his three best. And probably his most overlooked – hardly anybody saw that picture.'

All Hollywood could see at the time, however, was that none of the films made money. None of them had a run long enough to make any kind of impression on the public.

'He was never a star in anybody's eyes,' one industry insider said. 'Then he had this shot to be a star, with big parts in three movies. But the movies didn't make a dime. If you took the grosses of those three movies combined, it might be enough to buy you four hot dogs and a Coke.'

16

Hollywood, Keitel quickly discovered after the resounding flop of *Fingers*, was a fickle mistress, ready to cut your heart out at the first whiff of failure. As Yaphet Kotto put it, 'This business is a whore. You can caress her from behind and someone is over there sucking on her tits, getting her attention. If you're not grabbing the part that makes her come or makes her feel good, you're nowhere.'

Ufland said, 'We live in a completely reactive society. The thought process is nil. You're not a star until you become a star. Then you're a star forever. But Harvey's career became about fitting into his niche, in special pictures nobody sees.'

Robert Asahina went so far as to write a summation of Keitel's efforts for the *New Leader*, headlined "A CAREER GONE SOUR", in which he said, 'It is a noteworthy feat for any actor to have the lead in three movies opening in New York in the same month. Unfortunately, none of them advances Keitel's career one bit further.'

There is no chill in Hollywood like that experienced by an actor who suddenly loses his heat. It is a self-compounding phenomenon, one that spreads perniciously, almost like a computer virus. It seems to happen virtually overnight. One day, it suddenly pops up, implanted in people's minds as though the thought had been there all along: 'He no longer suits our needs.' Your phone calls go unanswered. Your agent is hard to reach. You suddenly start caring about auditions for mundane, meaningless work you normally wouldn't look at simply because you need to earn money.

According to one industry insider, 'It killed his career as a leading man. People start to say, "Harvey Keitel has had his shot." A year goes by and people say, "Forget it, we won't make a movie with Harvey Keitel."'

An agent told Yaphet Kotto around that time, 'Oh, Harvey Keitel, that's an old story.'

'What do you mean?' Kotto asked.

'Oh, he's been around,' came the reply, implying that he'd had his chance, he hadn't become a star and now his turn was over.

'Oh, Harvey Keitel, that's an interesting choice,' was the noncommittal response his agent during the mid 1980s – Michael Black of ICM – received from casting directors when he put forward his client. Interesting – but they were seldom interested.

'Sometimes an actor gets pigeonholed,' Ulu Grosbard, the director of *Falling in Love*, offered. 'He may have been pigeonholed as a supporting guy. It's hard to get a part in some movies for commercial reasons. You want someone with a box-office track record.'

And people in Hollywood decide they're tired of a particular face, observed John Badham, who directed Keitel in *Point of No Return*: 'So they'll start to look for a new Harvey Keitel. When he's been gone a while, then he becomes a fresh idea again. Of course, it's tough on the actor. You want to keep working. If you were a doctor, that would never happen: "Oh, you've got to take ten years off because your patients are tired of seeing you."'

If anything, it confirmed in Keitel a sense of being an outsider. He had fought it since he was a youth, when he didn't seem to fit in his parents' world. He had embraced it as a teenager, playing the outsider by dressing and acting the part of the hoodlum. Then he'd tried to conform by joining the Marines and learning to be a cog in the machine.

But the machine had eventually spat him out and back into life, where he again cultivated the world of the outsider as the silent court reporter, always watching without participating. He'd traded that for the life of the artist, someone outside the mainstream of everyday American life in the 1960s.

And now, as a professional actor, he was tormented by what seemed to have become true of his career: that he was an actor who didn't belong in this commercially oriented world of movie-making. It was like an electric jolt from a socket he'd been trying to unplug himself from, a flashback to that sensation of otherness he'd tried to overcome all his life. 'Many nights when I regarded the clock and it was three in the morning,' Keitel said, 'I felt it was over.'

'It comes from his life, his frustration,' said director Peter Medak. 'It comes from the alien refugee background, coming into America. Being repressed, underneath, desperate, trying to reach up. I feel he's always been on the outside looking in at life.'

It wasn't that Keitel didn't work. He just didn't work much in Hollywood. The parts Hollywood offered him were always supporting roles, frequently villains, seldom central to the story, sometimes – as in Brian de Palma's *Wise Guys* – little more than a walk-on.

But he had to work. He couldn't avoid experiences like *Saturn 3*; neither could he say no to films such as *El Caballero del Dragon* or *Nemo*, which did poorly in Europe and barely played in the United States. Yet he also managed to work with a few of Europe's best directors, including Ettore Scola (*La Nuit de Varennes*), Lina Wertmuller (*A Complex Plot About Women, Alleys and Crimes*, also known as *Camorra*) and Bertrand Tavernier (*Deathwatch*).

Keitel wanted interesting work – and the only film-makers

willing to offer it to him were independent and foreign directors. They alone gave him the chance at big, challenging roles,
even if in films few people would ever see. The work itself
became the ever-more-refined focus – which would shape his
choices once he rekindled his career in the 1990s.

It still offered little comfort to an actor watching his choices
dwindle away, taking with them his power to shape the
material, to find stories that touched him in ways he wanted
to communicate to others. 'He went through hard times,' said
Ulu Grosbard. 'It's hard because he started with contemporaries
who went ahead. I'm sure he knew he had talent. But it was a
hard way to the kind of parts he wanted to play. That's very
frustrating for an actor.'

As Jack Mathews pointed out, Keitel also suffered because
he was a serious actor who had emerged in the seventies, one
of the most daring and adventurous eras in modern film-
making, only to survive into the 1980s, one of the most shallow
and superficial:

> The eighties were tough for everybody who was doing seri-
> ous acting, because those films weren't being made. That
> generation that came of age in the sixties was anxious to see
> tough, realistic, naturalistic stories and they got them in
> the early seventies. That's when Keitel, de Niro, and Pacino
> became stars. Scorsese exploded during that period. When
> the eighties came, what I think of as the Spielberg-Lucas
> era, society had calmed down. During the Reagan years, the
> generation of the eighties was more interested in safer
> movies. Turmoil was not part of their generation.

According to Alan Rudolph, 'You're looking at historically
the shallowest period of American film history in forty or fifty
years, because they discovered the *Jaws* phenomenon, that one
movie can make more money than all the others combined. In
the eighties, the villains were the film-makers. The ones who

mattered picked your pocket. The film-makers who bought into the idea of trying to be honest and pursue truth were swimming upstream.'

If anything, Keitel stayed true to form, no matter how difficult things got. While he might play a nothing supporting role in *Falling in Love*, he continued to pursue the same kind of troubled characters he so clearly relished playing. As Roger Ebert said,

> He didn't play those characters who were heroic, positive, charismatic. He played complex, troubled, twisted, maybe. And you see him keep on doing that. Very few actors are consistent in their careers. It's almost like everything for Harvey was set by *Who's That Knocking at My Door?*: working in low-budget films with first-time directors with a lot of street savvy and authenticity. He had that experience and he kept looking for it.

Of course, the result, at least in the 1980s, was films that went nowhere commercially. His European films had trouble breaking even in Europe and barely warranted a release in American theaters. 'He did a lot of terrible stuff,' observed Janet Maslin. 'Some of his risk-taking went off the deep end, which is the nature of risk-taking.'

'There was a time when I couldn't get any work,' Keitel recalled. 'It was beyond weird – it was hell.'

17

Part of Keitel's problem was the way he was classified: though he could and had played lead roles, he was seen as a character actor. And while some character actors became leading men, more often they were stuck in character roles: the particularly intense gangster or the oafish sidekick.

Actor David Dukes recalled sitting around in the make-up room with the entire cast of *The Men's Room* – including Keitel, Richard Jordan, Roy Scheider, Treat Williams and Frank Langella. Someone told a story about *Mean Streets* and made a reference to 'Harvey Keitel, the character man.'

Keitel looked up from his make-up chair and said indignantly, 'What do you mean, character man? I'm a leading man.'

Dukes commented, 'It became clear that he was a leading man in his own mind, though everyone thought of him as a character man. But he doesn't think of himself as doing characters. In his mind, every film is about his character's story.'

While Hollywood in its early years would occasionally elevate a character actor to leading-man status – Wallace Beery, Edward G. Robinson – more often those actors were stuck in secondary roles. If you were in a hit playing a wiseguy bellboy, you were forever stuck in that role.

Had Keitel been making movies in the 1930s or 1940s, he might have been stuck playing gangsters and hoods. It's only since the 1970s that an actor like Harvey Keitel could even consider becoming a leading man, rather than being stuck in the character-actor lane for his entire career. Yet even today, the character actor has a hard time breaking out of the mold.

In Keitel's case, it was the complexity he brought to even the smallest roles. Too often, however, complexity is not what a casting director is seeking for a character role; he wants simple, easy-to-grasp traits so that he can plug the actor into a slot and not worry about him upsetting the balance of a film by actually bringing new ideas to a role. Which Keitel inevitably did.

'Harvey is much more than your conventional bad guy,' James Toback observed. 'He presents a sense of potential violence, emotional turmoil and sexual restlessness that makes viewers feel very uncomfortable.'

And according to critic Harlan Jacobson, 'He's not the all-American male – he's the urban ethnic male. He's not wishy-washy, he's concentrated firepower.'

Apparently Hollywood sought a more dilute variety.

For several months after *Fingers*, Keitel was unsuccessfully looking for work before landing a small role in a low-budget western, *Eagle's Wing*, being shot by director Anthony Harvey, who also made *The Lion in Winter*. A somber, often wordless drama, it was the story of an on-going battle between a deadly Comanche brave, White Bull (Sam Waterston), and Pike, a young trapper (Martin Sheen), for possession of a white stallion that belonged to a Native American warrior who dies near the beginning of the film. Keitel was cast as Sheen's partner, Henry, who is also serving as his guide. He was billed in the credits as 'Guest Star' and was gone in the second reel.

He managed a couple of solid scenes with Sheen before the Comanche killed him in a river. Both of them took place around a nighttime campfire, as Keitel and Sheen debated the nature of courage they'd experienced during the Civil War. Keitel tells Sheen, finally, that being scared is part of staying alive: 'I been spooked ever since I left my mother's tit. That's what keeps me from dyin'.'

He also had a line that could just as easily have been spoken about his dealings with the movie industry up to that point: when Sheen asks him why he's nervous about trading with the Comanches – 'I thought you traded with them regular' – Keitel replies, 'I walk in rattlesnake country too, but I'm careful how I do it.'

The film was shot for long hours in the desert outside Durango, Mexico. Anthony Harvey had also lured the French actress Stéphane Audran from France for a cameo role as a stagecoach passenger. 'I always had enormous admiration for [Keitel],' Harvey said. 'On this film, he took a nothing part and turned it into something so interesting. And then he was killed off in the second reel. The pleasure of the film was Harvey and Stéphane Audran playing tiny parts and making them absolutely brilliant. Harvey's character was remarkable and then he vanishes.'

'Harvey had a great sweetness, a great sense of humor,' Sheen recalled. 'He makes you like him instantly. He has a presence that's so strong and human.'

When he's on the set but not on camera, Keitel is a virtual recluse; even when he is not in his trailer, he creates a kind of self-sealing bubble, a silent perimeter in which he can lose himself in his character between takes.

But Anthony Harvey described Keitel as 'a funny character with a marvelous, zany sense of humor. He was always doing Douglas Fairbanks stuff, jumping off horses, things like that. Once he stuffed his mouth with tobacco to get the right feeling for a scene. He was improvising all over the place. He was enormously professional, a real shot in the arm.'

Released to glowing reviews in England, *Eagle's Wing* never made it into American movie theaters. 'Primarily an art film – resolutely romantic, high on production values, low on grit,' wrote *Variety*. 'Harvey Keitel, low-key but impressive as Sheen's companion and mentor, is lumbered with a lot of

THE YOUNG HOPEFUL

Right Keitel at the beginning of his acting career

Below Keitel discusses a scene in *Mean Streets* with Martin Scorsese and actor Cesare Danova (seated, left)

THE DIFFICULT YEARS

Left Ellen Burstyn, as Alice Hyatt, tries to ward off the advances of Ben Eberhart (Keitel) in *Alice Doesn't Live Here Any More*

Right Donning full Napoleonic-era mufti for *The Duellists*

Below left A rare moment as non-combatants on the set of *Blue Collar*: (from left) Keitel, Richard Pryor and Yaphet Kotto

Below right What happened to my voice? Keitel, as the villain in *Saturn Three*, subdues a runaway robot, little realizing that director Stanley Donen would use someone else's voice instead of his

Above left As Roddy, the sensitive filmmaker with cameras implanted in his eyes, in Bertrand Tavernier's *Death Watch*

Above Betrayer or hero? As Judas in Martin Scorsese's controversial *The Last Temptation of Christ*

Left Cigar and hairpiece firmly in place, as Mickey Cohen in *Bugsy*, for which he received nominations for both an Academy Award and a Golden Globe

Above Quick on the trigger in *Reservoir Dogs*

Right Going native as Baines in *The Piano*. Director Jane Campion and Holly Hunter praised Keitel for the tenderness and vulnerability he brought to the role

THE GODFATHER OF INDEPENDENT FILM

Above The directors' choice: Keitel works through a scene with Quentin Tarantino on the set of *Reservoir Dogs*

Below And soaks up the attention at the Cannes Film Festival with Theo Angelopoulos, director of *Ulysses's Gaze*, and co-star Maia Morgenstern

Auggie Wren captures the perfect moment of a perfect day in Wayne Wang's *Smoke*

Jim Jarmusch (right) decides to share his last cigarette with his old pal Auggie in *Blue in the Face*, the improv movie made in less than a week, for only $2 million

LOCAL HERO

Left Keitel and daughter Stella brave the crowd at 'Welcome Back to Brooklyn Day' in June 1996

Below Keitel accepts his award, after Brooklyn Borough President Howard Golden (rear left) had dropped it

Fellow honorees actor Daniel Benzali, Keitel, radio legend 'Cousin Brucie' Morrow and jazz drummer Max Roach accept the audience's applause

superfluous exposition dialogue, then killed by Waterston.'

But, as Harvey recalled, Universal sold the American rights to Samuel Goldwyn – who promptly panicked when he screened it for New York critics and heard that Janet Maslin had fallen asleep. Though Rex Reed wrote in the *New York Post* that *Eagle's Wing* was better than anything then showing in New York, Goldwyn shelved the film until it was finally released on home video.

Shot in early 1978, the film was Keitel's last before a dry spell of several months. He'd been unemployed so long that, when he was offered the ludicrous villain role in *Saturn 3*, he took it. It proved to be the nadir of his career.

A turgid sci-fi film greenlighted in the wake of *Star Wars'* success, *Saturn 3* was a dour little fable about planned obsolescence, set on one of the far moons of Saturn. There, scientists Kirk Douglas and Farrah Fawcett are performing research tasks, when a rocket arrives bearing Keitel, actually a psychotic who has murdered and replaced the real research scientist they were supposed to be getting. Dressed in a jumpsuit, his hair pulled back in a sleek little ponytail, he's brought with him a prototype for a new robot, Hector, and proceeds to put him together, then tries to take over the space station. But he gets into an Oedipal scuffle with Hector over Farrah, even as he's having similar tussles with Douglas.

Among other things, the film called for Keitel to engage in hand-to-hand combat with an aged, naked Kirk Douglas; to have his hand cut off by the robot Hector; then to have his head grafted on to the robot's body for the final encounter.

Written by Martin Amis from a story by John Barry, *Saturn 3* was to have been directed by Barry. But producer Stanley Donen was so unhappy with what Barry was doing that he replaced him less than a week into production. Unlike some of the young directors Keitel had worked with, Donen was a dictator of the old school, more interested in getting the film done efficiently and on schedule than in taking time out to discuss an actor's questions about his character or indulge his explorations.

'Certain directors tend to give him that room,' one friend of Keitel's said. 'If you don't, he's not a good person to work with. When he's not allowed to do that, he gets angry and frustrated. It's not petulance or ego. It has to do with being able to independently contribute to the role.'

It was immediately obvious that Donen thought Keitel was wrong for the part and felt that he was stuck with him. Donen wanted the character to have an upper-class veneer to make him seem both chilly and deadly. All Keitel could muster was a kind of affectless calm, which was not quite the same thing.

So Donen made life miserable for Keitel, making cutting remarks when Keitel tried to discuss what he was reaching for. Donen forced him to do takes repeatedly, losing his temper without condescending to explain to Keitel what he wanted, rolling his eyes and giving great sighs of dissatisfaction at the end of takes. He belittled Keitel's work behind his back; word eventually got back to Keitel, humiliating him further.

To add insult to injury, before the film was released, Donen went back and had all Keitel's dialogue dubbed by an actor with a deeper, more cultured tone to his voice.

But Keitel was broke: he needed a job to pay the rent, buy groceries, pay bills. 'I'm not going to sit here and cry about a movie I didn't really want to do,' he said. 'I did it and made $90,000. I'm not ashamed of it.'

'He hated everything and everybody on that film,' according to one friend. 'It was a movie he didn't want anything to do with.'

Nor did anyone else. Despite the presence of former *Charley's Angels* star Fawcett, the film drew ridicule from critics: 'Not much to recommend on this one,' *Variety* wrote. 'The audience at the Ziegfeld in NY hooted after it was over. So the indications are hit and run.'

'Out of despair come relationships and adventures that are chaos and hellish,' Keitel said. 'But I still have to work as an actor to make a living.'

18

It came like a love letter from a stranger.

Having seen Bertrand Tavernier's film *The Clockmaker* and admired it, Keitel came across a magazine interview with the French film-maker and began to read it with interest. To his astonishment, when Tavernier was asked, 'Who would you like to work with?' Tavernier responded, 'I would like to work with Harvey Keitel.'

Keitel had planned to visit Europe and travel with de Niro, who was on a hiatus from *Raging Bull*, eating everything he could see to make the startling transformation to the grossly overweight Jake LaMotta of the film's opening and closing scenes. Keitel, ever the physical fitness buff, watched with amusement as his friend devoured pasta and rich pastry in an effort to add the necessary pounds. And, when they reached Paris, Keitel arranged a lunch with Tavernier.

Tavernier was yet another director – like Toback, like Rudolph, like Anthony Harvey – who remembered the work Keitel had done in *Mean Streets*. Meeting him in person was a revelation. 'There was something of John Garfield in him,' Tavernier said. 'He had a wonderful smile, which he didn't use a lot. You never saw him smiling in a film.'

Though the 1960s and 1970s had seen a burst of interest in European films – at least in New York and other large American cities – by the early 1980s, that was on the decline. Even then, there remained a chauvinism: working in the movies meant working in Hollywood. It was considered a major stretch to act in a film made in England; to go elsewhere – France, Italy or Spain – was like a confession of Hollywood failure. True, Clint Eastwood had become a major American star only by making spaghetti westerns for Sergio Leone – but he was a distinct anomaly. If you wanted a career in Hollywood, you didn't work in Europe.

For Keitel, however, anxious for a decent part working with a director he admired, working in Europe didn't seem like a big leap. It was no longer a question of the prestige of Hollywood or nothing; it was a matter of going where the best offers of work were, in this country or elsewhere.

'If he's not huge in America, he's solid overseas,' said one long-time industry observer. 'Harvey will always be appreciated more overseas than in his own country. They have a different sensibility toward movies. In America, they want everyone to see every picture. Overseas, they accept the fact that a portion of the audiences wants to see one movie, while another portion will want to see another one.'

'I had the fortune of not being bankable in America,' Keitel said. 'I was looking for work and European directors wanted to work with me. Tavernier was the first.'

But the power of the Hollywood nay-sayers followed Keitel all the way to Scotland, where Tavernier was about to direct his first English-language film. 'It was a moment he was not very popular in the States,' Tavernier admitted. 'I had many people, as soon as I began working with an American producer, he said to fire him, to get someone more popular. I insisted on him. Getting him with Romy Schneider was something I thought could be powerful, yet with a lyrical quality. I fought to keep him on the film.'

Adapted by Tavernier and American screenwriter David Rayfiel from a novel by David Compton, *Deathwatch* cast Keitel as Roddy, an ambitious TV cameraman in some near-future world, who has just had video cameras implanted into his eyes. These beam whatever he sees directly back to the TV network, where he works for Harry Dean Stanton.

In this future world, disease has been all but eradicated. So when a doctor tips Stanton off that one of his patients has contracted a terminal illness, Stanton hits on the idea of turning her final days into a TV series called 'Deathwatch.' The woman, Katherine Mortenhoe (Romy Schneider), at first refuses, then agrees to allow her life to be filmed and broadcast for an outrageous sum of money.

When she takes the money and runs, Stanton sends Roddy after her. He tracks her down and befriends her, helping her on a journey to see her first husband before she dies. Although he gets her to trust him and talk about herself, he never reveals who or what he is, presenting himself merely as a concerned and caring companion. But the more he learns about her, the more he regrets what he has become a part of. She is sharing her personal thoughts with him – and he is uplinking them to millions of avid TV viewers around the world. In a moment of profound remorse, he blinds himself, out of guilt over deceiving and betraying her.

It's a spare, deftly told film, one that, having been made in 1980, predicted the media invasion into the lives of people caught in the news, sudden media celebrities whose tragedy attracts the entire world's focus, until there is no detail left that remains private. 'Everything's of interest and nothing matters, is that it?' Katherine wonders at one point.

Keitel gives a shaggy-haired boyishness to Roddy. He does impart a sense of cold-blooded menace, but also a breezy, easygoing quality not usually associated with Keitel. Yes, his smile is a winner, one that softens the slightly vulpine planes of his face, that takes some of the focus away from the proud, prominent nose.

To prepare for his final scene in the film (a dialogue between Katherine and the now-blind Roddy), Keitel visited an institute for the blind and made films for himself of people who were newly blind, to study how they moved. Then he would film tests of himself working at being blind and insist on showing them to Tavernier.

European directors tend to work more collaboratively with their actors than Hollywood directors because, while budget is always a concern, there is not the same kind of devastating economic pressure to produce a hit. Still, even for Tavernier, Keitel's devotion to detail and quest to fully explore the character occasionally became too much.

You tend to say, 'Harvey, it's enough already.' But when it came time to film the scene, he did it in one take. He controlled every movement in his face, every movement in his eyes.

He was incredibly dedicated. He asked a lot of questions and I was not used to that. When I work with Philippe Noiret or Romy Schneider, they don't like to psychoanalyze the character. They ask questions, but indirectly. Harvey was always asking a lot of things. When he's asking, you can't tell him you don't have an answer or dismiss him with a joke. You're there to discover a part by working on it. I was not used to all the questions, but it's a difference in culture.

He never does it to get the power of the director or to behave like a star. He's the opposite. There's a loyalty, a dedication, a desire to be good, to help the film and the character. But there were one or two times during shooting when I wanted to say, 'Harvey, stop.'

He did admonish Keitel once, after Keitel was less than diplomatic with the already highly strung Schneider (who would die before the film's American release in 1982). Schneider was working in English, her second language, and was having some trouble with the lines. But Keitel wanted freshness for his scenes; he liked to rehearse the day before he shot a scene rather than the day of filming.

So when Schneider asked to rehearse a scene just before they shot it, Keitel refused: 'If you need to rehearse, go rehearse with the continuity girl,' he told her, something you didn't tell a diva like Schneider.

'It was a rude thing to say to Romy and it upset her,' Tavernier recalled. 'Yet during the takes, he was helping and giving. When I'd say, "Action," everyone in the crew was impressed and so moved by him.'

For all his questions, Tavernier found Keitel more than willing to be directed, given the opportunity to try his own ideas as well: 'In terms of bringing ideas to the character, he was never competitive to me. There were a few times we would do two takes, to try his way and my way. If he saw that my way was better, he'd say so. He'd never question out of a power relationship.'

One example was the moment in which Roddy confronts a fellow in a bar and threatens to break his nose if he doesn't move so Roddy can have the seat next to Katherine. Keitel's instinct was to be menacing, to focus his noted intensity on this guy to make the threat a palpable one.

'No, try doing it quietly,' Tavernier told him, 'almost casually – and it will be much more frightening.'

Keitel tried the scene again, this time delivering the threat in an even tone with a slight smile on his face. Then he came back to Tavernier and said, 'You were right. That's the way it should be played. Don't even print the other take.'

Keitel felt that there was 'a common denominator among certain directors; it's called giving, it's called trust, it's called respect for another's work. Marty has it. Bertrand Tavernier has it. When the ingredient of trust, encouragement, support is present on both sides, wonderful things can happen.'

The key sequence in the film, however, was the actual blinding scene. The idea was that, because of the cameras, Roddy's eyes always had to have a source of light; he could never sleep or be in total darkness or the cameras would burn out. So, in his remorse over his betrayal of Katherine, Roddy closes his eyes and puts his hands over them until they short out permanently, causing him great pain and, ultimately, blindness. It's an excruciating scene, as Keitel, howling with agony, thrashes around on the ground in spasms of ocular torture.

The scene was a long one, filmed with handheld camera. It begins with Roddy standing in a pub and seeing the 'Deathwatch' TV show – evidence of his betrayal of Katherine – on the pub's TV set. He sees the crowd at the bar watching raptly and commenting on it. And he realizes that the relationship he has developed with her has led him to exploit and deceive her. Overcome, he runs out of the pub into the deserted streets, then to the deserted spot near a river where they are staying and blinds himself. Tavernier recalled that

Shooting the blinding scene was very difficult. Harvey wanted the streets totally empty for when he ran out, so there would be nobody there to damage his concentration. But he refused to tell me when he would go out. He was preparing himself, talking to himself, and then running out. It was a long tracking shot, beautifully lit, with the camera in the car.

But all he would say to me is, 'Be with me and I'll tell you when I'm going to go out. Then you can run to the car and jump in.' I said, 'No, I don't want to be a stuntman.' So it was a difficult night, getting everyone into the pub and keeping them there.

The next day, it was incredibly powerful and easy. He came to me and we talked for a while; he was telling me stories, getting himself ready. Then he said, 'I'm ready.' I told the cameraman, 'Follow him, be on him, no matter what.'

The cameraman followed him. Harvey banged his head and started bleeding a little, then went into the water. The whole thing was so strong that finally, when I said, 'Cut,' I knew we had it in one take. It was incredible. The camera operator said that, for all the trouble, it was worthwhile. It paid off. At the end, you forgive everything because he gives so much.

Deathwatch earned admiring reviews in both Europe and the United States, some of the best Keitel had received since *Mean Streets*, typified by Kevin Thomas of the *Los Angeles Times*, who wrote, 'Arguably, neither Keitel nor the late Schneider was ever better, which is saying a lot. Never has so much been demanded of Keitel, who progresses from relentless con man to thoroughly tragic figure.'

But the film took more than two years to find its way to the United States, then had an extremely limited release. Meanwhile, Keitel had already begun accepting offers from other European directors, who felt he could contribute to their uniquely personal or extreme visions. According to Harlan Jacobson, 'All the gritty guys found their way to Harvey.'

Unfortunately for Keitel, when he teamed up with the adventurous Nicolas Roeg for *Bad Timing: A Sensual Obsession*, he was catching Roeg on an off-film. The obsessive love story, about a young American psychiatrist in Vienna who falls for a free-spirited young woman, was resoundingly panned for the incoherent and tawdry mess it was. The story essentially focused on the shrink (Art Garfunkel), who falls for a good-timey American (Theresa Russell). He wants all of her time and sexual energy; she can't invest in a single relationship and is relentlessly promiscuous. When she overdoses on pills and alcohol, he finds her comatose form – and, as an act of revenge for her faithlessness, rapes her unconscious body before calling the ambulance.

The story utilizes the same fragmentary, non-linear story-telling technique Roeg used in *Performance* and *Don't Look Now*, flashing forward and backward in the story, from the couple's initial meeting through the grisly emergency room measures taken to save the overdosing young woman's life.

Keitel plays the Viennese police inspector (complete with baroque little accent) who is trying to figure out the sequence of events and who finally forces Garfunkel to admit his crime. With his longish hair slicked back but unfettered, dressed in a nondescript black suit and tie, he looks like a younger, hipper version of Mr White, the character Keitel played in *Reservoir Dogs*.

Critics were so busy savaging Roeg's film-making and Garfunkel's acting that they didn't pay much attention to Keitel, though David Ansen, who wrote in his *Newsweek* review that '*Bad Timing* is an oppressively bad movie,' made a point of calling the police inspector 'ludicrously played by Keitel.'

Critics generally focused on Garfunkel's lack of passion: director Joel Schumacher observed, 'If Harvey had played the Art Garfunkel role, it would have been a great movie.'

Keitel had slightly better luck with Ettore Scola's lush, knowing *La Nuit de Varennes*. Keitel played Thomas Paine in an international cast that included Marcello Mastroianni, Jean-Louis Trintignant and Hanna Schygulla. He recalled that

Marcello Mastroianni speaks English, Jean-Louis Barrault only spoke French. But the weight of the project and the people involved overcome any technical problems. I came to Rome to meet Ettore Scola and he asked if I wanted an interpreter. I said no, no interpreter, so we sat stumbling through three evenings without being able to understand each other. But, on another level, we were in the same place, especially as he had hired me to play Thomas Paine.

In the film, Thomas Paine is just one of a series of people (including Casanova) who cross the path of a writer named Restif. Restif is on the trail of King Louis XVI, who is trying to flee to the border and meet an army of Austrians, before returning to put down the French Revolution. As these travelers head for Varennes, they discuss the revolution, sex, death and anything else that comes to mind. And, in the end, the king is arrested and returned to Paris.

Though the film was praised, the reviews Keitel received for *Varennes* were non-existent. That may have been because the entire film was dubbed in French, though Keitel performed his lines in English. The most critics could comment on was his resemblance to Thomas Paine.

Keitel continued to work in Europe regularly during the rest of the decade, making films that were never or barely released in the United States and hardly made a dent in their own countries: *Une Pierre Dans la Bouche* (1983), *Nemo* (also known as *Dream One*; 1983); *Star Knight* (also known as *Knight of the Dragon* and *El Caballero del Dragon*; 1985); *A Complex Plot About Women, Alleys and Crimes* (also known as *Camorra* and *Camorra: The Naples Connection*; 1985); *The Inquiry* (or *L'Inchiesta*; 1987), in which he plays Pontius Pilate; *Caro Gorbaciov*, in which he played Bolshevik thinker Nikolai Bukharin (1988); and *La Batalla de los Tres Reyes* (1990).

So, though Keitel was able to find work that satisfied him, it gave him increasingly less exposure in the United States. To a Hollywood that paid virtually no attention to foreign films (except as a source of plots for weak American remakes), he might as well have been acting in his living room.

The most pervasive image of Harvey Keitel that lingered in

Hollywood still came from *Mean Streets* more than a decade earlier: the volatile young hoodlum, the kind of actor who can play gangster parts or bullies, but little else.

He took what work he could get, convinced that tenacity and dedication to the craft would lead him out of this black hole into which his career had fallen.

19

Keitel met Lorraine Bracco while walking in Paris in 1982. He was getting ready to do *Exposed* and was out with a friend one afternoon, when the friend stopped to talk to two women. One of them was a friend of hers. The other was Lorraine Bracco.

Keitel was immediately attracted to the angular, Italian Bracco. With her large, expressive eyes and brash Long Island manner, she struck a chord in him. Within a few months, they were living together, married by most standards except the legal one.

Until that time, Keitel was known as 'an actor-around-town,' as Pete Hamill wrote in *Vanity Fair* in 1984. 'Women arrived in his life, tarried a while, departed. It was as if they had supporting parts in a script that Keitel had written for himself.'

But Bracco, a decade younger than Keitel – who was forty-three – was different. The daughter of an Italian father – a wholesaler at the Fulton Fish Market – and a British war bride, Bracco was the second of three daughters who grew up in an upper-middle-class home in Westbury, LI. Raised in an insular and comfortable environment, she began modeling in her teens and, at the age of nineteen, had moved to Paris to become a Wilhelmina model, staying for ten years.

She married French actor Daniel Guérard and had a daughter with him, Margaux. She worked for a while as a disc jockey at Radio Luxembourg. But, by the time she met Keitel, she had divorced Guérard and was trying to launch herself as an actress. Keitel and Bracco went back to New York, where they began living together in a Hudson Street loft, though they never married. 'She calmed him down,' one friend observed. 'She gave him a focus, a center. He became more domesticated. He led a more ordered life.'

With his own career in something of a stall, Keitel concentrated his time on playing Pygmalion to Bracco's acting career. He encouraged her to study acting with his old mentors, Stella Adler and Ernie Martin. He got her a part in Lina Wertmuller's *Camorra* and persuaded James Toback to cast her in a small, one-scene part in *The Pick-Up Artist*. According to a friend, 'Harvey devoted himself to building up her career. I'm sure he took her to directors. He was a proselytizer.'

She continued to win parts with directors who had worked with Keitel, such as Ridley Scott in *Someone to Watch Over Me*, culminating in her Oscar-nominated role in Martin Scorsese's *Goodfellas*.

Keitel's career, meanwhile, was stationary: he was getting work in American films again – but he had to sit back and watch the truly meaty roles go to other (and, to his mind, lesser) actors.

'There are lists in Hollywood,' one long-time industry insider said. 'You go to the studio and they say, "We'll make the picture if you can get one of the actors on this list." And Harvey wasn't on anybody's list.'

Director James Toback discovered that when he tried to cast Keitel in a film he was about to make:

When I was doing *Love and Money* [in 1980], I wanted Harvey for the lead. But I was told, 'No way.' They would finance it if I could get Ray Sharkey or Jeff Goldblum for the lead – but not Harvey Keitel. So I did it with Ray. And Ray was not up to the part. The night before we started shooting, he said, 'I want to do a good job for you, Jimmy, but I just don't get this guy.' I look at that movie now and think, 'There's some terrific stuff in that script,' but then there's Ray Sharkey playing the part instead of Harvey.

All Keitel's insecurities came raging back. At one point, he was reduced to taking a role in a gimmicky mini-series for Italian television, *Baciami Strega (Kiss Me, Witch)*: 'I needed money. I was broke. I wasn't able to get work in the States. It was the second time in my life that I had been broke. The other was *Saturn 3*.'

'He was depressed,' said a close friend. 'He had a sense of humor, but he also had a general sense of unemployability. He kept saying, "I can't get hired. These fucking people. I don't fucking believe it. They'll use that guy but not me?"'

Yes, he was getting the chance to work with people he admired: Jack Nicholson and director Tony Richardson in *The Border*, director Ulu Grosbard and de Niro once again in *Falling in Love*. And he was still being offered the occasional role that allowed him to delve into his own darkness – such as the much-maligned *Corrupt* (also known as *Copkiller* and *Order of Death*). But the roles were either inconsequential supporting roles (as in *Falling in Love*) or leads in films that no one saw – and no one wanted to see (such as *Corrupt*).

So Keitel found himself still struggling for an opportunity to do the kind of work he wanted, to have the room to create a character – instead of merely delivering the performance a director demanded. 'I'd have more input if I had more power,' he said. 'Everything in Hollywood is power.'

But power derived from success; success was measured in terms of box-office totals. The movies he was in that did any business at all (*Falling in Love*, *The Border*) drew the perception of success from their stars (Nicholson, de Niro, Meryl Streep), not from Keitel's smaller supporting contribution. And the movies where he actually had the lead did no business, tarring him with the aura of failure.

Even his friend James Toback couldn't help. He cast Keitel in his film *Exposed*, as a terrorist bomber modeled on the real-life terrorist Carlos the Jackal. But the character didn't show up until the second-to-last reel.

'In *Exposed*, he felt he was part of a good movie,' Toback said. 'But it was only eighteen minutes of screentime. The frustration was that I think he felt that, if the role had been a lead, it would have been something he could really sink his teeth into. He kept saying, "Jimmy, when are we gonna do another picture like *Fingers*?"'

Those roles, however, were not forthcoming. So Keitel decided to circle the wagons and get back to basics. He would focus on his relationship with Bracco and return to where he had started: acting on the stage.

'The experience of acting is confronting yourself,' Keitel said. Which made the role of Phil in David Rabe's *Hurlyburly* a perfect fit: 'I know Phil very well. He was me a long time ago.'

In the fall of 1984, Keitel heard about casting for *Hurlyburly*, a new David Rabe play about Hollywood. Mike Nichols was directing; the cast would include William Hurt, Sigourney Weaver, Ron Silver and a few others. They would try the play out in Chicago, at the Goodman Theater, before coming to New York and opening off-Broadway at the Promenade.

Keitel got a copy of the script and read it, then tried to arrange for an audition to play Phil. But Nichols didn't believe Keitel was right for the part. Only after a hard-sell job by Rabe would Nichols agree to hear him. Keitel said, 'It really made me respect Nichols. He didn't think I was right, but he also didn't hesitate to change his mind after he heard me read for the part.'

Rabe found that he brought 'a tremendous sense of authenticity to the role. Very few actors are familiar with Phil's world and also have the talent to make it come alive. He is one of them.'

Hurlyburly was an ostensibly semi-autobiographical play about Rabe's experiences in Hollywood. Its central characters are Mickey and Eddie, who share a house that serves as headquarters for a group of friends and women (and never the twain shall meet). Mickey and Eddie are casting directors; one of Eddie's friends is Phil, a bit-part actor in an unhappy marriage. Phil has prison in his past, as well as a history of spouse abuse and a general tendency toward assault. During the course of the play, he tries to save his collapsing marriage and his own crumbling grip on the real world by agreeing to his wife's demand to have a baby. When she divorces him anyway, he sneaks into the house and steals the baby for his friends to see. Later in the play, on a date with a woman he has just met, he gets so angry at some perceived slight that he pushes her out of a moving car. According to Keitel,

> Phil is deathly frightened to confront himself. He's scared of seeing the reality that he's a failure. That's what kills him in the end. It's a disease. I understand that desire to escape from facing up. I've certainly struggled with the same problems, but thankfully with more success than Phil.
>
> In spite of the fact that Phil's a dangerous person, one feels sorry for him. I think we see something in Phil common to many of us. The trouble is, we're prejudiced against Phil. There are a lot of Phils walking around, you know, in white collars.
>
> One doesn't have to be married to understand Phil. One doesn't have to be a psychopath to play a psychopath.

The play began rehearsals in Chicago in December 1983. William Hurt had been cast as Eddie; Ron Silver, who had been cast as Mickey, had received an offer to star in Sidney Lumet's *Garbo Talks,* so Nichols replaced him with Christopher Walken. Keitel was Phil; Jerry Stiller was Artie, a producer friend of Eddie, Mickey and Phil; Sigourney Weaver was Darlene, a woman coveted by both Eddie and Mickey; and Cynthia Nixon and Judith Ivey were two women who drifted in and out of the story as virtual sex toys of the men.

A hit at the Goodman Theater, it moved to New York, where it opened at the Promenade in June 1984 and drew such strong reviews and a large advance that the producers moved it to Broadway in August, opening it there at the Ethel Barrymore Theater. Walken, who had a previous movie commitment, dropped out before the move to Broadway and was replaced by Ron Silver, who had finished *Garbo Talks*.

The ensemble was a blending of disparate personality types, each with a different approach to acting, each playing a role that, at certain moments in the three-act, three-hour play, could be considered the linchpin of the production. Director Mike Nichols called it 'an ensemble of highly accomplished soloists. There were more accommodations to be made than usual, with seven soloists finding ways to be together.'

'Although this is ensemble acting we are all very much dependent on each other,' Sigourney Weaver said in an interview at the time. 'We're all so different and have such different ways of working. We're not the kind of ensemble that works together as one machine. And the characters in this play are all at each other's throats at some level. The play does not encourage cohesion. It puts you out there on the edge and all kinds of dark feelings that are inside you come out when you're playing these roles.'

But that was exactly the point for Keitel: 'It's not that acting offers you so many different roles to play,' he said. 'It's that it offers you work that can take you deeply into a place if you choose to go.'

Still, given that many stars, that many styles, that many egos, things occasionally got a little wild. As Judith Ivey observed, 'Things changed on a nightly basis. We didn't talk about it. It just happened on stage.'

One day during a matinee, in the second act, Keitel began
to improvise. The scene was one of his key moments in the
play: Phil describes nearly beating to death a guy who looked
at him the wrong way in a bar. When he came back to the
script, he gave Ron Silver, who was playing Mickey, a wink.
Then, as Keitel was about to launch into his story about the
beating, Silver jumped in: 'Oh God, Eddie, now he's going to
tell you the story about the guy . . .' and proceeded to do the
entire monologue instead of Keitel, as though Phil had already
told this story to Mickey:

> It's not terribly professional for the president of Equity to
> be saying that he did this, but it was a matinee and I did his
> whole monologue, like five minutes. He gave me a look. He
> even looked at the audience, like, 'Do you believe this guy?'
>
> And when I was done, I winked at him. So there's some
> business and he crosses over near me and, upstage, steps on
> my foot. He's wearing cowboy boots. I'm barefoot. And then
> he winks at me.

The reviews for the show on Broadway were equally ecstatic
and the show ran for more than a year. John Simon, who once
had called Keitel 'that terrible actor,' came around this time to
call him 'awesomely right; he can even gain some legitimate
sympathy for a sick brute.'

Jack Kroll in *Newsweek* termed Keitel's 'complex, scary primi-
tivism' 'superb'; Frank Rich in the *New York Times* said Keitel
and Ivey 'rise highest in this illustrious crowd. Mr Keitel's
down-and-out actor, feral in appearance and gravely of voice,
is a dimwitted, tightly knotted animal who arouses contempt,
laughter and pity.'

Keitel finished *Hurlyburly*, then ran off to Europe to make a
couple of films: *Star Knight*, a piece of piffle about an encounter
between medieval Spaniards and an extra-terrestrial, and Lina

Wertmuller's *Camorra*, in which a by-then-pregnant Lorraine also acted.

'I have no choice,' Keitel said. 'I have to make a living. But also, I have to act to stay alive. Hey, I like money as much as the next guy and sure I'd like to be bankable out in Hollywood. Harvey would like to make millions. But what is bankable? All it really means is that you have wider choices.'

Then it was back to New York, where Keitel went into rehearsals with playwright-director Sam Shepard and his play *A Lie of the Mind.*

Once again Keitel was playing a wife-beater, this time named Jake; believing that he has beaten his wife to death, he goes back to his parents' home. The wife, meanwhile, survives, although she is brain damaged. Jake's brother, who has gone to check on her well-being, is shot by her brother. She nurses him back to health, even as Jake tries unsuccessfully to find his way back to her.

Keitel, according to castmate James Gammon, was 'one of the most dedicated actors I've ever met. He's constantly study-ing. Even after the show opened, he was always still involved in the study of his work. It's a constant kind of thing with Harv. I admired that greatly. He took his craft as an actor extremely and intensely seriously.'

Having two critical and popular New York theatrical hits would normally be enough to rehabilitate an actor's reputation, to strike the sparks that set the fire that lures the moths known as casting directors. Instead, Keitel's behavior on *A Lie of the Mind* worked against him, because of his health and the intense feelings about family that he was experiencing.

Part of that had to do with his impending fatherhood. All through rehearsals, Bracco grew increasingly pregnant. Five days after the play's opening, on December 10, 1985, Bracco gave birth to a daughter at 5 a.m. at Lenox Hill Hospital. She was named Stella – neither for the character in *A Streetcar*

Named Desire nor for Stella Adler, but for a square in a poor section of Naples he and Bracco had shot in while making *Camorra.*

'We were in a square and Lorraine was pregnant at the time,' Keitel recalled. 'Her daughter, Margaux, who was six, was with us and Margaux started playing with the children of the neighborhood. I was so touched by those children, knowing they could probably never get out of that poverty. They were trapped. That piazza was in the Quartiere Stella. And there for us was the name of our daughter. Stella. Those kids, in some way, could leave with us.'

His devotion to Stella caused a shift in his priorities, much to the chagrin of his colleagues in the play. While it sounds like a cliché, actors believe in the time-worn motto, 'The show must go on.' The only excuse generally accepted for missing a performance is an injury or life-threatening illness. But the evening after Stella was born, Keitel decided he couldn't face Shepard's richly textured play about family disintegration. So he skipped the performance, leaving an understudy to play his role with a script in his hand. 'I didn't want to be at the theater,' he said. 'I was feeling too good. That's not saying much for my great technique, but it's true. That feeling – joy – kind of overwhelmed me and I felt like doing something else, as opposed to being Jake in *A Lie of the Mind.*'

There may have been another factor at work as well: Keitel had actually doubted his art for a minute, in the face of a real-life tragedy that coincided with his and Bracco's happy time. A couple they had met in Lamaze class had their baby the same day as Bracco, but theirs was stillborn. 'I didn't feel like going onstage that night, because I felt, "There's the truth,"' he explained. 'And maybe what I'm doing is not the truth. I love *A Lie of the Mind* and yet I felt a truth in what happened to that couple that I hadn't reached yet in the play. That maybe we, in that production, hadn't reached yet. Maybe

I'm just being sentimental because I'm so touched by these people and their tragedy.'

The urge to be near his new child and a lingering bout of the flu that he couldn't seem to shake made Keitel a less-than-satisfied worker – and only a sometime presence at the theater. He complained publicly about the demands of the schedule, calling it 'a disturbing machination. I don't like doing eight shows a week. I think it's a mechanism created by the theater owners to make more money.'

The gossip columns of the New York tabloids took note when, in February 1986, Keitel missed four weekend performances, pointing out that he had missed twenty-one performances since the December 5 opening. 'Various ailments are said to be the reason for Keitel's uncommonly high absenteeism,' *Variety* reported.

Keitel was allegedly furious to arrive at the theater for a performance one evening and be greeted by a sign in the PROM-ENADE lobby that read: 'The role of Jake, normally played by Bill Raymond, will tonight be played by Harvey Keitel.'

Gammon, however, downplayed the notion of friction among the cast over Keitel's absenteeism.

It was not only the birth of his daughter. He had some illness himself that he was going through. That may be why things were blown out of proportion: because he was having a baby and he was sick. To a lot of people, the old 'show must go on' thing is pretty strong and a lot of people got upset that he missed several shows. But he came around. It was a sticky little time but it passed.

Having that daughter was the most exciting thing in his life. Every night, it was 'my daughter, my daughter.' It's exciting. I think he relaxed a lot after the baby was born. Once everything was fine with the family and his health, he relaxed a lot.

20

The movie work was picking up, in quantity if not quality. A job, after all, is a job.

And, to Keitel, acting was still acting, requiring the same kind of methodical, detailed preparation he had always believed in. It didn't matter if it was for TV (such as an episode – directed by Clint Eastwood – of Stephen Spielberg's *Amazing Stories*) or tiny roles in mediocre or worse comedies – such as Brian de Palma's dreadful *Wise Guys* or the bland *Off Beat*. A role was still something Keitel felt compelled to research, analyze and ask endless questions about.

'This wasn't a complicated part,' observed Michael Dinner, who directed *Off Beat* and cast Keitel in a minor role because of his long-time love of *Mean Streets*. 'But he's unpredictable and is always trying stuff. That's the kind of actor who makes work interesting.'

Despite the size of the role – as one of a pair of inept bank robbers – Keitel approached it with the same seriousness and intensity as if he were the star. Which put him at odds with a young, nervous director who had a schedule to keep to, despite his admiration for the actor: 'Harvey is a pretty intimidating guy. On the first day of shooting, I thought one of us would kill the other – and probably that it would be him that would kill me.'

But the next day, when a scheduling snafu necessitated improvising a scene to fill some time, Keitel and Dinner clicked:

'What I found was a complicated, intelligent, inventive actor,' Dinner said. 'At the core, Harvey is an intense guy.'

In the film, Keitel's partner in crime was played by his long-time pal Victor Argo, perhaps the single greatest beneficiary – outside of Keitel's own family – of Keitel's career. A character actor and bit player of limited range, he pops up in one Keitel film after another, eventually working his way up to the featured role of Vinny, the cigar-store owner, in *Smoke* and *Blue in the Face*. Keitel's street-smart wisecracks and Argo's dumb tough-guy act actually enliven *Off Beat* for a few minutes, but the role is insultingly minor, barely larger than a walk-on. The fact that Keitel is almost able to steal the film in its final minutes (away from a cast that starred Judge Reinhold, Meg Tilly, Joe Mantegna and Cleavant Derricks) is as much a testament to the film's flimsiness as to Keitel's screen power.

Keitel brought similar powers of concentration and earnestness to his role in Peter Medak's film version of Leonard Michaels's best-selling novel, *The Men's Club*. What's more, the film offered him the chance to do what he seemed to enjoy most: to rehearse and improvise, to dive headfirst into the process of acting before actually giving a performance.

'We came together with great bravado for two weeks' rehearsal before we shot the film,' recalled actor David Dukes, who was part of a cast that also included Roy Scheider, Richard Jordan, Frank Langella, Craig Wasson and Treat Williams. 'We started to do improvisations to talk about our relationships with women. We were all so excited because we were doing improvisation, developing very individual relationships to each other. Then the filming started and it ended up a very unfocused film. It was clear nobody knew how to do this.'

In the film, Keitel plays Solly Berliner, a real-estate agent who joins a group of friends for an evening of male bonding, discussing women and the problems they have with them. The film had the potential to be a thoughtful and provocative literary adaptation dealing with significant issues about women and men. In it, Keitel captures the lovelorn confusion of a man who has never and will never understand women because he'll never understand himself.

During rehearsals – and then during filming – Keitel blossomed under the patient hand of Peter Medak, a European director working in Hollywood. Medak gave Keitel the room he needed to develop his character and take him wherever the character would lead:

> Underneath the casual jokiness of his character in the film, you see the whole person opening up. It's a process Harvey goes through. He gives you more and more and more; he's very responsive to direction and he's there, hovering like a ghost. He's like a Rolls-Royce engine. Whatever comes up, it's always the truth of the character, he's gone through it so thoroughly.
>
> Harvey loves to rehearse and so do I. It was a very rehearsable piece. He loves to do it because he goes into all the directions with the character to find his background. Eventually it all adds up to the character. He's absolutely relentless. There's no stopping.

For Dukes, working with Keitel was like an acting class in how to focus on a part to the exclusion of all else:

> He's obsessed and self-possessed. Being obsessed is not a bad thing. It's absolutely necessary to film work. The focus is never about the actor or the character; it's always on the technical stuff. But Harvey is always so focused on what he's doing. It was just fascinating to watch this watchmaker; each moment reveals so much about his character. It's like a possession he goes through. By the time we were ready to film, he was so far beyond the words in the script. He's tremendously overprepared for the scene.

In the film, each of the friends has a tale to tell that is revealing about his character. Keitel, as Solly, tells how he had asked his wife to put her tongue in his mouth: she refused. Medak let Keitel do more than a dozen takes with the speech: 'In every one, the colors were different, as he sunk deeper into this guy's soul,' he said. 'It's like discovering Mount Everest in the clouds.'

But Keitel's self-consuming seriousness got on the nerves of at least one cast member: Frank Langella, a somewhat more free-wheeling actor. As the group sat around a dining-room table, listening to Keitel tell his story again and again, Langella took a paper plate and began using a knife to cut out eyes, nose and mouth for a mask. As Keitel finished his story, Langella popped the mask on his face. Dukes remembered that

> Harvey was ready to murder him. Frank is a wonderful actor, but he's the opposite of Harvey in attitude and work manner. Frank tends to be a bit naughty – he loves to tease. And Harvey is not teaseable. They almost came to blows twice, because Frank couldn't stand what he considered Harvey's selfishness. But it was Harvey's character being self-obsessed. That's how Harvey works. It was a clash of styles I've seldom experienced.

Medak recalled, 'Their characters were frustrated with each other in the movie and, through the characters, they were arguing. At one point they nearly blew up. Harvey said, "Wait, I'm not arguing with you. It's my character."'

Keitel was not above high jinks that upstaged a fellow actor. The late Richard Jordan had his own big speech midway through the film, as he paws through pictures of women he's known and talks about them. At the end of one particularly good take of his speech, Keitel, who was supposed to stand up and cross the room, did – and then dropped his trousers when he was halfway across the room. 'It was incredible watching everybody's face,' Medak said. 'Yet it was perfect for the character. I don't think even he knew why he was doing it. But it brings life into it.'

Keitel also offered brief instruction to Stockard Channing for her one scene, in which she conks her screen husband, Richard Jordan, over the head with a heavy frying pan. 'We didn't rehearse because he doesn't like to rehearse; he likes to improvise,' Channing recalled. 'He doesn't like to say the lines before he's on camera. Harvey was coaching me with the frying pan, like he was directing me. I came through the door and did it and Harvey nodded his approval.'

When he was offered a role in *Blindside*, a convoluted noir thriller to be shot in Toronto, Keitel leapt at the opportunity. Here, finally, was a lead role again – and one that gave him a chance to stretch in a new direction: playing a mostly passive and thoughtful, though troubled, character. As Penfield Gruber, the owner of a small motel who spies on his customers through hidden cameras in their rooms, Keitel shuffled around with short hair and a goatee (but no mustache), smoking a pipe. Though director Paul Lynch observes that this was ahead of the big goatee comeback of the mid 1990s, in fact it was the perfect touch for the character. At that point in the 1980s, only a creepy, pipe-smoking nerd would wear a goatee.

Lynch, who had interested Keitel in the role by sending him a script, found himself working with an actor whose attention to detail never let up:

I remember one shot in a park where we were filming him walking across the park with a long lens. As I was looking at him through the lens, he waved me down. Then he pointed to his shoes, which looked old and scuffed on top. He said, 'Look,' and showed me the bottoms. They were brand new.

So we had to take the shoes and scuff and wear out the bottoms before we shot. Every part of everything was part of the character to him. That's to be admired.

In the needlessly complex plot, Gruber is, in fact, a disgraced behavioral scientist who has won awards for his innovations in remote observation. In other words, he is able to spy on people without them knowing. But his wife has killed herself in their home, which he had bugged with cameras. He now spends his time watching her suicide over and over on videotape, even as he gets involved in a plot by a husband to kill his wife, using the wife's lover as the hitman.

For the scenes in which Gruber watches his wife's death, Keitel agonized over what Gruber should be drinking during his moment of gruesome voyeurism. 'It was fairly heavy stuff,' Lynch remembered. 'And he'd come up to me while we were setting up the shot and say, "I think I should be drinking tea," and walk away. Then, a little while later, he'd come over and say, "No, maybe I should be drinking soup." Then, a little later, he'd say, "No, it should be coffee." And I'd say, "Sure, Harvey." I figured I'd let him find it. He finally decided to go with water.'

One of Keitel's co-stars was a young actress calling herself Lolita David, who played a motel resident working as a stripper and trying to get Gruber involved in her life. She would later change her name back to Lolita Davidovich to play a stripper in Ron Shelton's film, *Blaze*. The two had a lengthy scene in her motel room, involving props and a variety of bits of business. But where Keitel had to make sure that each detail of the scene was right before he could begin, Lolita was a performer who acted on spur-of-the-moment impulses. According to Lynch,

It would drive Harvey crazy. She'd do what she did as a naturalistic actor who sort of drew inspiration from the moment. Harvey was very meticulous in planning, while Lolita just came in and did the scene.

At one point, he came over to me and whispered, 'I'm going to strangle her.' Yet he was very tolerant with her. He never blew his stack. He hung in and tried to help her as much as he could. He's such a fine actor that she became better because of it.

Keitel's devotion to process and professionalism in *The Pick-Up Artist* made him somewhat unique among that cast and crew. Another James Toback gabfest, the film cast Keitel as a vicious hood, the film's antagonist. He took the role for the money and for the opportunity it presented for a small role for Bracco. '*The Pick-Up Artist* he did for her,' Toback maintained.

Despite the role's lack of depth or screentime, Keitel attacked it with the same kind of concentration as a lead. 'I remember him being very focused and professional to the point of being a little bit aloof,' said Tom Reilly, first assistant director on the film. 'Some guys are loose and friendly; they'll goof around with the crew. Guys like Tom Hanks, Nick Nolte. But Harvey tends to be more serious, though he's got a good sense of humor and he's quick to laugh. He's very professional in terms of being available, knowing the work, being concerned about the details and focusing on the minutiae.'

That was particularly true when the production moved from New York to Atlantic City, where the film's final third takes place. The cast, which included Robert Downey Jr, Molly Ringwald, Danny Aiello and Dennis Hopper, tended to be distracted by the casino in which they were filming. According to Reilly,

There were four or five other actors we'd have to literally drag away from the craps tables. We were in a live casino, with seven or eight thousand people gambling. The casino had carved out a niche of four or five tables for us. And the guys with lesser roles would be like big kids, throwing dice or playing blackjack. We had to assign production assistants to the other actors, to make sure they'd come when we were ready for them. But Harvey was serious about stuff like knowing his lines and his blocking. In a way, he's very refreshing. A lot of actors are not so focused on their craft as they are on their career or the money. But Harvey was really there professionally.

21

When Martin Scorsese called Keitel to cast him as Judas in his film of *The Last Temptation of Christ*, it was the culmination of a project that had been in the works for half a decade.

Scorsese had originally tried to get *Temptation* off the ground in 1983 at Paramount. Working with executives Michael Eisner, Jeffrey Katzenberg and Barry Diller, he went all the way through casting (including Aidan Quinn as Jesus and Keitel as Judas) and pre-production before a nervous Paramount pulled the plug a month before filming was to begin on a misunderstood project they were convinced would only draw negative attention to the studio.

But in 1987, with the minor success of *After Hours* and a solid commercial hit in *The Color of Money*, Scorsese was able to persuade Universal to back a relatively low-budget production ($6.5 million) to be filmed in Morocco. Quinn was previously engaged; though there were rumors that Scorsese wanted to cast Robert De Niro as Jesus, his final choice for the role was Willem Dafoe, who had just received an Oscar nomination for *Platoon*.

Keitel, however, was still available to play Judas and took to the role with relish. Not the least of the attractions was the chance to thrash out age-old issues – good, evil, God, the devil – with his old friend Scorsese:

Marty and I spent hours and hours and days and days, discussing religion, discussing theology. These weren't just discussions about what the dialogue would be or the historical Judas. These were discussions about things we believed – things we didn't know, but felt. Our blood went into it. We felt we had to make a total commitment, because that's what people had given before us, thousands of years ago, up until the present time – their blood for these beliefs.

Keitel read the 1955 Nikos Kazantzakis novel from which writer Paul Schrader was adapting the screenplay: 'Kazantzakis put me into a world of reading I had not been in before regarding religion. His book was such an inspiration to me.' He found himself fascinated with this interpretation of Judas: not as a betrayer, but as a facilitator for Christ redeeming mankind's sins: 'I don't perceive Judas as evil,' he said.

Correcting that perception became one of his goals, as he struggled through the hot, dusty shoot in the deserts of Morocco:

I thought we were going to change the world – and we did in some ways. In the way religious people viewed the relationship between Judas and Jesus. There's more to the story of what made him betray Jesus than what I had read. People have been steered down a narrow, bigoted road. It was important to make the film to help people bridge the gap between Christianity, Judaism and perhaps to overcome their prejudices that exist because they've been fed the line that Judas betrayed Jesus.

Keitel had a particular interest in playing with stereotypes, in shaking up people's preconceptions about who this man – whose name has become a synonym for betrayal – really was:

Central to my desire to play Judas was my loathing, my abhorrence of prejudice. The notion that some man, woman or child's quality will be judged by the contours of their bones disgusts me and fills me with anger. That's why I had myself made up in the image of a stereotypical Jew: the hooked nose, the curly hair. Judas would have been a man of qualities who someone would point to and say, 'Look at that hooked nose, look at that protruding chin, look at that bone structure. There must go a low Jew.'

Kazantzakis believed that Judas was a patriot, that he believed in Jesus' work and that he was serving a cause they were both supporting and that they both would give their lives for. Judas was outraged at the injustices of the time: the economic inequality, the oppression of religious freedom, the rape of his people. What I saw was a man's spirit rebelling against that, willing to give his life for it.

Though they'd known each other for more than twenty years, Keitel still managed to surprise Scorsese and make him nervous with one of his requests. At the end of the film, as Jesus is dying on the cross, he has a fantasy: his last temptation, in which he sees how much easier his life would be if he was simply a man who fathered and raised a family. In the fantasy, he grows to old age but, on his deathbed, he is visited by an aged Judas, who condemns him for betraying his followers by not accepting death on the cross in order to redeem mankind.

The day before the scene was to be shot, Keitel went to Scorsese with an unusual request: When he was filming Keitel's portion of the shot, with the camera on Judas and Jesus out of shot, would Scorsese lie on Jesus' pallet, so that Keitel could deliver his lines to him?

Scorsese thought about the request for a while and grew increasingly skittish. Finally, he called Keitel that night from his hotel room. 'Can I talk to you a minute?' he said. He quickly scurried down to Keitel's room and asked, 'What is it you actually want me to do tomorrow?'

Keitel replied, 'Just lie on the pallet and be Jesus for me.'

'But what are you going to do?'

'I'm going to stand there,' Keitel said.

'Oh, you're just going to stand there?' Scorsese said anxiously.

'Yes,' Keitel said; 'I'm not going to move.'

Scorsese looked at him and muttered, 'OK, OK, OK, fine.'

The next day, Scorsese nervously took his place on the pallet as the camera focused on Keitel and he said his lines. In the final film, it is Scorsese to whom Keitel delivers his speech.

It's not hard to read the subtext of that moment: Keitel, the disciple and true believer, delivering a speech about betrayal to Scorsese, who hadn't given him a movie role in more than a decade – and who, to some, had squandered his gift on films such as *After Hours* and *The Color of Money*.

Right-wing critics of *The Last Temptation* didn't wait to see the finished film before condemning it. Released in August 1988, it stood as one of the year's most outrageous media events, with forces of the Christian Right aligning to attack the film before Scorsese had even finished editing it. Led by the Revd Donald Wildmon, the Mississippi nutcase whose American Family Association has staked out a fundamentalist position on American morals, the protests targeted Universal Pictures. The studio was inundated with letters and phone calls for weeks before the film was released; protesters acted out mock-passion plays, in which the very Jewish heads of Universal, Lew Wasserman and Sid Sheinberg, crucified Christ.

Even then, the outrage was based only on hearsay about what the film might contain – because no one had seen it. Indeed, Wildmon and his followers continued their attack long after the film opened – and still wore as a badge of honor the fact that they had not watched the movie.

The film, however, opened and played, in spite of the efforts of the lunatic fringe. It won mostly respectful reviews from critics, many of whom admired its seriousness and passion.

As Judas, Keitel knew exactly who he was. A tough, aggressive rebel, battling the Romans, trying to free the Jews from repression, Keitel imbued the role with a vigor that crackled. In a highly unconventional biblical tale, he was perhaps the most unconventional figure, with his curly red hair, his large prosthetic nose and his brisk, modern rhythms. To many critics (who claimed to hear the Brooklyn in Keitel's speech), he was distinctly out of place: 'They all looked like New Yorkers,' claimed Bruce Williamson of *Playboy*.

Keitel saw out the decade with three films: Pat O'Connor's limp ensemble comedy, *The January Man*; a portion of the horror anthology *Two Evil Eyes*; and Jack Nicholson's sequel to *Chinatown*, *The Two Jakes*.

In *The January Man*, Keitel plays the corrupt New York police commissioner with a sour look on his face. This look may be due to the weak script (by John Patrick Shanley), further aggravated by a writers' strike during production (though, according to one crew member, Shanley blithely ignored his union's admonitions against working and did rewrites during production; they didn't help). It's an unproductive supporting role in which Keitel can do little except what he does: appear uncomfortable. An odd-couple pairing has him married to an obviously impatient Susan Sarandon who, in the plot, actually has a yen for his brother, played by Kevin Kline. Who wouldn't?

It's a little easier to understand what Keitel saw in *Two Evil Eyes*, a gruesome but intriguing horror opus that is palatable in part because of its brevity. It's actually half of the film, a collection of two modern tales based on stories by Edgar Allan Poe. Keitel's section, directed by Dario Argento, is a loose modern adaptation of 'The Black Cat'; Keitel's role offered yet another chance to delve into the past of a dark and twisted soul, a guy who takes pictures of the violently deceased and displays them as part of his aesthetic vision. It's like a long version of an episode of *Tales from the Crypt*, without a sense of humor. But it might have been worse: he could have been forced to act with Adrienne Barbeau (who appears in the film's other story, directed by George Romero).

The role that put him on the road to a comeback, however, the role that once again had critics and producers beginning to pay attention, was Nicholson's *The Two Jakes* in 1990.

The sequel to the much-lauded *Chinatown* had been kicking around for a decade, as the notoriously fussy Robert Towne tinkered with and rejigged his screenplay about the continuing adventures of LA private eye J. J. Gittes, this time in a black-mail-murder plot involving a shady real-estate developer named Jake Berman, played by Keitel.

But Keitel nearly lost the part to studio pressure. He was still not considered a strong enough draw for audiences, and Paramount tried to get Nicholson to replace him.

This was nothing new for Keitel, who had suffered a similar indignity on *The Last Temptation*, with Universal pressuring Scorsese into dropping him from the role of Judas:

On both occasions, the studios objected to them using me in the film. Marty persevered. He told me, 'I'm going to go down the line with you on this. I want you in this film.' And he got his way.

With Jack – I discovered this, he didn't tell me – the same thing occurred. The truest thing I can say about Jack is that he stood up for me. When others wanted to fire me from *The Two Jakes*, he wouldn't allow it. What I'm trying to say is that I had their support. The studios were also right in their context. Now what is that other context? Economics? Popularity? Media exposure? They wanted somebody more famous. We need the Nicholsons and the Scorseses. I personally think too many of these directors give in too easily. Why? Perhaps because they lack the courage. Now that statement is probably going to cost me a number of jobs but I think they are jobs I wouldn't have had anyway.

I don't say these things lightly, believe me. I'm nervous. I need work. I have to depend on directors to get my work. I am not a bankable actor. I need directors to get a job and that's the long and short of it.

Nicholson, who had developed respect for Keitel while working with him on *The Border* much earlier in the decade, was equally insulted at having his judgment questioned, and fought to keep Keitel in the film. 'Harvey is an all-timer,' he said. 'He's given more than enough performances to prove it. How can you go to an actor of his skill and ask him if he can play this or that? It's like hurling coffee grounds in Van Gogh's face. Because Harvey's foundation is right, if you understand how to collaborate with him, then you get the best of him.'

Keitel was attracted to the role for a couple of reasons. For one thing, he keenly felt it had something relevant to say about the importance of families:

One of the main elements of it is the chaos that results from mankind not being in a family way. These people are in despair, hopelessness, agony. And they're all in search of a family: the Nicholson character, the Meg Tilly character, my character. We're all people without a family, without children.

The other thing that interested me was the question of law-of-ethics and morality. Where the issue of law of what is right and not right is raised, the question is, 'How far would you go to protect what you love?' It's a loaded film and it deals with issues that concern me.

He was also glad for the opportunity to work with Nicholson again, particularly as an actor working with a director:

Collaboration, support, respect, love, responsibility: I've had that with other people in my career and with Jack in spades. As a director and as an actor, Jack is one of the few around who understands the essence of acting and knows its importance. He knows the art of acting. He created the ground on which I could bring whatever I imagined into rehearsals, and into the actual execution, when we were shooting. He worked very, very hard on the film. He gave it his blood and his sweat.

None of which seemed to matter to critics or audiences. Critics found it distinctly lacking in comparison to *Chinatown*; audiences proved that a new generation carried no special brief for Roman Polanski's classic or for Nicholson.

Though David Denby in *New York* wrote, 'Keitel gives a solid, workmanlike performance as a Jewish gangster-businessman and husband,' he also described the film as 'one of the most impenetrably complicated movies I've ever seen.'

To Keitel, the reviews were needlessly harsh and too dependent on a long memory of *Chinatown* to be fair: '[Jack] did a great job of directing the film and I've wondered why that isn't recognized,' he said. 'I don't think it was the fault of Jack's direction. The script was in disarray. Robert Towne had left the project and we were working day and night on it.'

None of that seemed to matter, however, because, finally, the wheel was beginning to turn back in Harvey Keitel's direction. After years of taking what was offered, after years of the humiliation of seeing actors of lesser talent being handed roles that he could have done easily, Keitel was about to make a staggering comeback.

22

As 1990 was coming to a close, the film *Awakenings* was released to great fanfare, with the New York subways filled with the film's poster: Robin Williams standing on the shore while Robert De Niro, newly freed from the prison of his own paralysis, stands on a rock in Long Island Sound, arms lifted over his head in triumph.

In one of New York's many subway stops, some wag drew a balloon coming out of de Niro's mouth, filled with the words, 'I sure am glad Harvey Keitel isn't in this movie with me.'

In fact, Keitel could just as easily have played de Niro's role and done as good a job. But, by 1990, de Niro was a superstar – with two Oscars and several more nominations to his credit – whereas Keitel was perceived as an over-the-hill character actor whose time had passed.

How, then, does a career that had sunk as far as Harvey Keitel's suddenly turn around?

The answer is, of course, that it doesn't – at least not suddenly. Rather, it is a gradual process that, at a particular moment, comes to the attention of those who pay attention to such things – such as critics and entertainment writers – who then proclaim a return, as if they had made it happen.

Even then, a comeback isn't just one film. One film can start it, but it's up to the star to take advantage of that part and refocus on the work that made him a star in the first place. Otherwise, he will sink back into obscurity once more, yet another candidate for the 'Whatever happened to . . . ?' issue of *People* magazine.

No one was announcing Harvey Keitel's comeback at the beginning of 1991 – or even at the end of the year, for that matter. But the combination of films he made in 1991 put him in the right place to be comeback material. And the fuse was lit for the full explosion of his return with the initial screenings of *Reservoir Dogs* in January 1992 at the Sundance Film Festival in Park City, Utah.

If it didn't all happen in 1991, that first year of the new decade was a crucial year in terms of reigniting Keitel's career. It happened with three films: *Thelma and Louise, Mortal Thoughts* and *Bugsy*.

Thelma and Louise reunited Keitel with director Ridley Scott, who had gone on from *The Duellists* to build a reputation with *Alien* and *Blade Runner* as a director of both style and substance – only to squander it on such bombs as *Legend, Someone to Watch Over Me* (starring Lorraine Bracco) and *Black Rain*. Though he would have a huge hit with *Thelma and Louise*, he would flop again with *1492: Conquest of Paradise*, a misbegotten movie about Christopher Columbus starring Gérard Depardieu.

Scott knew he had his hands on dynamite, however, with Callie Khouri's script for *Thelma and Louise*, and milked it for all it was worth. The plot deals with two women – one unhappily married, the other in an unsatisfying relationship – who take off for a vacation break at a fishing cabin. En route, however, they stop at a bar; after dancing with a young man, Thelma goes outside with him, where he begins to rape her – until Louise shows up with a gun. When he shows no remorse, she kills him and they take off on the run, the target of a womanhunt that spirals out of control. Keitel plays the local cop who develops a sense of compassion for the two women he is pursuing, trying to save their lives from an overzealous FBI, but to no avail.

'The question popped in my mind when I read the script: Where are their daddies?' Keitel said. 'Callie Khouri had a great line in her script. It could be the guide phrase for the nineties: Love isn't something you fall into; love is something you do.'

Thelma and Louise became a cause célèbre, as the American media took up the pressing question: Was it or was it not male-bashing? Did it or did it not celebrate feminism? Did it condone lawlessness and vigilantism? It depended on who you asked. The commotion seemed unjustified, as did the Oscar for original screenplay: the movie had great style but no one could view its content as provocative or ground-breaking.

Still, Keitel believed the film had important things to say: 'Whatever brouhaha *Thelma and Louise* created, I say, "Good," ' he said. 'And I would hope it had some lasting effect in terms of relationships between men and women, knowing themselves and knowing each other.'

While stars Susan Sarandon and Geena Davis did their smart hick turns, Keitel provided a warm and bemused presence as the cop on their trail. He becomes their champion; examining their lives, he quickly understands what has pushed them to this dire pass. He is the picture of an Arkansas gentleman, soft-spoken and courtly, but with a relaxed and witty nature that he allows to show through.

Mortal Thoughts was like a matched set with *Thelma and Louise*: his second film in the same year that cast him as a sympathetic cop investigating a murder involving a dead man and a pair of women.

The story is told in flashback as a possible material witness to murder in New Jersey is questioned by two police detectives. Cynthia Kellogg (Demi Moore) works hard at not ratting on her best friend, Joyce Urbansky (Glenne Headly), who may in fact have murdered her husband, James (Bruce Willis).

The challenge here involved Keitel doing an entire performance sitting on a chair in a room. He and Billie Neale are part of the film's framing device: the police interrogation of Moore, who may be the key witness to the death. Keitel makes it compelling, playing Detective John Wood, who is called upon to solve the mysterious death of the boorish ne'er-do-well, played by Willis. Adapting his Brooklyn accent to New Jersey, Keitel plays it subdued and cagey, occasionally exploding for effect as the bad cop to Neale's good. He comes across as low-key and savvy, the cop who has seen and heard it all before. Almost from the moment he starts questioning Cynthia Kellogg, he knows that patience is the key to squeezing the truth out of an obviously nervous housewife who is out of her depth. Despite the limitations of her accent, this is one of Moore's better performances – and it's impossible not to believe that one of the reasons is having Keitel's steady and surprisingly compassionate presence to ground her in reality.

The project was being produced by Taylor Hackford and Moore's company. It was a relatively low-budget film for the time – $6.5 million – with only thirty-six shooting days budgeted. Written by NYU Film School graduate Claude Kerven and William Reilly, it was to be directed by Kerven, a first-timer. But when Kerven had a falling out with Hackford after production began, he was fired and Alan Rudolph was brought in to finish the film.

While some of Kerven's casting was changed (Peter Gallagher, who was to play Moore's husband, was replaced by John Pankow), Keitel was everyone's first choice to play the detective. 'He was an idea we had before Alan came on board,' said John Fiedler, one of the film's producers. 'We got him because we liked him. He was attracted because he didn't have to work that long and it was a New York-based production.'

Rudolph had barely arrived in New York when Keitel came to visit him at his hotel: 'It was some corporate tower on Third Avenue. Harvey said, "How can you stay in a place like this? There's nothing New York about this."'

Keitel had already spent time with police, doing research for his role; and Rudolph knew him of old:

> I just expect him to know everything about New York cops and gangsters and street life. I trust everything he learns will be skewed to what he has to do. So I was thrilled because I thought, I don't have to deal with any of this.
>
> His main complaint was about this white shirt he wanted to wear. He had to have the right white shirt. I saw I don't know how many white shirts. I loved the fact that a white shirt was so crucial to Harvey because it's typical of his commitment, his quest and his perception. When he was happy with the white shirt, that was it.

It took only two weeks of the six-week shoot for Keitel to finish all his scenes. But those scenes were charged with a kind of threat, because they were about what wasn't being talked about, rather than what was. 'Those scenes with Demi were intense,' Rudolph recalled. 'It was like a whole separate drama.'

The interrogation was the last thing filmed, after all the flashbacks were in the can. But Rudolph was having difficulty making sense of the film: 'I was still trying to figure out what the movie was about. The script literally didn't have an ending. It was missing the last twenty pages, which were being written while we shot.'

After three or four days of shooting the interrogation scenes, they came to the most intense moments of confrontation. Keitel filmed his side of the scene first. Then, as the camera and lights were being rearranged to shoot Moore's part, Keitel took Rudolph aside. 'I think I can push her further,' he told him. 'Do you want me to?'

'Do it if you can,' Rudolph said, figuring that this, in fact, was how the scenes should develop.

Rudolph turned the camera on Moore and began shooting the scene again, this time with Keitel off-camera feeding her his lines. Without warning, Keitel began screaming his lines at her, as though exploding with anger. According to Rudolph:

> You can see Demi jump in the movie when he does it – that was Harvey pushing her to the next level. The key to those interrogation scenes is Harvey's performance. Demi's key was Harvey. She may take a different view, but I think it's true. I was so proud of the guy, having his veins bulging off-camera, just screaming, for the love of the craft. And Demi gave it right back to him. She didn't falter at all. It shows the depth of his commitment, almost blindly, to his profession.

Despite grudgingly respectful reviews for the film, it did little business. Yet it added to a kind of growing realization: here again was Harvey Keitel playing something other than the edgy, explosive outsider. Though there were moments of heat in both these performances, at their core was restraint. He seemed almost relaxed, a word that has rarely been used to describe him. 'Does Harvey unwind? Well, he works at it,' recalled James Gammon about his experiences with Keitel in *A Lie of the Mind*. 'After all, he's a Marine. I thought his daughter would grow up to be a Marine, too.'

The final score of the year – the hat trick that won him more accolades than he had ever seen previously – was Barry Levinson's *Bugsy*, a lushly romantic, funny and violent retelling of the career of gangster Benjamin 'Bugsy' Siegel. Written by James Toback, it starred Warren Beatty as Bugsy and Annette Bening (who would become Mrs Beatty) as Virginia Hill.

Keitel played gangster Mickey Cohen. Wearing an oddly shaped bald cap and a false nose, he storms into this film as Cohen and almost takes it away from Beatty. Beatty's erudite Bugsy Siegel becomes a foil for Keitel's Cohen, a caustically funny and profane Jewish hoodlum who isn't above sticking up his own partners, if it serves his needs.

'As Bugsy sits before a sunlamp with more cream on his face than Lana Turner used,' David Denby wrote in *New York* magazine, 'cucumber slices covering his eyes, Mickey Cohen, a primitive local thug, shows up and begins cursing at him – surely one of the most incongruously funny confrontations in gangster-movie history.'

Still, other than his eye-opening entrance, the role is a small one. It was showy enough, however, to earn Keitel an Oscar nomination in a year when he should have had one for either *Thelma and Louise* or *Mortal Thoughts*.

The Cohen character, Toback recalled, was the easiest to write because he could treat him comically. Keitel, he said, studied newsreels and photographs of Cohen before having the make-up created for the role: 'He gets into roles both internally and externally. He made himself look a lot like Mickey Cohen. And he got the humor of the role.'

Keitel had even acquired enough heat to be asked to host *Saturday Night Live* at the end of 1991. Unlike his movie work, in which he fanatically focuses on every detail of the role, Keitel put himself into the hands of the writers and producers of the weekly skit-comedy show, offering to do whatever they threw his way.

'He was an absolute sweetheart,' recalled Tom Davis, who was then a writer for the show. 'He did everything he was asked. He thanked everybody at the end. He's right up on the top of my list of best people to host.'

He appeared in several skits, at one point playing a man on a date in a restaurant who has to use the restroom. The joke was that the facility was the size of a powder room in a small home – a toilet, a sink, barely room to turn around. But it was staffed with a solicitous washroom attendant played by Kevin Nealon, who refused to take a hint and leave, even when Keitel announced that he needed to move his bowels. Instead, Nealon stood attentively by as Keitel dropped his pants and sat on the commode, offering pleasantly after a couple of minutes, 'Air freshener?' then spraying anyway, even when Keitel declined.

He also played a castaway on a desert island who is joined by another castaway: Pat, the sexless character whose gender no one can figure out, played by Julia Sweeney. 'We've had sex eight times and I still don't know what you are,' Keitel told Pat after they'd been on the island a while.

In the skit that wound up winning Davis and the rest of the writing crew an Emmy that year, he was a subway station attendant whose announcements on the PA system are garbled and incomprehensible. But, as it turned out, that was in fact the way he spoke.

'He was funny and fun,' Davis said. 'He didn't question. He just went with everything. He's not a comedian but an actor. He's so sure of himself that he wasn't worried about what this might do to his career or anything else. He just went from piece to piece.'

As 1992 dawned, Keitel found himself nominated as best supporting actor for *Bugsy*, for both the Golden Globe Awards and the Academy Awards. Yet he downplayed the importance of awards in general, apparently unmoved after years of being ignored, by recognition that, to his mind, had not come in time to save him from a decade of wandering in the desert.

Asked about the Oscar nomination shortly after it was announced, he said sarcastically, 'I was so happy I went running down the street singing, "Zip-a-dee-doo-dah,"' then added, 'The only true recognition is the work itself. You don't need to be nominated for an Oscar to be recognized for your work.'

Keitel won neither of the awards. Both the Golden Globe and the Oscar went to Jack Palance for a comic turn in *City*

Slickers, a role, ironically enough, for which Keitel had aud-itioned and been rejected.

Keitel did win one award that year: as best supporting actor from the National Society of Film Critics, who honored him for his work in all three films: *Mortal Thoughts, Thelma and Louise* and *Bugsy*. Shortly after the award was announced, Keitel ran into Alan Rudolph and Robert Altman, entering a restaurant as he was leaving. Keitel was upbeat and magnanimous and made a point of saying to Rudolph, 'I'm getting an award and I want to thank you for it.' Which only goes to show that he may well have craved this kind of attention after all.

But it was the Oscar nomination that forced Hollywood to re-evaluate him. The imprimatur of the Academy Award, even if only as a nomination and not an award, carried weight. '*Bugsy* validated him with the vulgar Hollywood community that had written him off,' Toback said. 'It's a quintessential Hollywood movie of a certain type and Harvey was considered to be an integral part of that. All of a sudden he was not the outsider who did only aberrant movies. Then he was nominated for an Oscar. There's almost a pathetic respect for that. He was now someone they can't dismiss.'

Stardom, however, was a quality that would only take you so far, as Keitel discovered in late 1991, at a fundraising event for the homeless in Washington, DC. Mingling at a cocktail party, he found himself chatting with a homeless man who, surveying the celebrities in the crowd, looked at Keitel and asked, 'Who are you?'

'I'm Harvey Keitel,' came the reply.

The homeless man looked him over again and said, 'Well, you look like an old Martin Sheen.'

Even as Keitel was basking in the reflected glory that comes with a hit, he had already finished two projects for the coming year that would cement his place among contemporary actors.

Interviewed about them before they had embedded themselves permanently in the public consciousness, he described them with startling understatement. In one, he said, 'I play one of a group of professional robbers who are engaged in discovering what trust is about, what instinct is about and what the need for relationships is about.' In the other, the hero was involved in 'a personal story of finding what's good in himself after living a life of doing many bad things. He's on a journey for redemption.'

The films were *Reservoir Dogs* and *Bad Lieutenant*.

23

In 1991, Harvey Keitel played out a drama that sent him spinning into the dark nether regions of his soul. It was a story of trust and betrayal, in which an older, mentor-like character finds himself deceived by the protégé/confidant in whom he had placed his faith.

But this drama, unfortunately, was not a role he chose: it was his life. And the betrayer was his life partner, Lorraine Bracco.

In 1990, while working on a film called *A Talent for the Game*, Bracco became involved with her co-star, Edward James Olmos, who had the lead role. Though she went back to Keitel when filming was over, the sparks that had been struck were not extinguished and, by June 1991, Keitel had figured out what was going on. Bracco announced to Keitel that she was abandoning him for Olmos. She kept Stella and her daughter Margaux and forced Keitel to move out of the $1.2-million home they had bought together in 1989 in Snedens Landing, the pricey Rockland County enclave on the west side of the Hudson River that is also home to Al Pacino, Bill Murray, Mike Nichols and Diane Sawyer.

Keitel wound up living in their Hudson Street loft space in New York's trendy downtown Tribeca area, then sold it and bought one on North Moore Street, where he still lives, not far from the Tribeca Film Center, an old warehouse building that de Niro and partners had purchased and turned into a warren of offices and production facilities.

The split was an acrimonious one, with Keitel making more than one loudly rampaging visit to the house that sent Margaux and Stella scrambling to hide in closets.

'It came out of nowhere, as far as he was concerned,' said a friend who was close to him during this period. 'He said to me, "Can you believe she could be involved with somebody else?" It surprised him. Gradually, he heard, surmised, knew – and then knew the full extent. And then he realized this was going to cause a real breach in his life. It became about as devastating a combination of blows as you could go through.'

Publicly, Keitel tried to put the best face on the split, saying at the time,

> I'm learning to enjoy living because I'm learning to cope with sadness and loneliness. I'm learning not to run away from those things into other places. I don't want to pretend to know why, but living is difficult and living is beautiful. Without the difficulty, there would be no beauty. You have to surrender to love not being what you want, in order to find what you truly need, to discover your inner nature. Perhaps the institution of marriage is divine, but we're not. The suffering my children have gone through, it's difficult for me to say it's right. So let me just say that it is.

In fact, according to another friend, Keitel was shattered by Bracco's infidelity and decision to leave him for Olmos. It wasn't just that Bracco didn't love him anymore – but that she had left him for another man, that she had respected him and their relationship so little that she had violated it in this public way, carrying on behind his back and, he later discovered, in front of his daughter. It not only tore his heart apart; it hurt his pride as a man as well. One of his friends commented:

> He was totally devastated at the betrayal. And his mother died around that time. With the divorce, I think he went right out to the end. Given the way normal people function,

if there are 230 million people in America, I would bet you couldn't find a tiny percentage who would define their emotional state as being as miserable as he was. He looked at his life as agony. Harvey's attitude was, 'I am in the worst pain I've ever experienced, beyond whatever I could imagine.'

Perhaps it all fed into Keitel's own personal need to explore the darkest recesses of his own psyche: here was a pain he could only previously imagine. Now he was being forced to experience it.

In the past, when he confronted unhappy moments in his life, it was in the service of a role: by recalling the pain, he could imagine what the character he was creating must be feeling. True, Keitel often dug so deeply that there would be a residual feeling – depression, anger, anxiety – that bled into his life while he was making a film. Eventually, however, the production would be completed and, gradually, he would drop the character and the pain would dissipate and vanish as normal life resumed.

But this *was* normal life, not a movie. And the pain would not go away. It was there when he opened his eyes in the morning and when he went to bed in the evening. It was the first thing he thought about each day and the last thing he thought about at night. It haunted his dreams. It overwhelmed him every minute of every day. He was a man who was highly attuned to his own emotions – and now his emotions were blasting at him during every second of his existence, screaming with a pain that was almost unendurable. This wasn't a movie role he could leave behind; this was him and Lorraine, the woman he loved and had lived with, the woman who had borne his child, the woman who had cheated on him and left him for another man.

Still, Keitel tried to be philosophical: 'There have been times in my life I thought the pain would never stop, and I wanted to die. I learned that that changes. And from that I gained the ability to face any fear.'

Bracco won custody of Stella, then took Keitel to court in March 1993, complaining that he wasn't paying any child support. More to the point, he had stopped paying the mortgage on the house (which, with insurance and property taxes, was north of $11,000 a month). She sought $7,000 a month in child support.

Keitel responded that Bracco deserved none of it because she was the reason the relationship had been terminated. His deposition in New York Supreme Court stated that

> She lulled me into buying with her the Snedens Landing house just a year and a half before she broke up our relationship. Less than two years after that purchase, she took up with another man and threw me out. Not satisfied with destroying my romantic dreams and wrecking our home with her immorality, [she] now wants me to pay exorbitant sums in so-called child support, but which is largely support for her and her plans to get rid of me after buying the house at Snedens Landing. In short, she set me up.

To which Bracco replied in her deposition, 'I terminated my relationship with [Keitel] because I could no longer tolerate his abuse of me. Harvey Keitel is addicted to abuse. Even though our relationship terminated almost two years ago, [he] has continued to abuse me in front of my daughters, of professional colleagues and now in these court papers.'

All of which suggests that, even as he was trying to help her to launch her acting career during the early years of their relationship, Keitel still harbored a great deal of anger and resentment about the way his own career was going. Reading the trade papers, seeing other actors being offered roles that he wanted, not getting parts he auditioned for: all may have contributed to a personality that was dark and brooding to begin with, one given to occasional loud explosions of anger. To Keitel, these eruptions may simply have been a way to vent anger in a non-destructive way. To the people around him, however, to his partner and children, these sudden thunderstorms of temper may have been the kind of frighteningly unpredictable assaults that amount to psychological abuse. They raise issues of blame because, too often, they are ignited by some extraneous event, one that has nothing to do with the actual cause of the rage.

Yet, as Keitel reveals in his deposition, all he could see was the betrayal. As he lays it out, Bracco's relationship with Olmos was some premeditated plot to bilk him out of the house she'd persuaded him to buy – 'She set me up!' – rather than the response to an increasingly unhappy relationship.

Ultimately, the court ordered him to pay $6,200 a month and to make back payments on the mortgage.

After Bracco and Olmos were married in January 1994, Keitel went back to court to get his child-support payments reduced, claiming that Bracco was making more money than she claimed and being supported by a husband. He also called her a spendthrift who, despite receiving $6,200 a month from him, was still not making mortgage payments and was in threat of default. He derided her claims of poverty in the face of evidence of her extravagance: $4,900 for underwear; $2,100 for a pair of shoes; $1,300 for limo service within one two-week period in February 1994.

What hurt even more is that, in all likelihood, Bracco, with her decidedly limited acting skills, would not even have had an acting career – or not the career she had – without Keitel to push her into acting classes and to push his friends to give her roles. (And if you doubt that, rent the movie *Medicine Man* and try not snickering at her performance.) 'The irony is that Harvey was kind of a glorified agent for her,' said a friend of Keitel. 'He devoted himself to building up her career.'

At one point, Bracco publicly accused Keitel of just the opposite. She spoke out in a 1993 gossip column in the *New York Daily News*, accusing Keitel and Robert De Niro of badmouthing her to producers, who would think twice about offering her roles if de Niro said, 'I hear she's trouble.'

The irony was that, as an artist, Keitel found he could draw upon the pain of his split with Bracco to deepen and strengthen his acting. Suddenly, he no longer had to try and imagine the kind of unhappiness and torment his characters were going through, because he was living with it. It was eating him alive – and he was channeling that torture directly into his performances. 'Unfortunately, the pain he went through actually helped him as an artist,' said a close friend. 'He used this huge reservoir of pain he went through in the movies he did. It made him more compulsive about working.'

So it was that he went into *Reservoir Dogs*, the film that would introduce the world to Quentin Tarantino.

'I'm usually attracted to a role because it mirrors something I'm grappling with in my own life,' Keitel said, 'and I was impressed by the original way *Reservoir Dogs* addresses the themes of betrayal and the need to have a friend.'

24

Reservoir Dogs caused a sensation when it was screened at the Sundance Film Festival in January 1992. By the time it opened in October, it was a full-blown cause célèbre: the birth of a sizzling hot writer-director with a distinctive voice and a startling sense of how to tell a story. Though it made money, it was more of a succès d'éstime than a commercial blockbuster.

But it put Tarantino squarely on the map. And it further cemented Keitel's returning reputation as an actor – as well as casting him as a new sage of the American independent film movement.

Because, while Quentin Tarantino may have given birth to *Reservoir Dogs* out of his own fertile imagination and his insatiable urge to make movies, Keitel was the midwife to the film. It can be argued that, had Keitel not taken an interest in Tarantino's script, Tarantino's career might have taken a significantly different course.

'I always had Harvey in mind as the perfect guy to play this character but I never dreamed he'd do it,' Tarantino said. 'Not only did he take the part, but his attaching himself to the film gave it legitimacy and made it possible for us to get financing.'

'It's a really interesting question whether there would have been a Quentin Tarantino without Harvey,' said John Pierson, a long-time observer and participant in the independent film scene as the producer's representative who helped to launch the careers of Spike Lee, Michael Moore, Kevin Smith of *Clerks* and many more:

Quentin wound up on tour at the same time as *Laws of Gravity* [a film by Nick Gomez about street toughs, made without stars and a fraction of *Reservoir Dogs*'s $1.5 million budget]. And he'd look at it and how it was made and say, 'That's how I was prepared to make *Reservoir Dogs*' if he hadn't gotten Harvey. But it would have been Quentin instead of Steve Buscemi as Mr Pink and Lawrence Bender [the film's producer] playing the Michael Madsen role. Who knows what the film would have wound up being?

At the point when the script first reached Keitel, Tarantino was still a would-be writer-director, who had had limited success selling his scripts to other directors but who desperately wanted to direct one of his own. He wrote *Reservoir Dogs* and enlisted Bender, a would-be actor and sometime producer, to try to set up the financing.

Bender showed it to his acting teacher, who asked Bender who, out of all the actors in the world, he wanted most for the film. Bender mentioned a couple of names but focused on one in particular: Harvey Keitel.

Which just goes to show the power of a cult following. At this point, Keitel was not a star, at least not by any of the measurable standards Hollywood uses. But to film buffs like Bender and Tarantino – who reveled in the films and performances themselves, rather than their status as award-winners or box-office hits – Keitel was the real thing: an actor who had never stopped giving the kind of guts-on-the-line performances that connect viscerally to the viewer.

And, with the advent of home video, films that had made little impact at the box office, films that had disappeared before the mass audience was able to find them, were suddenly given a second life. Until the videocassette player became a staple of the American household during the early 1980s, the only people likely to have seen most of Keitel's films were film critics and the most rabid cineastes in major cities; many of Keitel's films of the 1970s didn't even play outside the major metropolitan areas.

But the following of a cult actor like Harvey Keitel suddenly grew exponentially when his films became available on video. An influential film like *Mean Streets*, which had never had a wide release, was now available to anyone who had the interest and a couple of bucks to put down at the corner video store. A cinema geek like Tarantino, stuck behind the counter at the video store where he worked in Los Angeles, could watch *Fingers* over and over at his leisure.

As it happened, when Bender mentioned Keitel as an actor he'd like to have for Tarantino's film, his teacher told him that his ex-wife was, in fact, a friend of Keitel's from the Actors Studio. And she could get the script to him.

The next thing Bender knew, he was retrieving a message from his telephone answering machine that said, 'Hello? Lawrence? Hello, I'm calling for Lawrence Bender. This is Harvey Keitel speaking. I read the script for *Reservoir Dogs* and I'd like to talk to you about it.'

Which blew Bender's mind: 'One, Harvey Keitel is like a god,' he said. 'He's not only a star but an actor's actor. Not just a personality. Two, the fact that Harvey was going to be in this movie, I knew that was the thing that would help us get this movie made. His presence gave us more weight. Suddenly we weren't two guys peddling a script around town. Now we had Harvey Keitel.'

Tarantino recalled, 'That was wild because Harvey was mine and Lawrence's, like, dream guy for the movie and Harvey is, like, my favorite actor. He's been my favorite actor since I was sixteen. I'd seen him in *Mean Streets* and *Taxi Driver* and *The Duellists* and stuff.'

When he'd read the script, Keitel told Toback, 'This guy wants me to do a movie. He's this nerdy guy but he's serious about his movie. I think he has great love and faith in me.'

To which Toback replied, 'It sounds like something you should do.'

And Keitel observed,

I'm always searching for an experience and Quentin came along and provided it. I read it and it was a profound, extraordinary piece of writing. His screenplay breaks up the structure of matter like a Picasso. It also explores issues that concern me in my own existence: the need to trust somebody, the need to love somebody, the need for redemption. I was very stirred that here was a new way of seeing these mythological themes, these universal themes of betrayal, camaraderie, trust and redemption. So I called Lawrence and told him I'd like to help the movie to get made.

There's a reaction to words on paper that provokes you. You're aware of being in a place you'd like to be. It's not the physical place. It's the universality of the ideas that are embodied by the text.

I just kind of presumed that Quentin's father or brother or uncle was associated with this kind of people – or a cousin or perhaps himself. I was astonished to discover that none of this was true because he had gathered it all by watching movies.

Before landing Keitel, Tarantino and Bender had scared up less than a half-million dollars for the film. With Keitel aboard, Richard Gladstein at Live Entertainment, who had been less than interested in the script, was suddenly offering a budget of more than a million dollars: 'The only reason Gladstein said, "Yes, I'm going to go with it," the only reason he read the script in the first place was because Harvey Keitel was attached to it,' Tarantino recalled.

Gladstein's first meeting with Keitel left a strange impression: 'I walked in and he's been a sort of icon to me and I was really looking forward to meeting him,' Gladstein remembered. 'We went into his kitchen and he was sitting there in a sort of cut-off T-shirt and he had this weird make-up on [from *Bugsy*] and a guy either taking off or putting it on him. In an attempt to make small talk, I commented on the make-up and asked what it was for.'

To which Keitel replied in a growl, 'See the movie.'

With his clout, Keitel was able to stave off suggestions that, perhaps, Tarantino should sit this one out, let someone else direct and settle for the writer-producer credit. But Keitel put his foot down: 'At one point, Quentin was going to drop out because we had run out of money and I said I didn't want to do it without Quentin directing. I put my name to it. I have a million dollars worth of power, I guess, because that's what we raised.'

Keitel sat in on casting sessions, reading with actors, offering advice to Tarantino and Bender. At one early casting session, an actor blew his audition because Keitel sat on the couch through the entire try-out, cleaning his toes.

But Keitel was having trouble making up his mind which role he wanted to play:

At first I wanted to play all the characters. A number of them attracted me. We dragged on for about four months about which character I would be playing. I began to ask Quentin to shift around certain monologues I liked to one character. Then I caught myself. What the hell am I doing here? I'm going to ruin the script. I told Quentin to go back to the original script and I'd pick out a part, no switching anything.

At one point, he suggested Tarantino and Bender fly to New York to audition some New York actors (they eventually hired Steve Buscemi for the role of Mr Pink from the Manhattan jaunt). Because they couldn't afford it, Keitel put up the money for their plane tickets and hotel and found a casting director to round up actors for them to see.

After the casting session, Keitel took his two young protégés to eat at the Russian Tea Room. During dinner, Bender said, 'Look, at this point, you've been so much help, we'd like to make you a co-producer on the movie.'

To which Keitel replied with a smile, 'Lawrence, it's about fucking time. What took you so long? I've been waiting to hear this from you.'

Keitel helped Tarantino to get into Sundance's director's workshop in 1990, so that he could try out what he wanted to do once he actually started production. Then, in 1991, with a cast that included Buscemi, Madsen, Tim Roth, Chris Penn and several others, Tarantino began rehearsal and production, with Keitel in one of the main roles – Mr White – as well as taking a significant role behind the scenes.

Rehearsing with Keitel was a new experience for Roth, an English actor who'd been selected for the key role of Mr Orange, a member of the gang who is, in fact, an undercover cop. There was the thrill of working with Keitel:

He's one of the reasons I became an actor. I'd seen all his films. Knowing he had casting approval on *Reservoir Dogs* and chose me was fantastic enough. Working with him was hysterical.

Harvey always likes to rehearse, but he just reads from the script. I don't know quite what goes on in his head but there's lots of thinking. It's very quiet the whole time he's reading it and nothing really changes until when he's filming and then it all comes together. And when the camera turns, that's it. It was very weird, but it all came together.

Keitel gives a gritty but sensitive performance as Mr White: tough, uncompromising in his commitment to a comrade after he is wounded. When that comrade reveals that he is, in fact, the rat within the organization, the betrayal cuts close to Keitel's own situation with Bracco, mirroring a relationship in which a steep emotional investment was repaid with deception. 'I play a man who's a skilled thief and has committed murder,' he observed. 'Yet he still has a profound need to care for somebody. It's very difficult to accept that need and say I'm not so tough after all. The real toughness is in admitting to the need for love.'

The mentor role of Mr White echoed the role Keitel quickly developed with Bender and Tarantino, who were relative novices in the film world. According to Bender,

> Harvey is a bit of a teacher in a sense and he likes to give his knowledge to people. We learned a lot from his working on *Reservoir Dogs*. I think there's something natural about him that's very giving if you give him an opportunity to promote what he feels film-making is all about and especially with directors who are really into actors. He really gave Quentin and me some weight behind us. He was such a wonderful source of inspiration. He would talk to us about acting and he would come to us when we were shooting scenes and he would say, 'Lawrence, this is a very important scene and Quentin's under a lot of pressure. If Quentin doesn't have time, maybe we can find time another day and cut something else out.'

Keitel had nothing but praise for Tarantino: 'To handle eight actors like this for anyone would be a task. For a first-time director, an enormous one. Quentin as a first-time director had enormous energy and enthusiasm, intensity and intelligence, vulnerability and a great willingness to learn, to want to be very open to the input the actors had in terms of their process to arrive at the characters he wrote.'

Keitel wasn't looking for special treatment, even though he'd added the title of producer to his résumé for the first time. 'It's not that anyone deferred to me,' he said. 'I just think I had something to contribute in terms of the process. I'm not sure I'd call that deferring to me because that implies they would be giving something up of their own. No, I think there was an openness on Quentin's part to work with me and take what I had to offer in terms of my experience.'

Critics were as polarized as audiences over *Reservoir Dogs*; it was a film in which neutrality was not an option. In particular, a scene in which Mr Blonde (Michael Madsen) tortures a captive police officer and then slices off his right ear and threatens to set him alight proved to be the dividing line for many movie-goers, who decided that this was the last straw and scurried out of the theater.

As Tarantino noted, 'My mother would not like this movie. But people who don't like it can go see *Sister Act*,' referring to a lame but popular Whoopi Goldberg comedy of the same year, in which Keitel incongruously played Goldberg's boyfriend, not so incongruously a vicious Reno Mob boss.

'If you don't leave this movie upset,' Keitel said, 'then we have failed in our job, which is to stir the audience to consciousness. Anytime reality is stirred, we are scared. Change is difficult. But without this journey into the ordeal by fire, rain and wind, there is no deeper awareness of the darkness.'

Reservoir Dogs is as visceral and witty a film as has come out in recent years, a no-nonsense crime caper in which the caper is never seen and the criminals are unlike any previously presented onscreen. Critics who did like it became early worshippers of the cult of Tarantino; others turned up their noses at its sometimes garish violence ('A good deal of *Reservoir Dogs* was difficult for me to watch,' Stanley Kauffmann wrote in the *New Republic*, while Terrence Rafferty in the *New Yorker* sniffed, 'It's a reasonably lively picture about nothing, and that's apparently all it was ever meant to be').

Roger Ebert maintained that 'Everyone got on the bandwagon for *Reservoir Dogs*. I thought it was an incomplete film. For Keitel, it was a fairly easy role. But it got a lot of attention because Tarantino got a lot.'

Still, that was truer in Europe, where the auteur theory developed, than in the United States. In the US, Tarantino didn't become a well-known personality until the success of *Pulp Fiction*. In Europe, however, the fascination with the brash young writer-director began with *Reservoir Dogs*, simmered for two years, then boiled over with *Pulp Fiction*.

25

If *Reservoir Dogs* did nothing else – and it did plenty – it firmly established Keitel as an actor willing to take risks on first-time directors and independent film projects, far away from more crassly commercial concerns of the Hollywood studio.

Yet it was only when *Reservoir Dogs* raised both Tarantino and Keitel's stock that people began to notice just how many first-time directors Keitel had lent his support to, how many independent films he'd racked up on his résumé.

Consider the first-timers Keitel had worked with: Martin Scorsese, Joel Schumacher, Alan Rudolph, Ridley Scott, Paul Schrader, James Toback, Quentin Tarantino, Danny Cannon (in 1993's *The Young American*). And examine the list of movies outside the Hollywood channels that Keitel has dragged into mainstream acceptance in the 1990s: *Reservoir Dogs*, *Bad Lieutenant*, *Dangerous Game*, *The Piano*, *Smoke*, *Blue in the Face*. 'Keitel is coming into his own, not only as an artist, but also as an enabling force in independent cinema,' Donald Lyons wrote in *Film Comment* in 1992.

Independent film in the 1990s has prospered – in part because Keitel showed other big-name actors that it was, in fact, safe to take a chance on something that paid a little less monetarily but a lot more creatively. As Ulu Grosbard saw it,

That kind of risk-taking in a career is unusual: working with first-time directors, working overseas instead of building a career in Hollywood. But Harvey's done that a number of times. It's admirable and it's highly unusual to work with that many first-time directors. Most actors try to protect themselves. A lot of first-time directors are not that good at directing. The guy who suffers is the lead because he's the most exposed. So it's real risk-taking. Clearly it's something he's prepared to do and does.

Yet it wasn't simple altruism on Keitel's part that drew him to untested talent. His impulse was always toward new and different material, something that was more readily available outside the mainstream of Hollywood. With the exception of something like *Thelma and Louise*, the best roles Keitel has had all came in films made outside the Hollywood studio system.

And, in a sense, there is enlightened self-interest at work as well: given his experience, Keitel knew that new directors, excited at making their first film, nervous about how it will come out, are looking for a reassuring presence somewhere in the production, an actor who can say to them, 'Don't worry – I know what I'm doing. Let me do it my way and things will come out just fine.'

In Keitel's case, that meant working in his own way: exploring the part, asking endless questions of the director during their collaboration, paying attention to the smallest details. It is the way that makes Keitel feel most assured about what he is doing; having Keitel exuding confidence and competence on the set, in turn, eased the anxieties of a novice director. 'Once you've directed two or three pictures, you start to think you know what you're doing,' James Toback said. 'You can't be as ready and open to letting the actor create a role. You don't have that fear where you feel better going with an actor who says he knows what he's doing.'

In carving out his unique career, Keitel has continued to blaze a trail begun by, among others, John Cassavetes and John Sayles. It is not a popular path in Hollywood, particularly among the talent agents who get a percentage of their clients' earnings: mainstream films bring in multi-million-dollar salaries, while independent films generally have tiny budgets and pay their actors scale. According to John Sayles:

> Usually what an agent says is, 'There might be a conflict.' Which means the agent is going to look for a conflict, because ten percent of scale is nothing. If his actor is off in Podunk making a little movie, he might miss the chance at a movie that would pay a quarter-of-a-million-dollar commission to the agent.
>
> Other actors see Harvey do that and think, 'Maybe I can talk my agent into letting me do that.' With Nick Cage winning the Oscar in a film shot in 16mm for three million dollars, the word is out now. It's almost chic to be in a low-budget film.

To Keitel, fashion has nothing to do with it; the script is everything. That, and the opportunity to work with someone who's willing to let him take chances, to trust his instincts, to work with him rather than trying to manipulate him:

> Working with first-time directors has never been frustrating. You meet the person, you get a feeling about the person. It's not just willy-nilly, every first-time director is so wonderful or that every experienced director is so wonderful. The first-time director experience we're talking about comes as a result of me reading a text or hearing an idea. Usually in reading that text or hearing that idea, I will learn something about the quality of the person.
>
> Independent film-makers have come on the scene because there was a hunger for something relevant to the struggle we are all a part of. You set out on a journey together as a team. One's lack of experience doesn't get in the way. You help each other along. That can even be inspiring. When you're flying, there's always the chance of crashing. You

have to know he'll help you up. And that is perhaps the most important ingredient a director can bring to the actor, along with an awareness of technique. A director needs to have the patience to create this environment for the actor.

While no one denigrates Keitel's role in the independent film world, producer's representative John Pierson pointed out that Keitel is not operating at the level of total no-budget novices:

Obviously, he's an activist, director-selecting actor who laid the foundation with Quentin for somebody like Travolta to take a flyer. Is he the godfather of this independent movement by virtue of being in these movies? Well, it's not like *The Piano* was Jane Campion's first film that she was making for $500,000 and sleeping in tents in the outback. Holly Hunter was already committed when they cast Harvey.

Sure, it's great when someone with some stature like Harvey agrees to be in your movie. Still, if you're somebody from nowhere trying to make an under-one million dollar film, you're not going to get to him and convince him.

Yet no one questions Keitel's daring in taking the leap into material that is provocative and controversial. As writer David Thomson observed at the time of the release of *Bad Lieutenant* and *Reservoir Dogs*,

If other actors did what Keitel's been doing lately, you'd fear for them. You'd wonder about suicidal urges. Harvey Keitel's face carries burdens of resentment, mistrust, coldness, intractability, selfishness, stubborn willfulness and unalloyed solitary meanness of spirit without which he would not, could not, be the remarkable actor he is today. He gives himself to the screen, helplessly. It is his one streak of generosity.

Few actors are more willing to portray the least flattering aspects of the human animal than Keitel. While he enjoys taking that leap, it bothers him that so few other actors are willing to take similar risks that he stands out in the crowd.

Asked how he felt about being called 'daring,' Keitel said, 'I'm more angry than complimented. I'm just upset at the way things are, the unwillingness to walk the razor's edge, because at the end of it are great rewards. The only way to do anything about anything has to involve risk. If there is no risk, you can forget about it. Just forget about it. Suck your thumb and sit home. There's a risk involved if you hope to evolve.'

26

If there was any more proof needed of Harvey Keitel's urge to move up the evolutionary ladder by playing the riskiest parts he could find, they were dispelled by his other significant role of 1992, the role that has all but defined his career in the 1990s: the lead in *Bad Lieutenant*, Abel Ferrara's envelope-pushing depiction of one man's descent into hell and his eventual redemption.

Written by Ferrara and Zoe Lund, *Bad Lieutenant* features Keitel in the title role, a man never identified by name and only referred to in the credits as 'Lt'. He is a New York City cop who, when first glimpsed driving his sons to school, is berating them for making him late. He stops the car, lets them out, then pulls out a vial of cocaine and quickly shovels a pair of hits up his bulbous nose.

It is a frighteningly realistic portrayal of a man pulling the plug on his own life and helping the water go down the drain faster. With his alternately deadened and self-hating expression, Keitel captures the sense of someone who has lost contact with everything that matters in his life, someone who has given up and is simply trying to numb himself against any experiences between now and the inevitable end.

Yet the role, which won him the Spirit Award as best actor of 1992 from the Independent Feature Project-West, was one he almost turned down when he first read the script. 'When I was given *Bad Lieutenant*, I read a certain amount of pages and I put it down,' he recalled. 'I thought, "I'm going to get a lead

role and it's this? There's no way I'm gonna make this movie."
And then I asked myself, "How often am I lead in a movie?
Read it. Maybe I can salvage something from it." And I read
on and when I did, I understood why Abel wanted to make it
and why Zoe Lund had written it.'

'When we were writing the script, we thought it was a real
long shot he'd do the film because we knew he was booked for
a long time,' Ferrara said. 'I think this story was something he
needed to do at this point in his life.'

Once he gave the script a chance and agreed to do the movie,
Keitel realized the film was exactly what he'd spent his career
working toward: a chance to say something profound about
right, wrong and redemption, an opportunity to delve into the
darkest recesses of his soul and his inner pain, recesses he had
recently been forced to explore by the humiliation of the divorce
from Bracco and the death of his mother.

The two events continued to eat at him, because of unresolved
feelings about his mother and the continuing agony he felt
about Bracco. He entertained all sorts of violent notions of
retribution toward her and Olmos, ideas he knew he could
never act on but which still haunted and energized him. It all
fed into the portrayal of a man who cannot control those
impulses, but knows there is a price to pay for his trans-
gressions:

> *Bad Lieutenant* came at a certain point on this journey. It
> seemed to me like a destiny to arrive at that place. I just
> know that [Lt] was waiting for me to discover him in me. It
> didn't happen at the moment that Abel said, 'Action.' He
> was struggling for life in me forever. And we found each
> other. I'm just glad that Zoe and Abel gave me the opportu-
> nity to go into hell and to discuss redemption and the need
> to do something good.
>
> I'd been looking for someone to come up with some idea

that had to do with the struggle between God and the devil. And this was *Bad Lieutenant*. I began to ask the questions central to this film many years ago. In a sense, it was destiny for me because it spoke directly to my own impulses to do bad – and this has been a hell of a struggle. The issue of forgiveness fascinated me because I was having a very difficult time in my own existence with forgiving and asking for forgiveness. I found it to be a wrenching struggle. It's a hell of a struggle and a heavenly struggle.

I wanted to play this part because I have a deep desire to know God and knowing God isn't just a matter of going to confession and praying. We also find God by confronting evil and this character gave me the opportunity to descend into the most painful part of myself and learn about that dark place. Call it what you will – the abyss, the holy void, the place where heaven and hell merge into the same experience – this is the place where man learns.

For Ferrara, Keitel was like a gift from God: an actor who would jump feet first into the most self-destructive scenes, such as one in which Lt stops a couple of teenage girls from New Jersey and forces one to show her ass and the other to simulate a blowjob while he stands next to their car and masturbates. Keitel never hesitated for a second to take the character to new lows. As Ferrara noted,

He's gonna go where the character goes. He's not afraid – he's an ex-Marine, for Chrissake. He said to me when we started filming, 'My sword is sharp, my boots are shined. Just point me to the hill and I'll take it.' He's worked with great people, he knows what great work is – and he demands it in himself and others. If you're not doing it, then step it up or get out of his face, baby. He's playing for all the marbles. You're either behind him or you're gonna get run over. It's like one continuous journey into the heart of

Harvey's darkness. You want to compare darkness? His wins
by a mile.

According to David Proval, Keitel's *Mean Streets* co-star,
'What Harvey had the courage to do is to reveal the demons,
the darkness. He has the courage to reveal the darkness, the
emotional nerve endings. He invites the pain; he shares the
pain. He's got a great emotional instrument. It's so raw and
he's been blessed with roles that let him do that.'

To Keitel, however, Ferrara's contribution to the film was
every bit as important as his own, if not more so: 'Abel is in
a place that is somewhere betwixt heaven and hell. He's a man
who's dealing with the chaos of existence in, I think, a profound
and divine way.'

The film was shot quickly and cheaply, with Keitel and Ferrara working closely together throughout the production,
rewriting and improvising to strengthen and deepen the character and the script. 'We had four weeks to shoot the movie,'
Keitel said. 'There are no excuses to be made. I wish to hell
someone had given us more money to shoot another month.
I'm very proud of what's on the screen. But me and Abel went
into it knowing we took some risks. We wouldn't cry over
spilled milk. We wanted to make this story.'

Did the film scare him? 'That's part of the journey – what
else counts?' he said. 'Without that fear, there'll be no reward.
You don't go into a film like this looking for approval.'

And has he ever gone further as an actor than he did in *Bad
Lieutenant* or, for that matter, *Reservoir Dogs*? 'No,' he said.
'No. You can't. You can't.'

Yet Keitel saw the film as a kind of gift to his daughter Stella,
who appears in it briefly as one of Lt's kids (she was six at the
time) and who was in another room near the set the day
Keitel did his scenes of drug-taking and nude dancing with
prostitutes:

I told her Daddy's going to be naked in the next room, there's going to be some women and that no actual sexual activity was going on and that we were telling a story I thought was important about a man's descent into hell. I told her that this man wasn't a very responsible father and that he should be paying more attention to his child. He should be looking at the picture she draws instead of being drunk and drugged. I explained to her that a man's absence of God can lead him to abuse drugs, alcohol, sex.

I'm thinking of my daughter seeing *Bad Lieutenant* when she's old enough. I think she's going to be proud of her daddy. At least we're trying to speak of conflicts that can help us live better and not inflict our sins on the children.

That descent into darkness, dealing with all the most dangerous and destructive emotions within, was and is a kind of therapy, a way to express those feelings in a constructive manner that does no damage to anyone else: not a catharsis, exactly, but an understanding, a coming-to-terms. It was frightening to Keitel, who harbored deeply antisocial urges inspired by the dissolution of his household and the loss of Bracco. Here was a chance to actually go crazy, in a way that wouldn't land him in jail. As he explained:

Man must descend into the darkness to find the light. If there is any new frontier, it is downward, not upward. What is fact or fiction? Sometimes art imitates life; sometimes it leads life. Hopefully we transcend the place we're standing in.

Without owning pain and rage, it's difficult to trust someone's sense of what is good. It seems to me that a person has the right to own that pain and to scream as a result of it. When I was a kid, I wish someone had said, 'You have the right to break any fucking thing around you because of the suffering you are going through,' instead of 'Shut up!'

Bad Lieutenant is, for me, a mythological journey. I had

to go into a place that was dark, deep, chaotic and wonderful, my razor's edge. There are, after all, no saints that have not been devils.

As Donald Lyons wrote at the time, 'Harvey Keitel takes us step by bloody step along the way of this guy's cross. Always angry, always unsatisfied by his many drugs, he yet lets us see the wreck of a decent man, in contrast to, say, de Niro's slime-from-the-get-go LaMotta in *Raging Bull*.'

Janet Maslin maintained that 'No matter what you thought of *Bad Lieutenant*, you couldn't take your eyes off of him. It grabbed you by the throat. He just makes you cringe in that film and yet you have to respect what he's doing. And he manages to be weirdly funny, too.'

The movie drew strong reactions on both sides: 'I really hated that movie,' recalled Jack Mathews. 'I felt for him it was a no-brainer. If Redford or any of a number of major stars had done it, it would have been earth-shaking. For me, it was something Keitel could have done in his sleep.'

But Peter Travers of *Rolling Stone* disagreed: 'I've never seen a movie that showed how hard Christianity was. It's one of the best performances I've seen by an American actor.'

Reservoir Dogs and *Bad Lieutenant* were both released in the fall of 1992: *Reservoir Dogs* in October, *Bad Lieutenant* in November. Even as this Keitel critical mass was forming, Keitel was already being honored: with a tribute at the annual Telluride Film Festival in Telluride, Colorado.

In the festival program notes, James Toback wrote, 'At first I thought Harvey Keitel was Italian and moodily humorless. Then I met him in 1976 and discovered him to be a profoundly hilarious Jew. Not to deny for a moment his darkness, ferocity, complexity, intelligence or restless curiosity, but what a capacity to laugh at himself, that historically indispensable instrument of Jewish survival.'

The one-two punch of the pair of vividly violent films within the space of a month provoked the kind of periodic hue-and-cry about violence in films generally reserved for an election year. Keitel too became a target for the controversy, because of his participation in the films.

'A lot of people asked me why I'm always playing violent characters,' he said. 'I said I've never ever played a violent character. I have played characters who were in deep conflict and despair and chaos. The lieutenant has a deep need. He's a family man; he has children. He knows he is bad. He has a deep need for redemption.' Indeed, Keitel questioned the way critics and other social commentators define violence in films:

> I've never made a violent film. A violent film is one that bares a woman's tits just to show them, instead of having it come from a place of some meaningfulness. There's a way to present the conflicts we have in our sexuality that has meaningfulness and there's a way to exploit sexuality without any meaning to it. There's a way to present suffering and violence that has a meaning to it and a way to go lopping off heads that is mindless.
>
> Frankly, I'm a little annoyed with the attention to violence in *Reservoir Dogs*. Yes there is a lot of bloodshed but, to me, *Reservoir Dogs* is more about the inner violence that the characters commit upon themselves in their need to have an identity, albeit in a criminal environment. Quentin and I were aware of our responsibility not to portray gratuitous violence. We were after what was real. As film-makers, we have an obligation to journey into this abominable place that violence possesses. How can we render its horribleness, its deadliness, unless we go into it ourselves? Hopefully, we've done that in a real way, never gratuitously. Never, never, never.
>
> And are the things we see in [*Bad Lieutenant*] really that

extreme? Do we all have the potential to sink to the level this man sinks to? I'm reluctant to speak for all of humanity, but all I can say is dear me, the sky is falling. Look around at the state this world is in for the answer to those questions. In the face of evil in the world and in the heart of man, we have to allow ourselves to be stirred and scared to death because that's the only way we can gain the knowledge we need to redeem ourselves.

Keitel's approach to violence in films mirrors that of the late film-maker Sam Peckinpah, who always said that he made the violence graphic in his films to show people the true horror of violence, rather than glamorizing or sanitizing it the way Hollywood always did. Peckinpah understood that violence is truly horrible – but that, in old westerns, when someone was shot and fell to the ground dead without suffering or pain, it was made to look simple and clean. In Keitel's view,

Violence should always be portrayed painfully. If anything is gratuitous, it's that people portray violence so that it is acceptable. The Tarantinos, the Scorseses, who are trying to portray the experience of humanity honestly – we must give these people our support, even if we throw up watching it.

A lot of people responded to the pain of the violence in *Reservoir Dogs*. It was vivid; that's the way it should be. It should be disgusting, the way that real violence is.

Goddammit, all this violence that's around us – where does it come from? Does it come from an opening up of one's spirit? No! It comes from a closing of the spirit, so that it's kicking inside your guts till finally you gotta pick up a chair and hit someone in the fucking head or put a gun to his head or rape someone or explode an atom bomb! It doesn't come from the openness of one's being.

So, to Keitel's way of thinking, the excesses of *Bad Lieutenant* are justified by the effect they create in the audience: revulsion at the behavior and, with luck, to drugs and violence as well. 'I was very proud when someone said it was the best anti-drug film they had ever seen because there was no moralizing in it,' he said. 'I believe it's a religious film, because hell is here now and so is the opportunity to know heaven.'

Still, he wasn't surprised at reports that people were walking out of both films, in horror and disgust at the blood-letting in *Reservoir Dogs* and the degradation in *Bad Lieutenant*:

> One of the great problems in our civilization is the way we try to avoid suffering. We want to avoid it with a passion. We will kill to avoid it. I understand that. There have been many moments in my life where I've walked away from difficulty – sulked, looked for a rock to hide under. But if I turn away from suffering and violence in life, I dump it onto my children. I say, 'I'm too frightened to cope with it. I haven't got time for it. I haven't got patience for it. I'm scared of it.'
>
> But if we do that, we are condemning our children to the hell we are not willing to face. Let other parents do what they think is right. My girls will be taught about that.

27

As Keitel's banner year of 1992 was closing out, word leaked to the press: Keitel would shortly be a father again.

The *Detroit Free Press* reported in October that Keitel had a new daughter 'due for release in December.' And *USA Today* claimed that he was 'about to become a father again with his thirty-years-younger companion, an acting student.'

Keitel was excited at the prospect. He'd met Heather Bracken at de Niro's Tribeca Grill, where she worked as a coat-checker (when she wasn't trying to break in as an actress). He even started preparing Stella for the fact that she was about to have a new sister.

It was an old and familiar pattern: the much older Keitel and the much younger, would-be actress. It allowed Keitel to pursue the role of mentor yet again, as he had done with Bracco. And it gave him the chance to show Bracco that he had moved on, that he was over her, that he was able to attract younger, attractive women. Perhaps she had left him for Olmos but his life had gone on; he was even starting a new family, one with an attraction – the new baby – that would draw Stella back into his orbit.

But when Bracken gave birth to a baby in December, de Niro had a conversation with his old friend. Equally skittish about marriage and paternity, de Niro had faced paternity-suit problems of his own. Moreover, as owner of the restaurant where Bracken had worked, he may have known more than Keitel about her.

So he urged Keitel to take a blood test to determine if he was, in fact, the father of Bracken's child. It seemed insulting to Bracken, Keitel thought, but de Niro pointed out that this tactic had saved him from at least one set of child-support payments in the past.

To Keitel's chagrin, the blood test came back negative. Not only was Keitel not the father of Bracken's child – but obviously, he also wasn't the only man in her life. It was yet another betrayal for a man who, in exploring his own inner darkness to provide insight into the characters he played, had failed to intuit what was actually going on in the lives of the people around him.

With *The Piano* in 1993, Keitel began an impressive streak: for the next three years, he would appear in the winner of one of the top two prizes at the Cannes Film Festival. *The Piano* won the Palme d'Or in 1993; Quentin Tarantino's *Pulp Fiction* would win the same award in 1994; and Theo Angelopoulos would win the Grand Jury Prize (essentially, second place) in 1995 for the film known variously as *Ulysses' Gaze* and *The Gaze of Odysseus*.

But it was *The Piano* that proved to be the most startling transformation for Keitel. As Baines, a Scotsman transplanted to New Zealand in the nineteenth century, he played, for one of the few times in his career, a romantic lead, a man of gentleness and grace, despite a kind of forceful inarticulateness. It was a watershed role for Keitel, one that finally revealed a tenderness and vulnerability, minus the kind of macho posturing his characters usually seemed forced into. It even transformed him into an unusual sex symbol.

It was, given his output the year before, an almost contradictory role for Keitel: 'But the essence of Harvey is contradiction,' Alan Rudolph noted. 'Harvey has made a career out of his potential to break your bones. But his real success will come when he can break your heart.'

Which he did in *The Piano*, the story of Ada, an English-woman, and her daughter, who move to the opposite end of the earth for an arranged marriage. Once she arrives in New Zealand, however, her new husband refuses to carry her piano over the mountain from the shore to their home. Instead, the husband's neighbor, Baines (Keitel), who sees a soulmate in this fierce little woman (played by Holly Hunter), trades her husband some land for the piano. Then he offers to sell it back to her, one key at a time, for lessons. The lessons, however, gradually reveal his feelings for her, until they become lovers.

If Keitel seemed an unlikely choice for such a role to some, that wasn't the case with writer/director Jane Campion, who cast him:

> His work is tender and masculine. I had always admired him, his curious work and curious choices, that interesting intensity. I wasn't intimidated by the screen Keitel, his tough guys with crimson cocks. I thought the strong physicality would be intriguing in a girl's movie. What I found was a very sharp mind and a very sophisticated person, interested in the politics of relationships. I don't think of him as macho at all. He's much more complex than that. He's very comfortable with women and he's very comfortable being directed by a woman. It's some sort of a heart-soul thing that makes Harvey what he is. It's the depth of his inquiry into life that makes Harvey so interesting.

Keitel returned the compliment, referring repeatedly to Campion in interviews as 'a goddess: She's mystical. She's a little girl, she's a friend. She has all the qualities of being a great guy . . . There's a lot to be learned from her. She's an extraordinary woman, extraordinarily dynamic. Her sensitivity, her insight, her courage.'

The role had parallels with Keitel's life, which he used in the preparation for it. Here was Keitel, who had discovered twice in the space of just a few years that the woman he loved had in fact betrayed him with another man: first Bracco, then Bracken. And he was playing a man in a similar situation: alone in the world, coveting a woman who belongs to someone else.

> I think I attracted *The Piano* and Jane attracted me. So I was put into this place where I had to take a look at being alone, the elements of the character: at being alone, at not having a woman, what that was like and why I didn't have one, why I wanted one, why I needed one.
>
> And not only that but to stop being a manipulator. If I need to be alone, I'm going to suffer the fear of being alone. I can almost say it's been a lifetime journey for me.

According to Holly Hunter, 'Harvey is quite vulnerable. And I think he brings a vulnerability to almost every character that he does. There was so little spoken in the scenes between Ada and Baines. Harvey and I were looking for the unspoken mystery that enveloped each scene. And I don't think Harvey has to work hard to have access to that. I think Harvey is just a really tender guy.'

But it comes at a price, Keitel said: 'You've got to do your homework. I'd say that ninety percent of it is homework and the other ten percent is bringing your ideas to life in a rehearsal. It's always a painful process. I haven't yet been in a situation where it wasn't painful. Painful.'

He found himself drawn by the film's depiction of a woman taking control of her own sexuality in a straightforward manner:

> For one of the only times that I am aware of, Jane has done what I have often seen men do – i.e., a woman gathering herself up, taking responsibility for herself and her sexual needs and her spiritual needs and taking action to fulfill

herself. That has usually been the domain of the man. Jane has gained access to that domain. Here we have a woman. We're examining her sexual desires, her needs, her sensuality. I don't know about you but I'm tired of the burden. How wonderful to have a woman come forward and say, 'We have these thoughts, we have these feelings.' Jane has helped me to come closer to an understanding of myself and women.

That depiction of sexuality included nudity – for both Hunter and Keitel. Baines appears nude to Ada, then removes her garments and makes love to her, breaking through the barrier of fierceness she uses as a shield against her husband to reach the passionately fiery woman beneath.

It was considered noteworthy that Keitel, for the second year in a row (after *Bad Lieutenant* in 1992), had shown his penis to the camera. While women routinely do full frontal nudity, male genitalia are not often shown in Hollywood films. Stars such as Mel Gibson, Kevin Costner and even Clint Eastwood will bare their butts in a film, but the penises of the stars are so rarely seen that, when an actor willingly shows his willie, it's noteworthy, commented upon and joked about. Richard Gere had the bare-it-all reputation in the 1980s. And Keitel became known for it in the 1990s. 'The joke was, "Oh, we don't want to see Harvey naked again,"' Peter Travers said.

It was all the more noteworthy because it came when he had reached an age when other actors are lucky to be working. Here was Keitel – fifty-two when he made *Bad Lieutenant*, fifty-three for *The Piano* – baring a physique that, despite the slightest thickening of the middle, still looked as hard and well-muscled as when he showed us a slightly leaner version in *Mean Streets* and *Who's That Knocking at My Door?* twenty and twenty-five years earlier.

It turned him into an unlikely sex object for female viewers:

'He's a guy in his fifties who takes off his clothes and has thirty-year-old women swooning,' observed Harlan Jacobson.

For Peter Medak, it brought 'a reality. It's his search for the truth and the reality that makes him do that. He works out hard to keep his body like that. He feels it's his acting instrument. It brings a tremendous truth and honesty to a character.'

Keitel, however, refuses even to acknowledge the idea of a nude scene. He draws a sharp distinction between what he does as an actor and what his character does as part of its life before the camera. Ask him about it in any form in an interview situation – even something as innocuous as 'Why do you think there is such a taboo about male frontal nudity?' – and the answer inevitably is the same.

'I've never done a nude scene,' he'll say. 'An actor tells a story the way his conscience dictates is best to tell it. Actors do not do nude scenes. They play events in the story. They should tell stories that mean something to them. Whether they're dressed or undressed is up to their conscience and their artistic sense.'

The Piano was an instant hit on its debut at the Cannes Film Festival in 1993, sharing the Palme d'Or as the year's best film with *Farewell, My Concubine*. It was selected to close that year's New York Film Festival and opened shortly afterward to rapturous reviews, perhaps the best Keitel had received in his entire career.

David Denby wrote in *New York*, 'Harvey Keitel, now over fifty, gives an immensely tender performance as this man who asks for love. Perhaps only a woman director would now photograph a man in this way, and when Holly Hunter, with rounded breasts and rump, joins him in bed, the sensuality becomes overpowering.'

Not that there weren't skeptics: 'I think the praise he got for that part came out of surprise,' observed Jack Mathews. 'Like, "Geez, that's Harvey Keitel doing that." He went against expectations. It's not a bad performance. I just think too much was made of it. I think a lot of people could have played the part in *The Piano*. He did a great job in a role that was pretty ordinary.'

The Piano went on to be nominated for a host of Academy Awards and Golden Globes, with Oscars going to Hunter as best actress; to Anna Paquin, who played her daughter, as best supporting actress (beating Hunter, who was also nominated for *The Firm*); and to Campion, for her screenplay. The New York Film Critics Circle gave awards to Hunter as best actress and to Campion as best director and for best screenplay. Hunter also won the Golden Globe Award and the Los Angeles Film Critics award.

Though Keitel won the Australian Film Institute Award as best actor for his performance as Baines, he was not even nominated for a Golden Globe or an Oscar. Peter Travers commented, 'They nominate him for *Bugsy* but not for *The Piano*. It shows that Hollywood still resists accepting him as something more than his gangster image.'

Yet Keitel was pleased that *The Piano*, an art film, enjoyed the kind of success and popularity it did in the United States. He also knew that this kind of visibility would only increase his offers of work. But he was less interested in cashing in on his success with a big pay day than with the increased freedom to take on tougher, less commercial fare and get it seen:

The broad success of a movie always brings change. Aside from the obvious – opportunities for more work – it opens up a perspective on the worker that was not present before. I look for something that's going to challenge me to struggle and take me someplace else, because of something it offers that I don't know. The work itself is a great motivator for me, a vehicle for descending into the self. In it is a religiosity, if you will.

28

'There is, so far, only one Harvey Keitel "type" and like Nicholson or Eastwood before him, he will have to impose that type on the industry and public, a process that could take a long time,' the late Stuart Byron wrote in *Film Comment* in 1978.

But when it finally happened, it happened in a big way.

Keitel's filmography currently stands at more than sixty movies – probably more by the time this book is published. Granted, that covers a period of twenty-five or thirty years (depending on whether you count from *Who's That Knocking at My Door?* in 1968 or *Mean Streets* in 1973). Aside from the large timespan, it might not be all that noteworthy a figure: even playing the lead in two movies a year, that's six months of actual work a year at most (being generous and allowing for twelve weeks of shooting per film). As Keitel is the first to admit, this isn't exactly digging ditches. 'The average guy works a lot more days and hours than I do,' he acknowledged.

The figure becomes a little more amazing, however, when you consider that Keitel made a third of those movies during the years 1993 through 1996. That's five movies a year, though, as Keitel himself admits, 'I didn't have a lot of leads, because if you do, you don't do that many films.'

Yet, unlike some actors, who wear out their welcome because of the limits of their talents and appeal, Keitel has increased and enhanced his reputation with his prolific film output. James Toback noted that 'As you get older, people are not more inclined to give you a shot at a lead. So his turnaround was a

miracle. It's just about unprecedented. He went from promise
to oblivion to stardom.'

Peter Medak said, 'It's a very hard thing to make three or
four movies a year, which he does. And they're all interesting
characters, which are hard to find. It's admirable what he does.'

It may be that he is driven, inevitably, by a sense of both
creeping mortality and lost time, given the dearth of meaty,
provocative roles he found in the 1980s. Once his star rose
again and his bankability gave him the clout to attract enough
money to finance modest independent films, he waded in up to
his hips, taking on role after role in a spurt of activity that is
noteworthy for the variety and, frequently, the quality of the
work he was involved in.

Consider that, in 1993, the same year *The Piano* was released,
Keitel also appeared in *The Young Americans*, *Dangerous Game*,
Rising Sun and *Point of No Return*. Or that, in 1994, the same
year he appeared in *Pulp Fiction*, he was also in *Imaginary
Crimes*, *Monkey Trouble*, and the still-unreleased *Somebody to
Love*. 'The older you get, anything you want to do you get the
feeling you better do it now,' James Toback observed. 'Harvey
thrives on working.'

Roger Ebert maintains that 'The great actors worked constantly. Today, actors who wait for deals and packages may
take a year or two between films. By working all the time, you
get better. It's a gift that does not improve with disuse.'

'My career has really picked up steam all of a sudden,' Keitel
remarked around the time of *The Piano*. 'I wish I knew what
made that happen, because if I did, I would've made it happen
ten years ago.'

Keitel reteamed with Abel Ferrara to play a role that was a
custom-fit: the actorspeak-spouting director in *Dangerous
Game* (originally titled *Snake Eyes*), which was released shortly

after *The Piano* at the end of 1993. According to Keitel: 'It's a story about the complete failure to cope with life's problems. The problems are dealt with in a destructive way.'

Ferrara referred to it as 'a cross between *Bad Lieutenant* and *Day for Night*, with Harvey playing Truffaut and Madonna as the actress.' In the film, Keitel is cast as New York director Eddie Israel, who travels to Hollywood to make a film (starring actors played by James Russo and Madonna) about a couple whose marriage is on the verge of collapse. It is threatened by the husband's urge to abandon himself to hedonism in all its forms: drugs, sex, liquor, even violence. But, as filming progresses, the leading man begins to take on characteristics of the character he is playing, threatening the film. Meanwhile, the director begins having an affair with the leading lady (and, in the film's most uncomfortably funny scene, nearly gets caught by his wife's unexpected arrival).

The film is presented as a documentary being shot about Israel and the filming of his movie, *Mother of Mirrors*. Keitel sits for interviews as Israel, discussing the actors' (and the characters') need to make a journey within to find the resources and the personal emotions to handle these challenging roles. At another point, trying to motivate a blocked Russo, Israel says, 'I need you to dig down to fucking hell!'

Pretentious and slow, the film still offers intriguing performances by the three principals. Keitel, his hair long and shaggy, looks like some biblical boho, or perhaps like a stand-in for William Hurt in *Kiss of the Spiderwoman*.

If *Bad Lieutenant* divided the critics, *Dangerous Game* united them. Reaction was typified by Leah Rozen of *People* magazine, who wrote, 'This is a stupefyingly bad movie. And boring. And pretentious . . . Even Keitel can't surmount such scenes as the one where he has to seduce Madonna by warbling Harry Chapin's "Taxi."'

Keitel defended the film, particularly Madonna, a perennial

target of film critics: 'I thought Madonna was excellent,' he said. 'She's committed to her work.'

But he wasn't blind to the movie's shortcomings: 'I can't say that I'm shocked that it disappeared,' he said. 'There were brilliant things in that film, but the central story was lacking. It needed some work, which we failed to do.'

Michael Crichton's *Rising Sun* was his controversial follow-up to *Jurassic Park*, though both wound up being released as films the same year. Ostensibly a murder mystery, the book also served as a polemic about the way America was losing the trade war to Japan, at a point when Japanese acquisitions included such quintessentially American icons as New York's Rockefeller Center and Columbia Records and Pictures.

As Lieutenant Tom Graham, Keitel had the unenviable task of playing a symbol: the ugly American espousing xenophobic attitudes about the way the Japanese have co-opted and under-mined the American economy. He wears a snide smirk, barely masking what is obviously a simmering hostility to all things Oriental. With only a few scenes and about ten minutes of screentime, Keitel manages to set a baseline of American know-nothingness about the Japanese, from which Wesley Snipes, as the hero, will grow. Clad in a blond wig and California-esque casual clothes, Keitel would seem to be playing a stereotype: the bigoted, small-minded, spiritually corrupt cop. His character embodies everything that Americans have come to believe about Los Angeles police after the Rodney King incident and the Mark Fuhrman tapes. Unfortunately for the movie, the character barely figures in the story after his initial appearance in the opening half-hour.

Still, Keitel poured himself into the role as deeply as if he were playing co-star Sean Connery's role. As always, it was the details that counted. Right off the bat, he decided he needed a blond wig, in order to look more Californian. He also decided that his character was a gum-chewer. Matthew Carlisle, the film's first assistant director, recalls,

> There was a difficult scene in the boardroom where they're all looking at the body and they just couldn't get it right. Phil [Kaufman, the director] was not content with what they were doing, take after take, and neither was Harvey. Then someone noticed a huge continuity error: Harvey had been chewing gum in the scene before but he hadn't been chewing during this scene. The moment we gave him the gum, Phil got what he wanted. Once he had his prop, he was able to slip right into the character.

Keitel had strong ideas about what that character should be. According to Carlisle:

> We did tend to do more takes with him – he wanted to try it a bunch of different ways. I'm not sure he and Phil always agreed on what the character should be. Phil wants to make his own decision in his own time, but Harvey has a really strong belief system about what his part should be. Phil was not always given the space to come to his own conclusions.
>
> Harvey accepted his part less easily than Wesley or Sean. He'd question the character a lot more than they would. He'd want to take time to discuss why his character was doing this, to the point where it might be considered an annoyance. Phil is a lovely guy, but he had his hands full with those three guys.

Keitel's internal manner of working – to hold back during rehearsal, processing and shaping the role in his mind before assaulting it fully in front of the camera – initially had some people worried that he might not be right for the role. 'I expected a much younger, Joe Mantegna-type cop, a beefy guy,' Carlisle said. 'We wound up with the shorter, more squat, more

New York Harvey. That's why I thought it was a strange casting choice. But it was good for the movie.'

Line producer Ian Bryce said, 'The rap on him is that, in pre-production, he was ill-prepared. But the way he works is very deceptive. When shooting began, he was completely ready.'

Even in a small role, observed Steve Rotter, the film's editor, Keitel invested his character with nuance that compels the audience: 'He has this tension in his performance. You never know what he's going to do. And that's not just as an editor but as the audience. That's what makes him great as an actor: that underlying spontaneity. He's slightly different from take to take, in terms of shadings. Though he may be doing the same thing, it still has that same feeling of surprise. He's full of surprises.'

Despite any professional tensions there may have been on the set, Carlisle said, Keitel was not what he anticipated. 'I was expecting somebody difficult and volatile, based on things I'd heard from other people in the industry,' he said. 'I was expecting more of a Jim Woods. But he was nothing like that. He was a really nice guy. I think a lot of people are a little bit afraid of him because of the parts he's played. But I found him to be really gentle and nice to be around.'

Bryce added, 'He's a busy actor making three or four movies a year. A lot of actors don't need or want to take the time to learn the names of the crew. But Harvey does.'

If Keitel had had his way, his role in *Point of No Return* would have been a virtually silent one.

'I'm Victor. I'm the cleaner.'

That's almost all the dialogue Keitel had in a small but juicy role in the American remake of the French action hit, *La Femme Nikita*. And he tried to get rid of that.

Director John Badham recalled:

I had to talk to him quite a bit to get him to say the words, 'I'm the cleaner.' He didn't want to. I said, 'It's a funny term.' He finally said OK. He's probably the first actor I ever worked with who wanted to cut out dialogue, rather than add it. He kept going through the script, saying, 'We don't need this, we don't need this, this is not necessary.' He understood that the impact of the character was visual, that his presence said more than most of the dialogue. And this was a character who was laconic to begin with.

Playing a part originated by Jean Reno in the French version, Keitel enters at the tail end of the film to clean up after professional hitwoman Bridget Fonda botches a job. He turns it into a small but gruesomely funny turn; working with the flattest affect imaginable, he cuts a swath of death through the picture that barely registers on his face. What's most striking is the variance between the character's actions and his appearance: with horn-rimmed glasses, short blond hair and a nerdy lab coat, he could just as easily be managing the local Kinko's or working as a computer programmer. Though the film itself is a rather formulaic exercise in style and violence, it gets a jolt of blackly comic juice for the few minutes that Keitel's Victor is on the scene.

Keitel's fetish for research led Badham's lieutenants to track down a real professional assassin, through the author of a book they'd found in a north Hollywood survivalist bookstore about ways to kill people.

'This is amazing,' Keitel said after chatting with the hired killer. 'You talk to him and it's like talking to an electrician or a plumber or someone like that. He's a quiet, soft-spoken, neat, tidy man. He even wears a pocket protector with pencils lined up in it.'

To producer Art Linson, making the character look like an unprepossessing dweeb was an inspiration: 'What Harvey does is he always makes the unpredictable surprising choice. He was playing this vicious killer and suddenly he appears dressed like a nebbish owner of a 7-Eleven. His appearance and his choices were the exact opposite of what you'd expect a big, scary, tough killer would be. And, as a result, he becomes even more terrifying.'

To first assistant director David Sosna, however, Keitel took the characterization too far: 'Badham was looking for a little more juice – and Harvey played it like an insurance agent. He pulled it in so tight that there was not a whole lot an audience could hold on to. It was like having a DMV guy be an actor.'

Keitel saw the character as a blackly comic mix: the killer nerd, so seriously all-business that he's not even aware of how funny he is – or how funny he'd be if he weren't also a murderer.

That vision of the role's comic potential led to one of the film's funnier sight gags: as Victor enters the apartment building where he will meet Bridget Fonda, he approaches an elevator. The doors open and he bumps into a nervous security guard, who asks him a question. In response, he pulls his gun and shoots the guard, who falls into Victor. Victor catches him, then casually pushes him backwards into the elevator and follows him in.

But in Badham's original staging of the scene, the guard fell backward into the elevator after being shot. When he explained it to Keitel, Keitel offered his own solution: the guard falling into him, him shoving the guard backwards into the elevator.

'It doesn't work that way,' Badham explained. 'When you shoot someone, they're hit with an object traveling at tremendous velocity. So they tend to fall away from the bullet.'

'No, he should fall toward me,' Keitel said, 'because it's funnier that way.'

So Badham tried it Keitel's way: 'It was funnier – and it's in the picture that way,' he admitted. 'He had in mind an image that was an amusing point: it makes the character even more brusque than if the guy just fell away from him. And he was very dead-set on that. It was very important to him. When an actor has something that's that important to him, you give it a try.'

Keitel's character ultimately tries to kill Fonda after they've performed a hit together at a mansion high in the hills above LA. (The target was Richard Romanus, Keitel's *Mean Streets* co-star.) When their car gets hung up on the lip of a cliff, they end up struggling underneath the car – until it falls on Keitel and carries him away, down the steep hill.

When it came to looping the dialogue during post-production, the last segment to be dubbed was the grunts of exertion followed by cries of pain of that finale. Keitel watched himself being crushed by the car a couple of times, then turned to Badham and said, 'I think you could do this. I've gotta go,' and walked out the door, leaving the ultimate groans to his director.

Of his 1993 films, *The Young Americans* was probably the least significant. Released in Great Britain that year, it eventually appeared on video in the US the following year, without gaining a theatrical release.

The film is a stylized look at club life and the criminal underground in London, where a new American drug lord (a feral megalomaniac played by Viggo Mortensen) is upsetting the old order among gangs by killing off his rivals' dealers in gruesome ways. Keitel arrives from the US as John Harris, a DEA group leader who has been after this same dealer for a number of years.

Keitel brings a certain sorrowful restraint to the role, obviously finding resonance from his own life in the character of a divorced cop whose kids live with his wife in New York. But he's mostly a strong, grim presence following a trail; much of the story focuses on a young bartender (Chris Kelly) – at a club used by the drug lord as a base – whom Harris persuades to help him trap the drug lord. Keitel does have a few nice bantering scenes with veteran British character actor Terence Rigby, as one of the old Cockney gangsters on the verge of being made extinct by the new breed. But, as Derek Elley wrote in *Variety*, 'Where the pic's reach exceeds its grasp is in the script department.' Despite a story that includes racial issues, interracial love, the intergenerational crime war and the British club scene, there's not much there for Keitel in a film that's at best an adequate crime tale.

29

The streak that had begun for Harvey Keitel in 1991 – with *Bugsy* and *Thelma and Louise* – and continued through *Reservoir Dogs*, *Bad Lieutenant* and *The Piano* – was sustained in 1994 with the year's most talked about, most envied, most hyped and most emulated film: *Pulp Fiction*.

While *Pulp Fiction* saw the deification of Quentin Tarantino, the validation of Bruce Willis and the rebirth of John Travolta, the beneficent presence shining over the whole proceeding was Keitel's, in his role as the Wolf, who is summoned to aid Vincent and Jules after they've blown the head off of their captive. It was a nifty bit of casting, lifted, Tarantino admitted, from Keitel's role in *Point of No Return* as the cleaner. Winston Wolf is a cleaner of a less violent sort than Victor, but a cleaner none the less.

And a cleaner with some of the best lines and reactions in the movie. His take when Travolta asks him to say please is priceless, as is his reading of the line, 'Pretty please with sugar on top, clean the fucking car.' When they've finished cleaning up the car and Tarantino's Jimmie starts marveling at how different it looks, Keitel says sagely, 'Let's not start sucking each other's dicks yet.'

There was also a certain resonance in the roles he and Tarantino were playing. Wolf rides to the rescue ('It's thirty minutes away; I'll be there in ten') of Jimmie, whose wife Bonnie will divorce him if she finds a body in the garage. Wolf says calmly, 'I solve problems,' just as Harvey Keitel once solved Tarantino's problem of getting *Reservoir Dogs* the finance it needed.

But the impact of the role goes even farther, according to Janet Maslin: 'He had that little part in *Pulp Fiction* and it was almost like a benediction, him giving his blessing of a long career unto a new generation. The thing I like best is this new authority he has.'

Peter Travers also felt his new influence:

He does mean a lot to that new generation. When I go to Sundance and see the young directors and actors and writers, they all have a tremendous respect for him. The younger generation wants to have that same kick-ass, I'll-do-what-I-want attitude they see in him. Many of them, by comparison, think de Niro has sold out or degenerated into self-parody. But Harvey seems able to take risks that young people, who are starting out, admire.

Writing in his journal in 1994, James Toback described a party he attended:

Harvey Keitel invites me to a gathering at his Malibu beach house, rented from Freddie Fields. It is one of the accoutrements of Harvey's late-found, newly arrived fame that actors and directors pay court to him now – or, more precisely, come to his court. Actors and rock musicians have formed a cult fan club since *Mean Streets*, but not in nearly the numbers nor with the unadulterated intensity that is now evident. Christopher Penn, Bruce Willis, David Caruso, Quentin Tarantino, Wayne Wang – are all happy to be in Harvey's orbit.

Keitel made three other films for 1994: *Monkey Trouble*, *Somebody to Love* and *Imaginary Crimes*. While *Monkey Trouble* was a mild hit among kids (more so on video), *Imaginary Crimes* was a serious film that never found an audience.

Somebody to Love has yet to be released – and may wind up as a straight-to-video entry.

Directed by Alexandre Rockwell, *Somebody to Love* centered on a taxi dancer in modern LA played by Rosie Perez. She is having an affair with a married actor named Harry Harrelson (Keitel), but it's going nowhere. So is this part, though Keitel seems to enjoy playing an actor who starred in a hit TV series in the early 1970s and is still trying to cash in on that fame. Up for a spot in a new Tarzan film, he recites mock Shakespeare to Rosie – clad only in a pair of leopard-skin bikini briefs – shortly before chasing her out of his house when his wife comes home unexpectedly. And, as it turns out, the part he's being offered is that of the gorilla. Keitel is relaxed and playful – but that may be because he doesn't have to carry this soggy little film.

Imaginary Crimes, on the other hand, was an earnest and tough-minded effort, based on an autobiographical novel by Sheila Ballantyne. Ballantyne had written the book as a kind of reminiscence of her father. After eleven years of options and no production deal, the script was passed to Keitel, who promptly connected with it. He was just the latest star to be mentioned for the role – Dustin Hoffman, Harrison Ford and Robert Duvall's names had been dropped in the past – but he was the first one to say, 'OK – when do we start?' even though the director, Anthony Drazan, was young and had only one low-budget film, *Zebrahead*, to his credit. 'Harvey was very influential,' Drazan commented. 'He's a determined man on some things, in a medium that tests your patience. After Cannes and *The Piano*, he had heat.'

Keitel went to San Francisco to meet Ballantyne and rummage through her old photos of her father, and to get her to plunder her memory for her thoughts on him. 'Harvey has a young daughter and I think that's why he was interested in playing the part of a young girl's father,' Ballantyne said. 'He's the one who pushed the whole project; he was the driving force. Without him, there would be no movie. For so long, it seemed like just a rather pointless waiting game, the book and the screenplay falling through every conceivable crack.'

Keitel took the view that 'I have been a son and I am now a father, so the story Sheila Ballantyne wrote, I found myself experiencing all the characters. I don't think I'm going to judge this man. He kept the family together where other people might have given up.'

In *Monkey Trouble*, a wan kiddie comedy, Keitel played a gypsy organ grinder who performs with his little Capuchin monkey – which actually has been trained to steal, picking pockets and snatching jewelry with great deftness. Keitel, always one for heavy make-up prosthetics, still wears the long hair from *The Piano* and *Dangerous Game*, though he's let it go lank and greasy. He's supplemented that with a mouthful of metallic teeth (shades of James Bond's Jaws!) and a Sergeant Pepper jacket. He also rides a bike and a skateboard and cries crocodile tears in playing the cartoonish gypsy.

For Keitel, there was one compelling reason to do the film: his daughter Stella:

When I told my daughter Stella I'm making a movie with a monkey, I can't describe to you the look on her face. She turned her head to me and broke into a grin and said, 'Daaaddy.' That was worth everything. It's for children and it discusses an ethic and it's a beautiful story, a children's fairy tale. There's a morality to it. It's as important to my mind as *The Piano* or *Bad Lieutenant*.

30

Keitel's feelings for his daughter Stella were much on his mind at that point in 1994, as he launched a fierce court battle to retrieve custody from Lorraine Bracco and Edward James Olmos. The struggle carried them all into the news and gossip columns, in a spat that saw nasty allegations from both sides.

In his suit, Keitel alleged that Olmos had molested a teenage friend of Bracco's daughter Margaux, a girl who was the daughter of friends of Keitel and Bracco's. The event had allegedly been kept from Keitel by Bracco for more than a year after the girl supposedly told her parents, who confronted Olmos and Bracco. According to Keitel,

> There is evidence in court that he paid $150,000 to the alleged victim's family and of a secret agreement that he entered into with the parents of this child who made the allegation of molestation. My suit for custody was not brought until I found out about the money Olmos paid. First I called the parents of the child. They wouldn't speak to me. I was stunned because I knew these people. Then I called Lorraine. She wouldn't speak to me. I ensured the safety of my daughter as best I could, given that I do not have custody.

'He's insane about his daughter,' said a close friend. 'To have her hooked up with someone with that going on – it's a nightmare.'

Keitel was able to get a court order prohibiting Olmos from

being alone with Stella. Olmos, however, claimed the charges were all false. According to one account from the Olmos camp, the girl in question was actually sleeping with Olmos's son, who subsequently dumped her. In anger, she concocted the story as a form of revenge, abetted by Keitel.

'Keitel is vicious and disturbed,' Olmos said. 'This man is out of control. He doesn't want Stella. The accusations originated from a vicious vendetta against me and Lorraine, which obviously has no limits. He's using the whole situation to hurt Lorraine and myself. These destructive smears are the hideous work of a sick mind. I have never, ever molested or abused anybody.'

And Bracco added, 'Harvey Keitel is motivated by jealousy and hatred at my happiness in my new marriage. He is both a destructive and self-destructive person. Suffice it to say that I do not believe the allegations.'

But Keitel remained adamant: 'It is incredible to me how Lorraine Bracco could allow a man she knew was accused of sexually abusing a young girl to sleep in the same bed with our daughter,' he said. 'I have an obligation to protect my daughter and I'm going to live up to that.'

After hearing testimony in a closed hearing from the girl Olmos allegedly molested, the judge ultimately gave custody to Bracco. However, he let stand the restraining order against Olmos, barring him from being in the same room with Stella unless another adult was present. But he also put a condition on Keitel's visitation rights: that Keitel could continue to see Stella only if he never asked his daughter if Olmos had violated the restraining order: 'From all evidence,' he wrote, 'including the court's in-camera interview with [the girl Olmos allegedly molested], there is no indication whatsoever that she has been abused, accosted or improperly approached in any way.' The judge also noted that there was no third-party witness or physical evidence and that the girl's sister had never had any problems with Olmos. He also noted that the alleged victim had a close relationship with Keitel.

After the ruling, Bracco issued a statement: 'After several years of accusations, gossip, litigation and countless trial delays, the court has decided that my daughter is safe and sound, and belongs in the home she has had for the past several years, with me, her sister and her stepfather. I can only hope that [Keitel] will accept the wisdom of the court's decision and, in our daughter's best interest, obey the court's orders.'

According to one insider, 'Olmos and Bracco actually agreed [to the ruling] because the big issue was getting custody and they were finally ready to agree to anything to get it resolved.'

Stella also figured strongly in Keitel's thoughts late in 1994, as he traveled to Europe to make *Ulysses' Gaze* with director Theo Angelopoulos and wound up filming in the war-torn Balkans.

He had been to the region earlier, traveling to Sarajevo with Vanessa Redgrave at the request of UNICEF, and wound up as a spokesman for the book *I Dream of Peace* (HarperCollins).

When his daughter found out he was traveling to the dangerous section of eastern Europe, she asked him why he had to go. Keitel recalled, 'I said to her, if she were there and her life was in danger and I wasn't around, I would hope someone would go for her. And she understood that.'

Keitel walked the streets of Vukovar and Mostar, then went to Sarajevo. What he saw there devastated him.

What can you say about a town that's been destroyed by bombs and hand grenades and house-to-house fighting? It's different than seeing it on TV. Our Serbian crew came with us and, by the looks on their faces, I understood the horror of what had happened there. That certainly stays with you

for the rest of your life. It certainly is a great device for
cleaning the bullshit out of your mind. It instills a sense of
despair about humanity.

Most importantly, I showed up. People need to be there
and I went. An American citizen showed up to listen to the
children. To hold their hand. To tell them there are people
who remember them and that they're not forgotten.

Keitel found himself drawn back to the region by the script
of Tonino Guerra and Angelopoulos, a Greek film-maker whose
thoughtful, studied work had barely been released in the United
States but had won a following in Europe.

In the Angelopoulos film, he plays a Greek expatriate movie
director, who returns to Greece after thirty-five years of living
in America for a retrospective of his work. While there, he
becomes involved in a search for three missing reels of film by
a pair of brothers who had taken the first cinematographic
images of everyday life in the Balkans. His search takes him
across half Europe and through strife-ridden Bosnia:

I just read the screenplay – that's all it took. I guess I knew
from the very first page that I had to make this movie. The
story is the classic journey of the soul's search for the soul.
The stated premise was, 'The soul that wishes to know itself
must journey through the soul.'

I didn't know Angelopoulos' work previously, which is
quite outrageous in itself. I asked Scorsese and other directors
and they all revered him. I was stunned myself when I found
out about him. I wondered, 'How did I miss him?' It's become
only too apparent that, in America, we miss a great many
extraordinary talents from around the world. There's not
much of a forum for foreign film-makers to have their work
shown, unless it's going to make money. But they have
stories we need to share with them.

One person close to Keitel said that 'He was offered a huge

amount to play the second male lead in one of these huge action movies. But he said, "I can't get myself to do that. In the past, when I was desperate, I could justify it. Now I cannot justify doing things I don't want to do."'

Here was Keitel, for the first time in his career being offered the kinds of roles in Hollywood he would have killed for ten years earlier – turning them down to do the films he felt most committed to: stark, introspective, decidedly independent. The freedom that this new popularity brought him didn't mean seizing the moment and cashing in on it for all it was worth. Rather, he utilized this clout to make the movies he wanted to make, the movies that had always attracted him, the movies that moved and challenged him, mentally, physically and emotionally.

Peter Scarlet, program director of the San Francisco Film Festival, which screened *Ulysses' Gaze* as part of a 1996 Keitel tribute, said, 'The fact that he's got the balls to go and work with someone like Angelopoulos, who he didn't know anything about, is pretty impressive – and he was making a film under circumstances that were not exactly a backlot. He's an example to other performers.'

In fact, Angelopoulos didn't really know Keitel's work either, having only seen *The Piano* at Cannes when he offered him the role. 'Our initial relationship was a bit hesitant and complicated,' he said. 'But the more the film progressed, the more his American side receded and the more European he became. He plunged himself into the historical problems, trying to understand the very Europeanness of this war. I had taken several steps, but he had taken many more and we found each other.'

As the filming moved into Bosnia, the movie company found itself held hostage by the local customs: 'It was a case of when in Rome, do as the Romans do,' Keitel said.

You have to pay the local gangs and mafias to have security. To stay alive, perhaps. You have to have contact with people who know what you need to know. I've never made a film anything like that before.

This was not a soundstage. It was not fake. These were real places, real events. These are places where people died in the thousands, children, women, men. Angelopoulos is a man of conscience, who amazingly goes to these places and tells a story about what it's like for us to try to evolve as human beings, the mistakes we make, the death we bring to us, if we don't venture into the unknown.

The finished film, nearly three hours long, was shown at the Cannes Film Festival in May 1995 and took the Grand Jury Prize, second only to another film about the war in the Balkans, *Underground*, by Emir Kusturica.

Jonathan Romney wrote in the *Guardian* of London, 'Angelopoulos has made one of the great landscape films, making stark beauty out of the dereliction of Albania and Sarajevo, but the landscapes are sometimes more affecting than the figures in them ... But Keitel is superb – he's taken on the mantle of gravitas that Burt Lancaster once wore, and he gives the film's vaporous tendencies the magnetic centre they need.'

Janet Maslin found the film

incredible, on the cusp of being absurd, but not quite. [Keitel] was playing this great brooding artist; the whole thing wouldn't work if he hadn't given himself over to the director's audacity. The director had decided to explore all of these classical themes right here and now; it could have been ridiculous, to have Harvey Keitel approach it with such total seriousness. And yet it's amazing – you can feel Keitel's leap of faith.

But the film never received an American release. Though it has been given an isolated screening here and there, no distributor was willing to step up to the plate for a three-hour film about a spiritual journey across the Balkans. Keitel was disappointed:

> *Ulysses' Gaze* has been shown extensively through the world, in every country – except in America. *Underground*, by Emir Kusturica, also has not found distribution in the States. I understand the reasons for it. Maybe they move a bit slowly, the film is the length it is, nearly three hours. But it tells an important story. There should be a place in this country where film-makers like Angelopoulos and the thousands of talents from other countries can find an outlet because people need to have their own opportunity to see these stories presented to them. No matter what they are, these works deserve to be seen.

31

'Imagine a film about Harvey Keitel, the actor so good, so persistent, yet so regularly denied at the highest table; ceaseless in his fury, his bitterness, forever hurtling forward in that cold, determined aura that is a mix of menace and resentment. What a role! And probably de Niro would get it,' David Thomson wrote in his *Biographical Dictionary of Film*.

In fact, Keitel wound up taking a role originally meant for de Niro: Detective Rocco Klein in 1995's *Clockers*. Based on the novel by Richard Price, it is a gritty, detailed story about the murder of a drug dealer and the struggle of wills between the investigating homicide detective and his chief suspect – a teenager named Strike – who is, in fact, not guilty.

Clockers was originally to be a Martin Scorsese film, starring de Niro. Then Scorsese and de Niro decided to do *Casino* instead – and Spike Lee took over *Clockers*, with Scorsese as executive producer. Lee, who, like most other film-school students of the late 1970s and early 1980s, revered *Mean Streets* and *Taxi Driver*, had unsuccessfully tried to interest de Niro in the Danny Aiello role in *Do the Right Thing*. But he felt he'd lucked out landing Keitel to play Rocco after de Niro decamped with Scorsese for Vegas.

Keitel approached the role as he always did: with research. He spent time with Newark police detective Larry Mullane, with whom he had done similar research for *Mortal Thoughts*: 'I've heard it said about detectives by detectives that they're great actors, that by the nature of their profession they have to be. To get information, you often have to put on a pretty good show. And the ones that are great detectives are, in a sense, great actors.'

Despite his admiration and respect for the police, he saw his role in *Clockers* as one that offered moral lessons about both sides of the drug war:

> There are important social and cultural issues in *Clockers* that are relevant to our well-being and evolution. One of the issues the story addresses is the danger we have of becoming self-righteous. Self-righteousness is a disease that can kill and does. The self-righteous aspect of Rocco is the same in all of us; it can blind us to other realities. I always felt that Richard Price was sending up a warning flag in the form of Rocco, saying, 'Beware of becoming self-righteous, beware of thinking you know everything, beware of that moment when you stop your discovery because you can lapse into self-righteousness.' And, in *Clockers*, a young boy's life is destroyed because of this self-righteous aspect of Rocco's personality.

But the relationship with Lee was a fractious one, in part because Keitel came to *Clockers* tired; it was his fifth film back-to-back. 'Spike felt like he'd waited all these years to work with Harvey and then Harvey sort of walked through the role with a kind of standard tough-guy grumpy performance because he was exhausted,' said a source close to Lee.

Still, to critics, Keitel's performance was the strong center to what was one of Lee's most accomplished and powerful films. 'He was wonderful in *Clockers*,' Janet Maslin said. 'The whole film was better than anybody gave it credit for being. It was a very tough role to pull off. You had to make the guy seem to be struggling with himself, confronting a confusing situation and still have the substance to do his job. And that all came through.'

Maslin pointed to Keitel's scenes with Mekhi Phifer, an inexperienced young actor Lee found to play Strike, the young drug-dealer: 'In the scenes with the kid, you could see him helping him, setting the tone for the scenes in a generous way. It looked to me like a sort of mentor arrangement. He wasn't trying to upstage him or to run away with the scene. There was a chance for the cop to dominate, strut and be a bully. But Keitel was kind of a teasing bully. You felt he wanted to get to know the kid, not overpower him.'

If *The Piano* revealed Keitel's penchant for dark romance, *Smoke* and *Blue in the Face* opened him up further, unveiling a new ease and charm, an earnest and easy-going confidence he had never before shown.

Smoke teamed Keitel with director Wayne Wang and writer Paul Auster, a Brooklyn writer writing about Brooklyn. The film was a loosely organized series of short stories involving a set of interlocking characters, connected by the Brooklyn Cigar Co., a corner cigar store in the Prospect Park area.

Keitel plays Auggie Wren, who manages the cigar store and whose story intersects with those of the film's other characters. But the final act of the film belongs to Keitel: a Christmas story he tells to William Hurt about stolen merchandise, a lost wallet and an elderly blind woman who mistakes Auggie for her long lost grandson, come to visit her on Christmas. It's an aria of compassion and wistful humor, with just Keitel in close-up, telling this mesmerizing tale.

The character of Auggie was based on someone Auster knew, who had supposedly told him a similar Christmas story (which ultimately wound up in the *New York Times*). 'Harvey was curious, wanting to know every detail of who Auggie Wren actually was,' Auster recalled. 'Little things mattered – like the fact that he had been in the Navy. Harvey decided that Auggie was neat, and so he was always cleaning or sweeping up. It's the peripheral habits that Harvey worked on that make the character richer onscreen.'

The conditions on location in Brooklyn were often difficult but the spirit on the set was upbeat and happy. They were filming in cramped quarters in an abandoned post office, remade into the Brooklyn Cigar Co. 'It was about a hundred degrees in that little smoke shop,' said Giancarlo Esposito, who played one of the guys who hang around the store, reading the racing form and kibitzing.

But, as Stockard Channing commented,

Wayne Wang was unflappable. We [Channing and Keitel] were in the car and we kept going around the block with the camera in the backseat, improvising and arguing. In terms of our characters, I had to make him up and vice versa. This had been a deep relationship twenty years earlier. But it's something we don't discuss, like an accident. Our unfamiliarity with each other was as potent as anything else. He was hostile to me and I was defensive. For the last scene on the promenade, it was like he was someone who was unknown to me, yet known. There was a certain abrasiveness. But there was a good chemistry. You could buy the fact that we were once together, that something had gone on. His rudeness to her was out of defensiveness.

Though Auggie was a talkative and outgoing character, Keitel tended to keep quietly to himself off-camera. Esposito remembered that he was

reserved, quiet, not trying to impress anyone. His work is rooted in truth. It's hard to hold yourself back, not to be 'On' or put on a show. But a couple of the actors were saying, 'What's wrong with the guy? He doesn't look at you. It's like you're nobody.' Everyone takes his attitude as non-friendly. But the guy is into what he's doing. The thing was, everyone wanted his attention and he was trying to create a character. Everyone knew if you had interaction with Harvey on camera, you'd get seen.

For me, it was just a pleasure to watch Harvey Keitel figure out his next action. There was this internal dialogue going on. And it was great to witness the work between Harvey and William Hurt. They're both very reserved but they've got inner demons crawling all over them.

For Keitel, working in Brooklyn was an instant trip into the past of Ebbetts Field and egg creams and Coney Island. 'There were a lot of memories evoked, sure,' he said. 'I take everything I am with me into that shop. It was great being in Brooklyn.'

While filming on a Friday night, the production drew a crowd of onlookers from the neighborhood, who turned the event into a kind of low-key party, drinking beer and having a good time. At one point, they watched the cast go through five takes of a scene before they got it right – which prompted one wit in the crowd to yell out, 'If I drove my bus the wrong way five times, I'd be fired,' cracking up both the crowd and the cast.

Keitel found himself drawn to the character of Auggie, seeing him as 'a philosophical story-teller,' about as venerated a calling as there is in the Keitel canon: 'He understands something about living that is quite unique. Which is that, on your own corner, in your own neighborhood, perhaps all you need to know will take place. And part of me believes that. I'm speaking metaphorically when I say on your corner. You might want to walk around the block.'

The film drew solid reviews and became a sleeper independent hit of the 1995 summer in the United States; its rambling structure and low-key performances also made it a cult hit in Europe.

'The success of *Smoke* was a particular joy,' Keitel said. 'It told a story – just a plain old simple story – without pyrotechnics on a budget of seven million dollars. There was good writing, good film-making and a good cast. And the story was a sweet, hopeful, uplifting piece of philosophy and mythology.'

Smoke's success was also good news for Miramax, the film's studio, which had already given Wang, Auster and Keitel the money to make another movie built around the same characters. Entitled *Blue in the Face*, the film was an experiment in storytelling: the film-makers took several of the characters from the film, added some new ones (including Jim Jarmusch, Lou Reed, Lily Tomlin, Roseanne and Michael J. Fox) and shot a series of barely scripted, mostly improvised scenes, then filled in the cracks with material about Brooklyn, its culture and history, much of it shot on video.

The idea for the film evolved from something that took place on the first day of *Smoke* rehearsals. As a way of getting into their characters, the cast began improvising a scene in the smoke shop. Keitel let the others take the lead, leaving Auggie to sit and observe at first. Finally, he interrupted the proceedings and said, 'Wayne, can I do something here?'

He then took one of the actors aside and gave him a direction: he was to go out and then come back in five minutes, needing to borrow money from Giancarlo Esposito.

'He started an improv that was more specific,' Esposito recalled. 'That led us into doing the scene. It was all over in about fifteen minutes. And then we had a three-hour rehearsal that felt like a half-hour. After that first day, Wayne said, "Wouldn't it be great to make a movie that was just about you guys at the smoke shop?" No one thought it could happen but Wayne was serious and started putting it together.'

Wang felt that 'we've got something with all these wonderful actors who have small parts.' He and Auster went to Miramax honcho Harvey Weinstein and told him that, for less than $2 million more, he could have another movie, shot in less than a week, after *Smoke* wrapped. 'My reaction,' Weinstein said, 'was, "Let's keep rolling the dice."'

So they did. The idea was to take ten rolls of film (each ten minutes long) and, for each roll, give the actors a different scene to play. There would be no multiple camera set-ups: just one master shot that would keep rolling until the film ran out while the actors kept talking until they were, appropriately, blue in the face.

According to Keitel,

Improv is a very important tool for the actor's technique in order to put him closer to himself. Improv is a way to discover how to get from here to there. It's also a way to bring you closer to what the character is going through. As a matter of fact, we improvise most of the scenes, even though they're written. We improvise scenes that never even took place in the movie, but took place the moment before the scene begins to again bring us closer to the character and to ourselves.

Improv is not play, however, as Marc Urman, the unit publicist on the film, discovered: 'I was a fly on the wall – for *Blue in the Face*, I spent three days on the closed set. My job was to observe and then create a press kit. And to keep the press away. Harvey was doing a scene and I was sitting absolutely invisibly in the corner, soaking up atmosphere. At a certain point, he politely asked me to leave because he couldn't concentrate with me sitting there.'

Not all the actors who played the smoke-shop guys had the same training as Keitel, however, and not all the improvs bore fruit. Though the directors (Wang was sharing the chore with Auster, and both had written the scenarios for the scenes) held up signs that said FASTER or GET TO THE POINT or BORING, not all the actors got the idea. 'Improv takes quickness, being facile and also some thought,' Esposito said. 'Some of the guys hadn't done their homework. There's this great focus put on being funny but that's a dangerous trap to fall into. The guys figured out how to be funny instead of how to be real.'

Still, some of the humor comes from real surprise, as in a scene in which actress Mel Gorham, as Auggie's on-again, off-again girlfriend Violet, comes into the smoke shop, angry that Auggie is trying to duck out on a date with her to go dancing.

'Paul told me to go there and convince Auggie that the most important thing in the whole wide world to me is to go dancing Saturday night,' Gorham recalled. 'So I went in and pushed Harvey up against the wall and I grabbed his crotch with all my might and I looked at him with my face about two inches from his face and I said, "I'm going to ride you like a big bull"' – the latter pronounced 'beeg bool' in Violet's exaggerated Hispanic accent.

On the other hand, when Esposito and Keitel got into a scene that produced strong emotions, Wang found it too heavy for the tone he was trying to set. Tommy (Esposito), a long-time habitué of the store and the neighborhood, comes in and tells Auggie that his older brother, a decade older than Tommy himself, has died. Because of the age difference, Tommy didn't know his brother well; he was coming to Auggie, who had been in the Marines with Tommy's brother, to ask him what he was like. As Esposito described it,

I found a picture of my own brother and me as kids. It was a wonderful moment. It was about how much I loved Auggie and how I knew he'd have words for this. So I came in and he didn't react. I broke into tears. He started to say, 'That fucking guy. What did he do to himself ?' and starts asking me, 'What happened to him? He got so fat.' And then he called him a nigger.

There was this incredible moment where I had to deal with sorrow and anger. I said, 'He wasn't a nigger.' There was a silence. Harvey kept saying, 'I can't tell you that – I can't tell you what he was like.' So the reel ran out. They changed it fast. Wayne said, 'Keep going.' So we did.

Harvey broke into tears. He was angry because he hadn't seen my brother in a long time and they used to be good friends. We wound up both in tears in each other's arms. When it was over, Harvey was wasted and I was wasted.

So Wayne, who was just back for his first day after missing the first two days because he was sick, came in and said, 'Do you think you can do that again? But a little lighter?' Harvey looked at me. I said, 'I don't think we can go there again.' We never did it again and it never got into the picture.

The unused scene, Esposito said, 'was a look into [Keitel's] soul, the sadness and bitterness in his life, the success he's had of late, the truth and honesty of a human being. It was a great gift to me, to know how deep I can go. He was throwing the ball back to me. A lot of actors think they're throwing the ball but they're just taking space, taking the spotlight. And it's about throwing the ball.'

Blue in the Face wound up less as a sequel to *Smoke* than a companion piece, sort of a guide to life in and around the smoke shop that had been only one facet of *Smoke*. It received mixed reviews, running the gamut from disdain ('What a bold notion for a movie and what a bust in terms of execution,' Peter Travers wrote in *Rolling Stone*) to enthusiastic praise for its experimental verve and loosey-goosey comic feel: Janet Maslin 'just loved [Keitel] in *Blue in the Face*. He had this fabulous screen presence. It was really a lovely star turn.'

Maslin had less kindly words about Keitel's next film, *From Dusk Till Dawn*, one that reunited him yet again with Tarantino, though she allowed that Keitel made her take it more seriously than she otherwise might have:

Even in that godawful *Dusk Till Dawn*, he gave it gravity. He gave the impression that he was doing something other than the usual special-effects vampire horror show. Under horrendous circumstances, he was very convincing. He was this soulful guy floating on the fringes of the movie that gave it another dimension. The fact that it was Harvey Keitel was so strange that you have to pay attention.

He does not seem to be doing these things frivolously. When he makes a decision to do something like this, you have to assume it's a serious decision and take it seriously.

Written by Tarantino, directed by Robert Rodriguez and released at the beginning of 1996, *From Dusk Till Dawn* is a wild genre-mixing film, full of garish and gory imagery, but delivered with a wicked sense of humor at a breathless pace. Keitel plays Jacob Fuller, a minister who has given up the calling because he lost his faith after the death of his wife in a horrible car accident. He and his two children are on a vacation, touring the country in a large mobile home, when they are kidnapped by a pair of vicious killers, Seth and Richie Gecko (played by George Clooney and Tarantino). Seth, who has just escaped jail, forces Jacob to take him and his brother to Mexico, to a rendezvous.

The rendezvous, a biker bar called the Titty Twister, turns out to be a haven for vampires, who kill all the customers. But the Geckos and Jacob and his children, along with a couple of bikers, are able to kill most of the vampires – until the army of the night comes pounding down the doors. In the end, only Seth and Jacob's daughter (played by Juliette Lewis) are alive. When he is bitten by one of the vampires, Jacob orders his daughter to kill him as soon as he begins to turn into one of the undead.

It's a gruesome romp, crackling with energy and bizarre visual ideas. It opened to strong business and went on to win the award as best horror film from the Academy of Science Fiction, Fantasy and Horror Films at the 22nd annual Saturn Awards.

Clooney, in his first serious movie starring role since attaining stardom in TV's *ER*, found working with Keitel enlightening and, at times, challenging. 'My character was supposed to dominate him,' he recalled. 'Now nobody, but nobody dominates Harvey onscreen. I did my best, but when I look at the result, I can see him throw in a gesture, raise an eyebrow or even take a pause – and he takes focus. That's why he's Harvey Keitel and I'm just a lucky guy with the best job in the world.'

Keitel seemed amused at being in a horror film: 'Growing up I loved movies like *The Day the Earth Stood Still* and the original *Blob*,' he said. But, for Keitel, *From Dusk Till Dawn* was more than a combination of action-thriller and monster movie; it was a movie about faith: 'I made this movie because it presents a theme that appears in many movies I do. It's about faith and the loss of faith and the journey through hell to regain it. It's perhaps the only valid theme there is.'

32

On April 28, 1996, Keitel was honored with a tribute and an award at the San Francisco International Film Festival. He was the first recipient of the newly created Peter J. Owens Award, given to him as someone 'whose work exemplifies brilliance, independence and integrity.'

Keitel arrived in San Francisco around noon from the set of *City of Industry*, a crime film directed by John Irvin in which he co-stars with Stephen Dorff, where an accident had left him in rocky shape. But he pulled himself together for a press conference at which, according to Peter Scarlet, program director of the film festival, Keitel was 'articulate but not hostile in delineating his work as a private area.'

The same was true when he appeared on the stage of the Kabuki Theater for the tribute, including a showing of relevant film clips and a question-and-answer session with the audience and a moderator from Cahiers du Cinéma. A clip from *Ulysses' Gaze* was interrupted at one point when Keitel stood up and started waving his arms, saying, 'It's the wrong clip.' When the clip was changed, only to be replaced by another wrong clip, he told the audience, 'I can see why you're bored, if you're bored.' Scarlet later took responsibility for a misunderstanding about which of the clips were to be included.

When someone asked Keitel whether the characters he plays stay with him after filming, he replied,

Part of coming to accept awards such as these is that it opens you up to questions that I as an actor never want to answer. Because . . . the place you are asking me to speak about is to a large extent a private place. I'm reminded of American Indians who didn't want their picture taken because they felt it would steal their soul. I have a similar feeling, so I'll try to answer your question as best I can. All those characters are in me, inside me. There's no shaking them off.

He decried Hollywood's inability to make films that have the kind of political content *Ulysses' Gaze* possesses, observing that 'there are people who will not pay attention to these issues, who refuse to confront them, and you can probably only do one thing to convince them to address those issues, which I'll demonstrate right now.' He then grabbed the microphone stand and strangled it.

He spoke passionately about the need for more outlets for foreign films such as *Ulysses' Gaze*: 'Why can't we put together a theater in this country where films like this could be seen, even if only once a week or once every two weeks?'

He urged young film-makers to grab the reins of their own destiny, to make their films themselves if no one else would help them: 'I can't urge people enough: MAKE YOUR OWN FILMS. Do not wait for Hollywood. Hollywood is a myth. It does not exist. We can be what we want Hollywood to be, but we need to take risks. Freedom comes with a price; you can never have it without sacrifice.'

And he told how he had appeared in an off-off-Broadway play at the Café LaMama and how the great surrealist painter Salvador Dali showed up in the audience one night – only to get up and walk out in the middle of the performance. 'I was thinking, "Who does he think he is? He thinks his hometown in Spain is the center of the world." Of course, everybody knows the center of the world is Brooklyn.'

Still, Keitel seemed evasive or oblique at times, whether responding to the moderator or the audience. To one question he didn't want to answer, he replied, 'We used to have a saying in the poolroom in Brooklyn. Which was, "I'll answer that question tomorrow at three o'clock."'

According to Scarlet,

A number of people said he was a difficult interview. The guy on the stage was not comfortable with him. But newspaper guys at the table of that evening's formal dinner said that's how he is. He was exceedingly articulate about what he wanted to talk about and what he wouldn't talk about. Once those parameters were laid, he talked provocatively and intelligently about things he felt comfortable with.

The dinner guests included Stockard Channing and Wayne Wang. By about 8:30 p.m. Keitel was ready to go. He had to catch a plane back to LA for another day of shooting on *City of Industry*. But as he left, he turned to Scarlet, his chaperone for the day, and said, 'You've been a perfect host, this has been a perfect day and I've enjoyed myself immensely,' and disappeared into the night.

These days, Keitel divides his time between a house in Malibu and his loft on North Moore Street in Tribeca, not far from the Tribeca Film Center, where he spends time reading in his airy, sunlit space, which is decorated with model sailboats and books.

Or at least he does when he's not working. That's not very often, judging by the way he moves from project to project to project. Besides *Somebody to Love*, Keitel has at least one other film in the can: *Head Above Water*. Written and directed by Jim Wilson (who wrote *Dances with Wolves*), he plays a judge on vacation with his young wife, when an ex-lover of hers turns up – and then turns up dead in her bedroom. In *City of Industry*, which opened in March 1997, Keitel jumped with both fists into film noir – yet another journey into darkness. As Roy Egan, a man out to avenge his brother, he plays a man of action and few words. A former stick-up man who has gone straight, he is pulled back into the criminal life by his younger brother Lee (Timothy Hutton), who needs him for a jewelry heist in Palm Springs. While the heist goes off without a hitch, one of Lee's partners double-crosses the crew, killing everyone but Roy and making off with the score. So Roy cuts a swath through the L.A. underworld to track him down and avenge his brother's death: 'I'm my own police,' Roy grunts at one point. It's a gutsy, subtly emotional performance in a stripped-down and propulsive film.

And he has projects stacked up like planes at LaGuardia: *Copland*, in which he appears with Sylvester Stallone and Robert De Niro; *Illumination*, a film to be shot in London in which he will play Houdini; *Dreaming of Julia*, which he is helping to produce, to be shot in Puerto Rico by director Juan-Gerard Gonzalez (he'll play a grandfather in pre-Castro Cuba who has an affair with a mysterious American movie star. The role, to be played by Mira Sorvino, was originally cast with Embeth Davidtz, a young actress in her twenties with whom Keitel had been involved briefly); and *Eyes Wide Shut*, an erotic thriller starring Tom Cruise and Nicole Kidman, directed by Stanley Kubrick.

At this point in his career, Keitel can, within a certain low-to-mid-level price range, do almost anything he wants. According to one observer, 'He's on certain kinds of lists for certain people now. Though not in the way that, say, Mel Gibson is. But Harvey can put together financing for certain kinds of films because he can guarantee pre-sales, European sales, video sales.'

Joel Schumacher feels that he is 'a great character actor. I'd put him in the category of actor whose greatest roles are still ahead of him. You can't say that for everybody at fifty-seven.'

Martin Scorsese maintains that 'Harvey's career has finally kicked into high gear because he's a damned good actor. There are a lot of hard knocks in this business but he hasn't let that get to him and has just kept working. That's the only thing you can do, and if you're any good, people eventually start to notice.'

For Quentin Tarantino,

Harvey's a throwback to a kind of actor that was big in the forties and fifties, but doesn't really exist anymore. Ralph Meeker, Sterling Hayden, Lee Marvin, Robert Mitchum, Aldo Ray – those guys had an inherent hardness that's a result of age, experience and environment, and most actors today don't have that quality because they haven't lived the life those guys lived. But Harvey has. If another actor were to play the part he has in my films, they'd have to spend the duration of the film trying to convince you they were as tough as Harvey is when he walks through the door.

Keitel is aware that his name is now worth something at the box office – but he has no interest in letting himself become just another 'element' in a movie 'package.'

'Today, when they want to make a movie, they start saying, "Let's get these two stars,"' he pointed out. 'Not the best actors. Two stars. They are bankable, they say, and will do good at the box office. There's no thought given to providing a deeper truth, to making something that will feed us, help us deal with the feeling of being lost in the world. The thrust has been to disregard the nature of the film itself.'

Despite the economic temptations of high-profile roles in big-budget studio films, Keitel seeks out the parts that will test him, take him to the limit, no matter where they might be. Which makes him a potent example to the rest of the film world, as Janet Maslin explained:

To a young actor, he means you can try anything and still have a brilliant career. To a director, he means you can hope to get him interested, if you've got an interesting story to tell – and it means he's got the clout to get it made. To young film-makers, he represents the fact that you can use an actor's personality to give a film a large amount of flavor, to set its coordinates by putting him front row center.

I'm sure there are people just writing parts for him, hoping to get his attention. Dennis Hopper had that and lost it. Christopher Walken had it and overused it. But Harvey is just getting better. He's really being pretty smart in how he's handled it.

33

Keitel's career in many ways resembles the stories of loss and redemption he discovered when, as a young Marine on a troop ship in the Mediterranean, he picked up a book of Greek mythology and began to read for pleasure for the first time in his life.

Imagine him as the young hero, who emerges from humble beginnings and, after a number of years and false starts, discovers his true purpose in life.

As he begins to learn the nature of this calling, he achieves early success. But, unable to repeat that success, he is labeled a failure. He shrinks from hero to has-been, forced to pursue this calling now with the added handicap of perceived failure smudging the badge of early success.

Yet, having truly focused his pursuit, he perseveres as he ages, concentrating on achieving personal satisfaction in his pursuit – and, as a result, comes to enjoy the kind of public acceptance he never knew as a young man.

And now Harvey Keitel does receive that kind of adulation – as the actor's actor and, among audiences, as someone whose very presence in a film is a signal about what to expect.

Have the movies finally caught up with Harvey Keitel? On the contrary, Keitel said: 'I think it's me that came around. I came around to a deeper understanding of myself, the work, myself and the work, the work and me. We call it evolving. So I think everything has been timely for me. I don't think I was overlooked. I think I was looked at and the reaction was the correct one. I don't think I was given short shrift.'

But it has taken him a long time to reach that realization. It has been an arduous and pain-filled journey, beginning in Brooklyn and taking him through the insecurity of adolescence, the education of the Marines and the near-wrong turn into being a court reporter.

Even after he discovered acting as an outlet, there were also years of indecision and uncertainty: Was he talented? Did he have what it took? For so many years, Keitel received so little encouragement and so many signs that this, too, was a wrong career move.

For Keitel, the goal remains the same: to pursue roles that will tell him about himself, to be in movies that challenge him as an actor, as a human being and as a man – and to impart to the audience the depth of that quest within himself to explore the most basic human questions, no matter how painful.

What has changed is his understanding of himself. For too long, he sought out the darker roles for their own sake, for the chance they offered to act a variety of strong emotions. Doing so made him feel better, though he didn't understand why. Eventually he learned to focus on the very real pain he had hidden within himself, to use that pain as a means of exorcising the demons that, even today, torment him in real life:

The reason I became an actor was to get closer to understanding myself – and I'm infinitely closer to it today. I've solved a lot of mysteries that have separated me from my feelings. It's not painful – it's bliss, it's enchanting. If there is pain, then that's the experience the actor has going through hell on his way to being enlightened.

It took me a long while to get to know myself, to understand who I was, a process I'm still engaged in. I had doubts, which always take the same form: 'I can't do it. I don't know how to do it.' I couldn't get the inside outside and it used to kill me. That's why I became an actor, to express who I am. We all have an inherent need to do that.

The fear never completely goes away. Never. But if you eat it, live in it, descend into it long enough, the sound of fear will change and you will in fact digest it. It will become a friend, something usable.

My early career was exactly what it should have been. I was ready to do certain things; I was not ready to enter into other places in my own soul that would have given me the materials that I needed in order to make my work deeper. It took time, it took experience, it took struggle to find out about who I am.

At this point in my career, everything that has occurred appears to be right. Because everything that occurred has provided an opportunity for me to see whether I'm going to run this way or run that way. Luckily enough I've chosen a path where I ran into myself. And knocked myself over many times. But I got up.

The only reason I see to make films is to descend deeply into something. I need to take more chances. To be like Van Gogh, who had the courage to face his own anxiety. That means being scared, being tired, being lonely, being hungry, being uncertain, being exhausted, suffering. It means trying to be more. It means being the most you can be.

Which doesn't mean the same thing as being happy. Asked to describe 'Harvey Keitel' to someone who doesn't know him, Keitel responded: 'Number one, he's not always angry. Number two, he is always in turmoil.'

harvey keitel filmography

MOTION PICTURE WORK

Reflections in a Golden Eye (1967; dir. John Huston;
Warner Bros.–Seven Arts)

Who's That Knocking at My Door? (1968; dir. Martin
Scorsese; Joseph Brenner Associates)

Street Scenes (1970; dir. Martin Scorsese; New York
Cinetracts Collective)

Mean Streets (1973; dir. Martin Scorsese; Warner Bros.)

Alice Doesn't Live Here Anymore (1974; dir. Martin
Scorsese; Warner Bros.)

That's the Way of the World (1975; dir. Sig Shore;
United Artists)

**Buffalo Bill and the Indians, or Sitting Bull's History
Lesson** (1976; dir. Robert Altman; United Artists)

Mother, Jugs and Speed (1976; dir. Peter Yates;
Twentieth Century-Fox)

Taxi Driver (1976; dir. Martin Scorsese; Columbia)

Welcome to LA (1977; dir. Alan Rudolph; United Artists)

The Duellists (1977; dir. Ridley Scott; Paramount)

Blue Collar (1978; dir. Paul Schrader; Universal)

Fingers (1978; dir. James Toback; Brut Productions)

Eagle's Wing (1979; dir. Anthony Harvey; Rank Films)

Bad Timing: A Sensual Obsession (1980; dir. Nicholas Roeg; Rank Films)

Deathwatch (1980; dir. Bertrand Tavernier; Selta Films/Gaumont)

Saturn 3 (1980; dir. Stanley Donen; Associated Films)

The Border (1982; dir. Tony Richardson; Universal)

La Nuit de Varennes/That Night at Varennes (1982; dir. Ettore Scola; Triumph Films)

Corrupt (1983; dir. Roberto Faenza; New Line Cinema)

Exposed (1983; dir. James Toback; United Artists)

Nemo or Dream One (1983; dir. Arnaud Selignac; Columbia)

Falling in Love (1984; dir. Ulu Grosbard; Paramount)

A Complex Plot About Women, Alleys and Crimes or **Camorra: The Naples Connection** (1985; dir. Lina Wertmuller; Cannon Releasing)

El Caballero del Dragon or Star Knight (1985; dir. Fernando Colomo; Cinetel)

The Men's Club (1986; dir. Peter Medak; Atlantic Releasing)

Off Beat (1986; dir. Michael Dinner; Touchstone)

Wise Guys (1986; dir. Brian de Palma; United Artists)

Blindside (1986; dir. Paul Lynch; Norstar Entertainment)

The Inquiry (1987; dir. Damiano Damiani; Italian International Film Releasing)

The Pick-Up Artist (1987; dir. James Toback; Twentieth Century–Fox)

Caro Gorbaciov (1988; dir. Carlo Lizzani; VIP)

The Last Temptation of Christ (1988; dir. Martin Scorsese; Universal)

The January Man (1989; dir. Pat O'Connor; MGM)

La Batalla de los Tres Reyes (1990)

Two Evil Eyes (1990; dir. Dario Argento; Taurus)

The Two Jakes (1990; dir. Jack Nicholson; Paramount)

Bugsy (1991; dir. Barry Levinson; TriStar)

Mortal Thoughts (1991; dir. Alan Rudolph; Columbia)

Thelma and Louise (1991; dir. Ridley Scott; MGM)

Reservoir Dogs (1992; dir. Quentin Tarantino; Miramax)

Bad Lieutenant (1992; dir. Abel Ferrara; Aries)

Sister Act (1992; dir. Emile Ardolino; Touchstone)

The Piano (1993; dir. Jane Campion; Miramax)

Dangerous Game (1993; dir. Abel Ferrara; MGM)

The Young Americans (1993; dir. Danny Cannon; MGM)

Point of No Return (1993; dir. John Badham; Warner Bros.)

Imaginary Crimes (1994; dir. Anthony Drazan; Warner Bros.)

Pulp Fiction (1994; dir. Quentin Tarantino; Miramax)

Rising Sun (1994; dir. Phil Kaufman; Twentieth Century–Fox)

Somebody to Love (1994; dir. Alexandre Rockwell; Lumiere)

Monkey Trouble (1994; dir. Franco Amurri; New Line)

Smoke (1995; dir. Wayne Wang; Miramax)

Blue in the Face (1995; dir. Wayne Wang and Paul Auster; Miramax)

Clockers (1995; dir. Spike Lee; Universal)

Ulysses' Gaze (1995; dir. Theo Angelopoulos; Fox Lorber)

Get Shorty (1995; dir. Barry Sonenfeld; MGM)

From Dusk Till Dawn (1996; dir. Robert Rodriguez; Dimension)

Head Above Water (1997; dir. Jim Wilson; Fine Line)

Copland (1997; dir. James Mangold; Miramax)

City of Industry (1997; dir. John Irvin; Largo)

Dreaming of Julia (1997; dir. Juan-Gerard Gonzalez; October Films)

Illumination (1997; dir. Charles Sturridge; Paramount)

Eyes Wide Shut (1997; dir. Stanley Kubrick; Warner Bros.)

TV APPEARANCES

Dark Shadows, 1966

Pueblo (TV movie), 1973

Kojak, 1973

The FBI, 1973

The Virginia Hill Story (TV movie), 1974

Dear America: Letters Home from Vietnam, 1987

acknowledgments

All quotes are drawn either from interviews by the author (with persons named elsewhere in this book) or from the following sources:

Ernest Leogrande, ' "Harvey who?" Well, not the invisible rabbit,' *New York Daily News*, 16.7.75

Elizabeth Stone, 'Harvey Keitel Is Trying to Get Out of the Poolroom,' *Village Voice*, 21.7.75

'Won't Wait for Brando, Keitel Fired,' *Variety*, 21.4.76

'Martin Sheen Heir to Keitel's Role,' *Variety*, 5.5.76

Charles Higham, 'When I Do It, It's Not Gore, Says Writer Paul Schrader,' *New York Times*, 9.1.77

Stuart Byron, 'The Keitel Method,' *Film Comment*, 1.78

Robert Asahina, 'A Career Gone Sour,' *New Leader*, 30.1.78

Excerpt from diary of Eleanor Coppola, reprinted, *New York Times*, 5.8.79

Lorenzo Carcaterra, 'A street actor in the desert,' *New York Daily News*, 16.2.82

Richard David Story, 'Harvey Keitel builds a name with angry roles,' *USA Today*, 2.8.84

Arnold Abrams, 'Harvey Keitel Moving Up,' *Newsday*, 15.7.84

Leslie Bennetts, 'Inside the Ensemble Play of *Hurlyburly*,' *New York Times*, 18.7.84

Jerry Tallmer, 'Edging up to Harvey Keitel,' *New York Post*, 7.8.84

Enid Nemy, 'Broadway,' *New York Times*, 20.12.85

Pete Hamill, 'Keitel on a Roll,' *Vanity Fair*, 8.86

David Thompson and Ian Christie (eds.), *Scorsese on Scorsese*, Faber and Faber, 1989

Julian Schnabel, 'Jack and Harvey,' *Interview* magazine, 8.90

Martha Southgate, 'Strong Moral Fiber Girds Harvey Keitel's Tough-Guy Image,' *New York Daily News*, 19.8.90

Alex Witchel, 'A Mafia Wife Makes Lorraine Bracco a Princess,' *New York Times*, 27.9.90

Mary Pat Kelly, *Martin Scorsese: A Journey*, Thunder's Mouth Press, 1991

Les Keyser, *Martin Scorsese*, Twayne Publishers, 1992

Lawrence Van Gelder, 'At the Movies,' *New York Times*, 17.1.92

Douglas Rowe, 'Harvey Keitel,' *Associated Press*, 26.2.92

Judy Gerstel, 'A Method to His Madness,' *Detroit Free Press*, 4.10.92

Kristine McKenna, 'Leaps of Faith: Harvey Keitel's Search for God Often Involves Confronting His Darker Self,' *Los Angeles Times*, 18.10.92

Stephen Schaefer, 'Harvey Keitel's Roles Delve into a Demonic Side,' *USA Today*, 19.11.92

Tim Appelo, 'Killer Elite,' *Entertainment Weekly*, 27.11.92

Donald Lyons, 'Scumbags,' *Film Comment*, 12.11.92

Julian Schnabel, 'Harvey Keitel, Zoe Lund and Abel Ferrara: The unholy trinity that makes *Bad Lieutenant* a religious experience,' *Interview* magazine, 12.92

Joyce Persico, 'Harvey Keitel: He's a Fine Actor, But Still Not a Star,' *Trenton Times*, 3.12.92

Peter McAlevey, 'All's Well That Ends Gruesomely,' *New York Times Magazine*, 6.12.92

David Thompson, 'Harvey Keitel: Staying Power,' *Sight and Sound*, 1.93

Annette Insdorf, '*Bad Lieutenant*: Harvey Keitel Sinks into Moral Mire as Corrupt Cop,' *San Francisco Chronicle*, 27.12.92

Minty Clinch, 'Method to His Madness,' *Evening Standard*, 7.1.93

Roger Ebert, 'Harvey Keitel, On the Edge,' *Chicago Sun-Times*, 17.1.93

Anne Thompson, 'The Soul of a Role: Probing the lower depths with Harvey Keitel,' *Chicago Tribune*, 24.1.93

'American Psycho,' *Face*, 2.93

Shawn Levy, 'Harvey Keitel: Beyond Face Value,' *Oregonian*, 7.3.93

Amy Longsdorf, 'For Harvey Keitel, Life's Dark Side Has Its Bright Spots,' *Allentown Morning Call*, 4.4.93

Nick Tosches, 'Heaven, hell, Harvey Keitel,' *Esquire*, 9.93

David Thomson, 'The face to watch,' *Independent*, 26.9.93

Karen Schoemer, 'Harvey Keitel Tries a Little Tenderness,' *New York Times*, 7.11.93

Bill Cosford, 'Harvey Keitel Out of Character,' *Miami Herald*, 21.11.93

Georgina Howell, 'The Gospel According to Harvey,' *Vogue*, 12.93

George Rush, 'Minor difficulties with Keitel, Bracco,' *New York Daily News*, 11.1.94

Transcript, *The Charlie Rose Show*, 24.1.94

Karen Thomas, 'Keitel's Cause: "Tough Guy" Actor Battles for Youngest Victims of War,' *USA Today*, 24.5.94

Nancy Jo Sapes, 'Keitel, Olmos and Bracco's Bitter Custody Battle,' *New York* magazine, 25.7.94

Lorraine Bracco-Olmos, Letter to Editor, New York magazine, 8.8.94

Matthew Gilbert, 'Harvey Keitel: His "Imaginary" Journey,' *Boston Globe*, 9.10.94

Transcript, *The Charlie Rose Show*, 14.10.94

Peter Stack, 'Writer's Journey into World of Film,' *San Francisco Chronicle*, 18.10.94

Stephen Hunter, 'Keitel Opts for "Presence" over Superstardom on Film,' *Baltimore Morning Sun*, 30.10.94

Jeff Dawson, *Quentin Tarantino: The Cinema of Cool*, Applause Books, 1995

Wensley Clarkson, *Quentin Tarantino: Shooting From the Hip*, Overlook Press, 1995

Jami Bernard, *Quentin Tarantino: The Man and His Movies*, Harper-Perennial, 1995

James Toback, 'Divisions and Dislocations: A Journal for 1994,' from *Projections 4*, Faber and Faber Ltd, 1995

Stephen Kinzer, 'Wait Let's Make Another One,' *New York Times*, 2.4.95

Wayne Wang quote from *Mr Showbiz* on-line magazine, 23.8.95

Alona Wartofsky, 'Dark Side of the Actor: Harvey Keitel, Plumbing the Depths of the Soul,' *Washington Post*, 13.9.95

John Anderson, 'Odd man in,' *Newsday*, 14.9.95

Peter von Ziegesar, 'Where There's Smoke: A Semi-Spontaneous Semi-Sequel,' *New York Times*, 8.10.95

Joan Anderman, 'Mel Gorham: A Real Person with a Real Life,' *Mr Showbiz* on-line magazine, 18.10.95

Lawrence Grobel, 'The *Playboy* Interview: Harvey Keitel,' *Playboy*, 11.95

Ron Dicker, 'Risky business: On the razor's edge with Harvey Keitel,' *Salon* on-line magazine, 13.1.96

Patrick Stoner, George Clooney interview, WHYY radio, 1.96

Jamie Portman, 'Keitel finds religion in vampire flick,' *Montreal Gazette*, 13.1.96

Andrew Pulver, 'Harvey Keitel is the king of character actors,' *Guardian*, 29.1.96

Hugh Barnes, 'Head on the Block in Bosnia,' *Sunday Telegraph*, 11.2.96

Barry Walters, 'Show-stopper afternoon with actor Harvey Keitel,' *San Francisco Examiner*, 29.4.96

Karen Hershenson, 'Harvey on his terms,' *Contra Costa Times*, 30.4.96

Mick LaSalle, 'Reel to Real With Harvey Keitel,' *San Francisco Chronicle*, 30.4.96

Sarah Allen, 'S.F. film fest honors Keitel,' *Oakland Tribune*, 30.4.96

Elisa Leonelli, 'Harvey Keitel's Journey,' *Venice* magazine, 5.96

'Harvey Keitel Interviewed,' *Roughcut*, 10.5.96

Leah Griesmann, 'Harvey Keitel Talks at SFIFF,' *Release Print*, 6.96

Tim Rhys with Brian O'Hare, 'Harvey Keitel: The Ecstasy of the Agony,' *MovieMaker*, 6.96

'Strange end to Keitel custody row,' *New York Post*, 16.9.96

index